Youth, Class and Education in Urban India

I0124997

Urban India is undergoing a rapid transformation, which also encompasses the educational sector. Since 1991, the important new market in private English-medium schools, along with an explosion of private coaching centres, has transformed the lives of children and their families, as the attainment of the best education nurtures the aspirations of a growing number of Indian citizens.

Set in urban Kerala, the book discusses changing educational landscapes in the South Indian city of Kochi, a local hub for trade, tourism and cosmopolitan middle-class lifestyles. Based on extensive ethnographic fieldwork, the author examines the way education features as a major way the transformation of the city, and India in general, are experienced and envisaged by upwardly mobile residents. Schooling is shown to play a major role in urban lifestyles, with increased privatisation representing a response to the educational strategies of a growing and hetero-geneous middle class, whose educational choices reflect broader projects of class formation within the context of religious and caste diversity particular to the region.

This path-breaking new study of a changing Indian middle class, and new relationships with educational institutions, contributes to the growing body of work on the experiences and meanings of schooling for youths, their parents and the wider community, and thereby adds a unique, anthropologically informed perspective to South Asian studies, urban studies and the study of education.

David Sancho holds a British Academy Postdoctoral Fellowship and is currently carrying out research on transnational educational trajectories with Indian-origin pupils in Dubai.

Routledge Series on Urban South Asia
Edited by Henrike Donner
Goldsmiths, University of London, UK

The series showcases a wide range of disciplines that study processes of urbanization in globalizing South Asian cities and towns. It encompasses monographs as well as edited volumes, which address urban issues including urbane lifestyles and subcultures, urban politics and economies, as well as planning regimes and policies in the context of contemporary South Asia.

Youth, Class and Education in Urban India

The year that can break or make you

David Sancho

Routledge
Taylor & Francis Group

LONDON AND NEW YORK

First published 2016
by Routledge

2 Park Square, Milton Park, Abingdon, Oxfordshire OX14 4RN
711 Third Avenue, New York, NY 10017

Routledge is an imprint of the Taylor & Francis Group, an informa business

First issued in paperback 2018

British Library Cataloguing in Publication Data
A catalogue record for this book is available from the British Library

Library of Congress Cataloging in Publication Data
Sancho, David.
Youth, class and education in urban India : the year that can break or
make you / David Sancho.
pages cm. -- (Routledge series on urban South Asia ; 2)
Includes bibliographical references and index.
1. Youth--India. 2. Social classes--India. 3. Urbanization--India--Social
conditions. 4. Education--India. I. Title.
HQ799.I5S256 2016
305.2350954--dc23
2015021333

ISBN: 978-1-138-78586-1 (hbk)
ISBN: 978-1-138-32022-2 (pbk)

Typeset in Times New Roman
by Fish Books Ltd.

For Iris

Contents

Illustrations

Figures

Tables

Acronyms and abbreviations

BVM	Brahmacharya Vidya Mandir
CBSE	Central Board of Secondary Education
CSL	Cochin Shipyard Limited
EC	entrance coaching
ECE	educational and cultural exchange
EIC	East India Company
GPS	Global Public School
HIG	high-income group
HSS of Jesus	Higher Secondary School of Jesus
ICSE	Indian Council of Secondary Education
ICT	International Container Terminal
ICTT	Vallarpadam International Container Transhipment Terminal
IIT	Indian Institute of Technology
INP	Indo-Norwegian Pilot Programme
ISA	International Schools Award
IT	information technology
ITC	industrial training course
ITES/BPO	information technology enabled services/business process outsourcing
ITI	Industrial Training Institute
LIG	lower-income group
LMS	London Mission Society
MIG	middle-income group
NKC	National Knowledge Commission
NRI	non-resident Indian
NSS	Nair Service Society
OBC	Other Backward Class
PDC	pre-degree course
PIO	people of Indian origin
PPP	public–private partnership
PSS	Private Secondary School Scheme
PTA	Parent–Teacher Association
RSS	Rashtriya Swayamsevak Sangh

SC	scheduled caste
SJPS	Sadhujana Paripalana Sangham
SNDP	Sree Narayana Dharma Paripalana
SNHSS	Sree Narayanan Higher Secondary School
SSLC	Secondary Schooling Leaving Certificate
TTC	teacher training course
UDF	Indian National Congress Party

Acknowledgements

In the process of completing this monograph I have accumulated many debts. First, I would like to thank the Fundacion Caja Madrid, who generously funded my doctoral studies. Second, I would like to express my gratitude to the Royal Anthropological Institute, who gifted me with the Sutasoma Award in 2012 and the Leach/RAI Research Fellowship in 2013. Third, I am extremely grateful for the guidance and support of my doctoral supervisors at the University of Sussex, Filippo Osella and Geert De Neve, and my mentor at Brunel University, Peggy Froerer. Thanks for illuminating my way through fieldwork and the writing-up period, for sharing books, ideas, contacts and friendship. You have made my doctoral and postdoctoral experience a remarkably enjoyable and swift one. I would also like to thank Dr Raminder Kaur for her support and encouragement.

This book has benefited greatly from the collaboration, advice and input from individuals in both India and in the UK. Above all, this work would not have been possible without the generosity and openness of my friends and informants in Ernakulam. I am infinitely grateful for the help I received from the students and staff of BVM and HSS of Jesus. I would like to especially thank Sachin, Bimal, Viswa, Swathy, Sathya, Neelanjan and the rest of the eleventh and twelfth STD students at BVM. In Kothad, I would like to thank Neelu, Jinu, Shillu, Ainsteen and Phil, as well as the rest of the students at HSS of Jesus. I would like to thank A.D. Paul and Joseph Job for their support; without it, fieldwork would not have turned into the enriching experience it was. I am infinitely indebted to Asma, Salma, Jafer, Sinan, Rikas, Rizu and the rest of their family for their love and hospitality, and to many others who helped me as I carried out my enquiries over the course of a year. I would like to thank Mrs Laly Roy, Geetha Mathen, Dilip Narayanan, Dr V.J. Varghese and Dr J. Devika for their support.

I would like to thank the support and encouragement from friends in Brighton. Especially I would like to thank the companionship and help received from Miguel, Vesselina, Shrikant and Ana. Miguel's continual support through the writing-up and editing stages of the PhD was invaluable. I would also like to thank the support and encouragement of Dr Kaveri Qureshi, my gratitude goes to you.

Finally, thanks go to my family who have been extremely supportive during the fieldwork and writing-up process. Writing this book has been the culmination of a dream that began over ten years ago, which above all would not have been possible without the love and patience of my dear wife Iris Villarrubia. Iris, I dedicate this book to you. Thank you for staying by my side all these difficult years and for making this project your own. Finally, I would like to thank my tiny ones, Simone and Marion, whose smiles washed away any sorrows produced by the writing process.

1 Introduction

Making 'the year that can break or make you'

Application in youth makes old age comfortable
Nothing ventured, nothing gained
Work is worship
No pain, no gain
Strive like a race horse, govern your attitude towards work
and never slacken your efforts

These messages decorated the walls of the staircase at Brahmacharya Vidya Mandir (BVM), one of the schools where the research, on which this book is based, was carried out. The messages were directed to the students in their final year of school, who were reminded that life-long 'success' was being forged there and then. They were also reminded that 'failure' was just around the corner. This level of cruciality so early in the lives of young people was not unusual in Kochi. The notion that the final year of school can, to a great extent, unleash, or at least forecast, success or cast failure upon the lives of young men and women is a marked feature of middle-class urban India. Throughout twelve months of ethnographic fieldwork in Kochi, many parents and young people told me about how much was at stake in this crucial year, that working hard was of the foremost importance, suspending all forms of 'leisure', putting themselves under 'house arrest' or being 'like a bird in a cage'. Parents, students, teachers, tutors, all imagined this to be, quite literally, 'the year that can break or make you'.

This craze was linked to celebratory understandings of India as poised to claim its rightful place as an international superpower, a general conviction that, since the 1990s, has come to dominate the imagination of many, including my informants (Nigam 2004). Many of my young informants held the belief that the phenomenal growth of the Indian economy over the last two decades has transformed the employment prospects for the new generation. They envisaged the economy as providing a wide range of 'avenues' and opportunities for lucrative employment, while depicting the past as being shackled by public sector and old-economy jobs. 'The sky is the limit' in India today, I was told on several occasions. They dreamed of themselves leading urban and globalised lifestyles, generally not in Kochi, but in cities such as Bengaluru or Mumbai, which were considered to be at the centres of the new 'rising' India. Much of this optimism and pride revolved around India's rapidly expanding information technology (IT) industry, where many of the young men and women I met in Kochi aspired to be employed in the near future. However, their lives and professional success in this new context were seen as being tied to their capacity to acquire highly competitive professional degrees and other forms of global knowledge and skills to be sold in the new global labour market, crucially, English and IT credentials.

School education was deeply ingrained in the furore around the final year. Lifelong and professional success amongst middle-class urban students was seen as being inextricably tied to their performance in secondary education. They preferred private schools – thought to offer higher standards of English-medium education – over state-funded institutions, and school subjects (science stream, especially the computing variant) thought to lead sons and daughters into engineering (or medical) careers. In Kochi, as elsewhere in urban India (see Jeffery *et al.* 2005), the inadequacy of government-funded schools in meeting these changing demands, together with a host of other key factors, such as increasing middle-class purchasing power, compressing public expenditure on education (Kumar and George 2009: 10) and the Indian state's endorsement of privatisation, has fuelled a rapid transformation of the schooling sector over the last couple decades.

Figure 1.1 Billboard publicising one of the most popular coaching centres

Notably, since the late 1980s there has been a rapid growth in the number and proportion of children schooled in private schools, which in Kerala have had consistently better results in all of India competitive examinations for admission to higher education when compared to the weak performance of Kerala government and aided schools (George *et al.* 2002: 57). Private providers of education are not new in Kerala, or elsewhere in India; in 1951 they accounted for half of the schools available in Kerala. However, between 1950 and 1990, schooling came to be largely subsidised by the government, with only 4.5 per cent of the total number of schools in Kerala being private schools in 1991. Since then there has been a gradual yet important emergence of a new private English-medium sector of schools, now comprising more than 13 per cent. Private schools and some reputed government-aided schools catering for the middle classes contributed to the craze around the final year of school. A substantial portion of the academic year in such institutions is routinely turned into strict training regimes for final year exams or boards. Private schools' reputations, in turn, are build largely on their capacity to put students through the examination hoop successfully.

The physical landscape of Kochi contributed to the fad around the final year of schooling, too. Advertisements for private coaching institutes[1] were omnipresent in roads and billboards, often featuring the headshots of dozens of students who had attained the highest rank in final year and entrance examinations, the so-called 'toppers'. In urban India, coaching institutes, combined with private schooling, have become a definer of middle-classness (Kumar 2011). The tremendous popularity and demand for these centres comes down to fact that they have tapped into and reproduced the middle-class desire for making children successful in the competition for particular kinds of tertiary education and employment. In particular, coaching institutes cater for the middle-class aspiration to access the highest-ranking careers: engineering, management and medical professions. Offering programmes of study especially tailored for the entrance examinations leading to the training courses for each of those professions, coaching institutes have come to be increasingly relied on as a crucial component to middle-class success.

Even the research I present here faced somewhat of a crisis at its initial stages when I attempted to gain access to schools, as a result of the craze and anxieties surrounding the final year of schooling in middle-class Kochi. Although the schools were generally forthcoming about the idea of me conducting research on school premises, institutions were deeply apprehensive or outright prohibiting when it came to allowing me to spend time with the year 12 students. I was denied access to a reputed aided school catering to the lower spectrum of the middle classes on the grounds that final year students and the school could not afford any sort of 'distraction' in such a crucial stage. To me, that testified to the pressures, uncertainties and anxieties experienced more intensely by those whose prospects of downward mobility seemed almost imminent.

The practices, discourses, aspirations and even institutions that gave meaning to and turned the final year of schooling into 'the year that could make or break you' were amongst the most important cultural processes through which the urban middle class created itself. This book builds precisely on a sense of middle-class culture as a constantly under-construction cultural project that grows out of shared practices, values and aspirations. It is one of the core objectives of the book to draw attention to the critical role that practices and aspirations centred on education, such as those described before, played in the production of middle-class culture and the successful middle-class subject for the Indian and global economy in Kochi. Middle-classness was being forged in the actual performance of the final year school; a performance that was simultaneously as inextricably bound to the bedrock of economic resources as it was to the everyday practices and aspirations around which young people and families of different socioeconomic backgrounds converged and jointly negotiated their identities. Not everyone could afford what it took to participate in giving this particular meaning to the final year of school.

In the current context of economic recovery, more and more families take part in this melodrama. While domestic income in the 1960s, 1970s and 1980s ranked Kerala low amongst Indian states, the late 1980s witnessed steadily rising per-capita incomes in the state. This was due to a number of factors: crucially, the expansion of employment markets overseas with the concomitant inflow of remittances from the 1970s onwards, and a long history of widespread education, which in spite of very high levels of unemployment had enabled many to access stable employment and enter the middle ranks of society. In Kochi, as in many Indian cities, a complex and changing middle class has sprung up, comprised of families of markedly different histories, caste ranking and financial capabilities. With their mounting incomes, their expanding global connections and the arrival of new consumer goods, they have become most evident through the consumer-oriented lifestyles that have recently transformed Kochi and many other Indian cities (Bloch *et al.* 2004; Dickey 2013; Osella and Osella 1999; Rajagopal 2001; Upadhya 2011). Education is crucial here: private schooling and coaching are amongst the primary 'consumables' through which families and individuals assert their class identities. Increasingly varied families converge in buying privilege through private schooling, and more and more families and youth converge on the aspiration to attain a particular kind of success defined by being urban, professional, global, wealthy and in a privileged relationship with the globalised economy. More and more middle-class households reoriented parenting towards supporting children through their education and the enhancement of marketable skills acquired in educational institutions (Donner 2006; Kumar 2011).

This is not to say that these distinctively middle-class aspirations and educational strategies are never pursued amongst people in lower social strata. They are, indeed. Their participation in middle-class practices and discourses reveals the extent to which this middle-class culture has spread across communities in India and the ways in which its values and aspirations have captured the minds of a widening range of social groups (Baviskar and Ray 2011; De Neve 2011; Deshpande 2003). Not all middle-class families and young people understand and value these dominant educational practices equally. For many parents, for instance, lower- to middle-ranking communities from rural or semi-rural areas, investing in valued private English-medium education in urban centres may primarily respond to a desire to give their children the social connections and sophistication (of urban and higher caste middle-class peers) they lack themselves (Jeffrey *et al.* 2008; Wilson 2011). This book documents the educational experiences of young men and women (and their families) in their final year of schooling across different class groups.

In seeking to explore class formation and its relationship with school-level education in urban India, my research sought to straddle two groups of youth who inhabited very different structural positions: one attending a private English-medium school (BVM), which was nearly at the top of the educational hierarchy; the other attending an aided Malayalam-medium institution towards the bottom of the educational ladder. My initial plan was to concentrate on two schools in the urban centre, however, as a result of the usual vicissitudes of ethnographic field-work I ended up conducting research in very different environments: one school physically at the heart of the city; the other on the fringes. The latter was located not only at the geographical edges of the city, but also on its educational and social outskirts. BVM was situated in a middle- to upper-middle-class neighbourhood in the centre of Kochi. I spent a year engaging, observing and making friends with young men and women inside and outside both schools, whose aspirations and strategies of mobility, and how the city featured in these, were markedly different. This research was augmented with visits to students' households, interviews and conversations with parents, teachers and school directors, and observations of other educational institutions, including coaching and language centres, all carried out over twelve months between 2009 and 2010.

This introductory chapter begins by examining the theoretical frame I use when seeking to understand processes of class formation and in particular middle-class life in Kochi. It is Liechty's (2003) suggestion to look at class formation as both a material *and* a cultural project[2] that I follow here. In this book I argue that formal education and the cultural production of 'youth' as a social category are amongst the most important cultural processes involved in the creation of the middle class as a social entity. Importantly, I attempt to highlight the role of education, not just as a key consumable generative of middle-class lifestyles, but more crucially as a locus of middle-class aspirations and strategies of mobility. I argue that these are ultimately oriented towards cornering a prime relationship with the economy as *producers*, which are in turn historically specific. If a job in the Indian Adminis-trative and Foreign Services was seen as a pre-eminent position in the middle-class imaginary under the developmental regime, today the middle classes locate their aspirations in the private sector – iconically in the IT industry – and the manage-ment and engineering professions are the most sought after (Kumar 2011: 238). It is specific forms of education and 'youth' that are pursued as the most important factor improving one's children's or one's own chances in the competition for jobs and future education. Thus, in this book I attempt to show how class, education and youth are mutually constitutive cultural processes. Finally, by placing education at the centre, this books charts a path towards an understanding of the middle class that opens up current media portrayals of the middle class and academic debates about the meaning of becoming and being middle class in India, which have been narrowly dominated by consumption-centric representations.

These themes are taken up in Chapter 2 (and throughout the book), where I trace the development of modern schooling in Kerala and examine the social processes that went into making Kerala the most literate state in the Indian Union. Attempting to go beyond the dominant narrative on the development of education in Kerala – the so-called Kerala Model literature,[3] which is celebratory in nature – I describe the prolonged relationship between education and class formation, highlighting how in spite of laudable achievements, modern education has, since its emergence in the nineteenth century, served as a key resource for the reproduction and transformation of patterns of inequalities. It links modern education to the eruption of class-based identities amongst high-caste elites in the late nineteenth century. The processes that led to the emergence and consolidation of an English-speaking elite in the nineteenth and early twentieth centuries have remained in place following Independence in 1947. The mastery of English, the language of power, continues to be a preserve of urban elites. Simultaneously though, education is strongly linked to the emergence of the 'new middle classes' in the last few decades; those who, coming from castes of low hierarchical position, have recently experienced social and economic ascension often as a result of agrarian reforms, positive discrimination policies or the opening of employment markets overseas prior to economic liberalisation. This chapter shows that rather than displacing caste hierarchies, education has complicated the ways in which caste and class continue to be entwined in contemporary Kerala. Therefore, the underlying contention of this chapter, and the book as a whole, is that a focus on education allows us to historicise our understanding of the middle class, which previously has tended to emphasise 'newness' through a focus on consumption practices. Education allows us to trace the continuities and to capture the transformations in patterns of inequalities. If the present desire for English-medium education is the same as that found amongst the privileged social groups who first defined themselves as middle class in the late nineteenth century, the contemporary drive for private schooling and coaching institutes speaks of the consumer lifestyles, cultural orientations and the aspirations of the twenty-first century middle class.

In his recent survey of urban theory[4] John Rennie Short (2006) writes that the twenty-first century has witness rapidly increasing numbers of 'wannabe cities' in both the developed and developing worlds, which seek to achieve a world-city reputation and command a function of centrality. Kochi is no exception: following the embrace of liberalisation reforms in the 1990s, aspirations to transform the city into a hub of global trade and tourism, and a rival to established South Indian 'metros', are running high. Local residents, the state government and the private sector are all imbricated into a wider project to achieve what is locally referred to as 'international standard'. As Short notes, wannabe cities – or rather, wannabe metros in the Indian context – are sites of spectacle and intense urban redevelopment (2006: 115). Kochi's urban landscape is being transformed by the sprouting of high-rise apartment buildings, lavish shopping malls, multiplex theatres and the growing choice of Italian-style ice cream parlours, cafes, restaurants, bars and posh supermarkets, all catering particularly to the desires of the rising middle classes and the non-resident Keralites who have a particularly keen interest in the city's transformation. Growth is being promoted aggressively in a number of sectors, primarily its trade and transport infrastructure, with the development of a major trade hub port for the Indian Ocean region and the city's IT industry. These changes have been accompanied by a powerful growth rhetoric; Kochi is being touted as 'today's symbol of Kerala's progress and promise of prosperity', while local inter-locutors depict it as a serious rival to Bangalore. This book reflects on how Kochi's metro status is still very much a matter of debate, while the use of the term 'metro' (metropolis) has become part of the popular lexicon in the city.

Linked to this desire to achieve a world-city reputation, Kochi has recently witnessed the emergence of new exclusive schools marketed as 'international, modern and secular', and offering internationally recognised curriculum and cred-entials (Hayden 2011), a trend emerging in cities across the developing world. Expanding beyond their historical niche of catering to the children of elite expatriates, these international schools have been propelled by local elites' demand for cutting-edge education. They are largely the result of drawn-out migration processes across the Indian Ocean, through which Indian educational entrepreneurs have acquired substantial expertise at establishing schools modelled on 'western' educational institutions (in Persian Gulf countries), but adapted to the cultural requirements of the middle-class South Asian expatriate population. In an already fragmented and stratified schooling sector, divided into a mass of underfunded[5] government schools catering for poor families, large numbers of aided schools fragmented according religious/caste affiliations and a small but growing number of private schools catering to very different economic capabilities, these schools have further augmented the stratification of the school market, allowing the elite to reinstate privilege and distinguish itself from the rising middle classes. Simultaneously, though, these schools have fuelled an emerging desire for 'internationalised' forms of education amongst the middle classes in urban India who aspire for their children to gain the English competences and the personalities, skills and credentials that will make them competitive in globalising labour markets in India or abroad (Qureshi and Osella 2013). To capture this expanding market, curricula and pedagogies in India are being reformed to include an 'international' or 'cosmopolitan' flavour, seeking to provide students with 'exposure' (Fuller and Narasimhan 2006; Narasimhan 2009).

In Chapter 3 I concentrate on a group of families whose children attend BVM. I present a set of common parenting practices around school education, coaching and higher education that shows the way in which middle-class parents aggres-sively endeavour to control and structure their children's schooling experience, ultimately training them to pursue predetermined career paths regarded as safe for income generation and economic mobility. The high level of parental intervention stands at odds with the images of self-driven, competitive and ambitious youth and students that now circulate India and form an integral part of middle-class culture. This chapter examines parents' efforts to construct this new youth's competitive and ambitious identity in the domestic realm, which disguises their role of producing an employable and skilled middle-class workforce.

Chapter 4 examines how a private school, BVM, catering for the middle classes in Kochi responds to the establishment of international schools and reorients its pedagogical project in response to the shifting educational orientations of the hegemonic fraction of the middle classes and the elites. The chapter shows how BVM attempts to simultaneously emulate and differentiate itself from such schools. BVM has become successful by advertising itself as offering the best of international education – offering exposure to world culture and English-language skills – while championing 'true' Indian values and culture, thus claiming a certain moral superiority to the new international schools catering for the upper classes. The chapter argues that while the school's practices are still focused on satisfying the core aspirations of the bulk of its middle-class students – centred very much on India and on gaining access to reputed higher education institutions – contributing to the rise of 'international' education as a middle-class demand, there is a shift that amounts to the transmutation of particular elite interests to a national ideology.

Chapter 5 seeks to complicate the argument that private schools have become spaces in which young people come to see themselves less as representatives of one ethnic or caste community and more as indices of their own family's economic standing and as members of a class group. I argue that a closer look at the way in which students experience and narrate private schooling reveals a much less straightforward process. Schools, I argue, are mobilised by youth as flexible tools in complex and competing strategies to construct a middle social space for themselves. The chapter tries to address a dearth of research on the complex and severely contested processes of transformation of the self-implicated in strategies towards urban educational opportunities.

Chapter 6 concentrates on the fringes of the city, and shows how as Kochi expands and is transformed into a South Indian metro, the urban poor and marginalised peri-urban populations become objects of exclusionary processes. In particular, it documents how schooling has become a new arena for the production of difference amongst the inhabitants of a backwater islet to the north of Kochi after the construction of a bridge linking it to the city. I describe the flows of students between the islet and Kochi, and show how such circulation of students is the outcome of new educational policies and physical linkages – roads, terminals, connections to boost India's global trade – and old inequalities. I demonstrate how these inequalities respond to both old spatial gaps – between the coastal backwater region and the urban centre – and social differences, which pit low-status Latin Catholic groups against other higher-status communities.

Chapter 7 focuses of the formulation of life and professional aspirations as cultural practice. I compare the dream life projects of two distinct groups of young people as an arena in which to explore class formation and the reproduction of social and economic inequalities. The chapter brings out how different visions of the future engender different ways of experiencing the final year of schooling across social groups.

In conclusion, this book argues that within the context of social changes resulting from India's integration into the global economy, and the rise of the idea of the middle class as an aspirational model, education has become more than ever a contradictory resource: offering a widening site for cultural capital and contestation of older and more established middle-class power, as well as a pervasive apparatus of power and domination that reproduces old inequalities.

The goals of this book are three-fold: to describe the historical relationship between modern education and processes of class formation in urban Kerala, to provide a detailed account of the important role played by secondary schooling in the reproduction and transformation of patterns of inequality amongst the contemporary middle classes in Kochi, and drawing on these ethnographic insights, to offer a novel perspective in the understanding of middle-class culture in India. The book attempts to argue that education is one of the most crucial dynamics through which the middle class has always created itself. I will endeavour to produce a novel perspective that brings specific forms of education at the centre of middle-class aspirations and strategies of mobility, while, at the same time, paying attention to the emergence of new forms of inequality based on differential access to private education.

The rest of this introductory chapter gives a brief look at the theories and debates within the three themes central to the book: class, education and youth. Following this overview, I describe the locations and the various methods of data collection I used during fieldwork.

Middle-class culture

Local communities

Although this book seeks primarily to examine class as the main framing paradigm for many people in Kochi, it is crucial to remain mindful of the powerful influence of caste, and of the way these intersect in everyday life. By caste, I mean not an unchanged survival of ancient Indian nor a single homogeneous system that reflects a core cultural value, but a product of a concrete historical encounter between India and British colonial rule (Dirks 2003). The population of Kerala includes Hindu, Christian and Muslim communities. Unlike how caste has evolved in other parts of India, modelled according to the four-fold division of society into Brahmins, Kshatriyas, Vaisyas and Shudras, in Kerala Hindu communities are grouped in three clusters: high-caste Hindus or *savarnas*[6] including Nambudiri and Tamil Brahmin as well as Nair;[7] non-caste Hindus consisting mostly of *avarna*[8] groups, such as Ezhavas classified as 'Other Backward Class' (OBC); and Scheduled Castes of Kerala, such as Hindu Pulaya or Parayas (Aiyappan 1965: 5). In other words, Nambudiri Brahmins occupy the summit of the hierarchy, while Nairs are ranked below Brahmins, and Ezhavas below Nairs, the last two being the most numerous Hindu communities in Kerala (Fuller 1976). Brahmins in Kerala have traditionally treated and considered the numerous groups in the Nair sub-cluster as Shudras, as a result of which Ezhavas and other groups in the second cluster fall outside the four-fold division of Hindu castes. However, throughout the twentieth century, Ezhavas pursued mobility in many social arenas, both as a newly united caste and as individual families. Through a strong imperative in education, respectable employment, the accumulation of wealth and entry into the mainstream

Hindu fold, Ezhavas have, to a large extent, succeeded in redefining themselves as non-untouchables (Osella and Osella 2000).

Although technically outside the caste hierarchy, Kerala Christians and Muslims are ranked with respect to each other and surrounding Hindu castes (Fuller 1976; Mathew 1989). As Fuller explains, Christians can be divided into Syrian, Latin and New Christians groupings, distinguished according to two criteria: the caste to which the original converts from whom the members of each grouping claim descent belong, and the date of the original conversions (Fuller 1976: 54). Syrian Christians most commonly claim to be descendants of Nambudiri Brahmins, said to have been converted by St Thomas the Apostle after his alleged arrival in India in AD 52. Other Syrian Christian groups trace their origin to the descendants of a merchant of Syria, Thomas of Cana, who is said to have led a migration of Syrian Christians from the Middle East to India between the fourth and ninth centuries. While some Syrian Christians claim Nambudiri rank, it is generally accepted that their ranking is somewhat equal to that of Nairs. They are classified by the modern state as a 'forward' caste. Latin Christians (or Latin Catholics) are the second major group of Christians. They are the descendants of various waves of conversion to Christianity speared by the missionary endeavours of St Francis Xavier in the sixteenth century. Most of his converts came from Scheduled fisher Castes (Mukkuvans and Arayas), while there is also a small minority of Latin Catholics who are descendants of high-caste Hindus (Klausen 1968). Although they are officially classified as OBC, they are generally seen by others as ranked either as Scheduled Caste (those who descend from Hindu fishing caste converts) or as Forward Caste (those who claim to be descendants of high-caste Hindus). A third group are the descendants of those converted in the missionary wave of the nineteenth and early twentieth centuries (Fuller 1976: 55). New Christians are also classified as OBC by the state government, however, they are most commonly perceived to be ranked with Scheduled Castes. Finally, Muslims are also classified as OBC. Like Hindu castes, these groups are strictly endogamous.

Theorising class

Pinning down the concept of 'class' has remained an exceedingly difficult endeavour for all modern social science disciplines that have attempted to write about it, not as an 'objective' or natural category that is accounted for in terms of universal and taken-for-granted indicators, but as a constantly re-enacted cultural project that never exits outside its actual practice or performance in everyday life. In developing a conceptualisation of the cultural production of class in urban Kochi, this book draws primarily from the recent work of Mark Liechty (2003) in Kathmandu and Pierre Bourdieu's analysis of French society. Liechty's approach to the cultural production of the middle class in urban Nepal starts from an attempt to reconcile what he sees as the rather sketchy theories of class produced by Karl Marx and Max Weber, the two most influential theorist of modern capitalist society. He brings together Marxian emphasis on interclass antagonism – the product of the unequal distribution of economic power and resource – and Weberian concern for the role of social status (to do with lifestyle, education, occupational prestige) in determining a person's relative position amongst the 'intermediate' groups (Weber and Henderson 2012). He proposes an outline of a theory of middle-class cultural practice that incorporates both a concern for social complexity and intra-class status competition, and larger spheres of cultural practices and interclass power imbalances.

The work of Pierre Bourdieu and his analysis of class reproduction (Bourdieu 1984) is particularly relevant when seeking to understand middle-class cultural life as internally differentiated. He showed how everyday practice and the 'ordinary choices of everyday existence' that made class fractions possible and reproduced inequality depend on a combination of the varying degrees of cultural, social and economic capital (Bourdieu 1984; Donner and De Neve 2011). In other words, for Bourdieu, people's class positions vary according to their possession of varying amounts of the various species of capital (Bourdieu 1984). Class position is simultaneously dependant on a person's economic resources, social capital – the sum of the resources that accrue to an individual or a group by virtue of possessing a durable network of more or less institutionalised relationships of mutual acquaintance and recognition (Bourdieu 1992: 119) – and cultural capital, the symbolic credit, which one acquires through embodying and enacting signs of social standing. The latter derives from three sources: material possessions, institutional recognition (for example, in the form of education credentials) and certain styles of behaviour and competences, such as 'intelligence' and 'taste', or the mastery of a language, primarily learned from early childhood (Bourdieu 1986). It is his emphasis on cultural capital, which for Bourdieu accounted primarily for the internalised, deeply rooted and long-standing sets of dispositions of one's class position, in myriad combinations with other forms of capital (educational and economic) that I find most useful in the study of class as contradictory positions vis-à-vis other classes.

Bourdieu also stressed that the various types of capital must be understood according to his concept of 'field'. Bourdieu viewed society as an ensemble of relatively autonomous fields of social competition where agents' positions vary according to their possession of a combination of varying amount and weight of cultural, social and economic capital (Bourdieu 1984). Agents then compete to gain control over the species of capital that are most effective and hold a high value in the particular field of play, which in turn provides each field's own internal logic and regulatory principles that govern the game in the field. Therefore, people with the right combination and volume of capital resources and with *habitus*[9] – 'internalised orientations to action inscribed in people's demeanour reflexes and tastes that both reflect people's histories and shape their futures' (Jeffrey 2010: 19) – that match a particular field will outmanoeuvre people who lack the resources and attuned habitus.

While Bourdieu allows us to understand the middle class as an internally differentiated social field, Liechty's approach enables us to grasp middle-class culture as a process shaped by internally competing cultural strategies and status claims (Liechty 2003: 15). In particular, I take his concern with how class-based identities and class culture at large are actually constructed through everyday practices. Thus, like Liechty, I pay crucial attention to both performances and narratives as ways through which class culture is actively produced by people. Adopting ideas of performativity to class theory, he proposes an understanding of class as a reality 'that exists only in its perpetual sociocultural enactment' (Liechty 2003: 23). Performances, he then suggests, are best understood when combined with 'narrativity'. Narrative, 'helps us conceptualise, analyse, and ethnographically represent what it is that is being performed in sociocultural life' (Liechty 2003: 23). I draw inspiration from recent works such as *Telling Lives in India: Biography, Autobiography, and Life History* (Arnold and Blackburn 2004) to show how stories are revealing of the ways in which people cope with society and how individuals seek to create their own 'versions of truth' (2004: 5), which, importantly, includes creating representations of people's notions of themselves. Simultaneously, the book also seeks to show that competing performances and narratives are nevertheless imbricated in a wider middle-class project geared towards the construction of itself in opposition to its class others, above and below. In this latter project the cultural domination and privilege of the hegemonic fraction of the middle class is concealed behind seemingly non-economic rhetorics of merit, individual achievement and so on. This wider middle-class project then has the effect of reproducing and concealing the inequalities and power imbalances amongst different middle-class positions. This is particularly relevant in post-liberalisation India, where new social groups and individuals have acquired (or increasingly aspire to acquire) the trappings and the self-identifications of middle-class life (Donner 2011).

The power of the middle class as social construct

Looking beyond middle classness as a lived experience, many scholars – mainly sociologists and political scientists – have stressed the need to supplement empirical accounts with 'an analysis of the ideological work performed by the "middle class" as a social construct' (Baviskar and Ray 2011: 7). This move has become compulsory since the 1990s, when economic liberalisation brought this social category into prominence (Deshpande 2006). A notion of India's 'middle class' now dominates much of the public imagination, as well as government discourse and policy, media, advertisement and business. Many have noted that the 'middle class' is often presented as the protagonist and primary driving force of India's rapid economic growth, not only as a result of its size and financial strength – making it a sizable market for consumer goods that flooded India's market – but importantly for its intellectual and attitudinal strengths. The iconic figure in media representations is that of the urban IT worker, or the young entrepreneur whose virtues of risk-taking, innovation and creativity, as well as pragmatism and the capacity to turn adversity into opportunity in the quest for wealth, profit and success are the key to growth and development in India today (Gooptu 2013). The *Times of India*'s 2007 campaign, Lead India, has become a classic illustration of this point. The stated aim of this campaign was to inspire enterprising, middle-class youth to direct their talents to the task of public governance, to rid India of corruption, just as they had applied their expertise and abilities in the private corporate world to successfully establish India as a major economic power. Last, but not least, an important feature of this imagined middle class is its diasporic disposition. Media and the government – through the NRI (Non-Resident Indian) categorisation or the recent establishment of the PIO (People of Indian Origin) card, for example – hail diasporic subjects, especially those who migrate to western countries as privileged members of the Indian nation (Vora 2011). So, while common sense tells us that there are a diverse set of actors in the postcolonial Indian middle classes, the 'middle class' that has come to dominate public imagination connotes specific characteristics: urban, white-collar worker, entrepreneurial, oriented towards consumer and globalised lifestyles.

Sociologist Satish Deshpande (2003; Deshpande and Yadav 2006) stresses that the power of the 'middle class' resides in its capacity to articulate hegemonic values, beliefs, aspirations and trajectories as those of the nation as a whole. In this way, the category 'middle class' performs the cultural task of concealing inequalities (Baviskar and Ray 2011: 7) and the ways in which one or more groups within the middle classes exercise a cultural dominance over the rest.[10] The daily lives of the members of the middle class that I describe in this book are, by definition, oriented towards specific ideas of educational/occupational and economic success, which most of the time turn out to be an illusory quest for the vast majority (Ferguson 1999). To a large extent it is only the upper tiers (Fernandes and Heller 2006) of the middle classes who are actually benefiting from cutting-edge schooling and the new, highly remunerated employment opportunities made available after liberalisation (Fuller and Narasimhan 2007; van Wessel 2004), except their lives mirror the idealised images of prosperous urban Indians, leading transnational lives and residing in expensive suburban homes equipped with all modern conveniences increasingly in circulation in Indian media (Jeffrey 2010: 8).

Many, including this book, have highlighted how the trope of 'merit' has become a central piece in the ideology of the middle class in post-liberalisation India. This narrative, which holds that success in one's career or business is, or should be, purely a matter of individual talent and hard work has been specially examined with reference to the IT industry. Carol Upadhya, for example, notes how the industry depicts itself as a champion of merit-based recruitment and a source of employment opportunities for socially disadvantaged groups (Upadhya 2011: 186). In contrast, the public sector is portrayed as a place where only connections and bribes can garner jobs and promotions. These claims are often supported by the circulation of stories of rapid upward mobility of the founding member of key companies such as that of Infosys' Narayana Murthy. This discourse is also invoked by most industry leaders to oppose job reservations or affirmative action programmes on the basis of caste, which are seen as impinging upon their capacity to hire the 'best' and contravening the principle of equality of opportunity. But as Upadhya (2011) rightly notes, the ideology of merit and the resistance to reservations permeates the middle class in general. IT professionals, as well as many of the students and parents at the heart of this book, see reservations on the basis of economic status as acceptable, but not on the basis of caste, thereby overlooking the fact that this approach only serves to reinforce the congruence of caste and class status. Ultimately, reservations based on economic criteria would tend to benefit 'poor Brahmins' like Narayana Murthy, who would possess the attitudes, demeanours, personalities, communication skills (Fuller and Narasimhan 2006) and even family names recognised as 'meritorious' by the industry. The 'merit' trope is based on a very simplistic and partial understanding of inequality in Indian society. The pervasiveness of the ideology of merit amongst self-defined middle classes conjures a unifying 'middle class' identity that denotes not just specific socioeconomic status and aspirations, but also a particular set of social and cultural values and orientations, such as the notion of individual achievement underpinning 'merit' tropes (Upadhya 2011: 187). In India, more and more young people imbibe the dream to have successful and well-paid careers in the IT industry, while empirical accounts corroborate the systematic upper-caste and class monopoly over higher education and private-sector jobs (Fuller and Narasimhan 2006). In addition, more and more people uphold the belief in hard work and individual achievement, allowing those who are already well off and gainfully employed to believe that middle-class status is not just inherited and can be acquired. Thus, the 'middle class' as a social construct allows for the simplification and reproduction of inequalities. It is through the language of merit, for example, that inequalities are concealed, and through which particular elite interests and trajectories are turned into widely encompassing class aspirations. In short, the cultural politics of the 'middle class' performs the dual task of distinguishing what 'middle class' is from those above and below it, and concealing the fact that such cultural politics works in favour of a middle-class elite and not so much to the benefit of others in more precarious middle-class positions.

My aim is to examine how these values and orientations towards individual achievement and merit permeate secondary schooling. Private schools catering for the middle classes in Kochi, and urban India in general, contribute vastly to the spread of the middle-class values of individual achievement by framing education, especially in the final year of school, as being about an equal quest to demonstrate merit and achieve specific social and economic rewards. Today a disproportionate number of families and youth imbibe the middle-class dream that in India, through sacrifice and merit in education, 'the sky is the limit'. In the final year of schooling students actively unite and orient themselves towards a common struggle to improve their prospects in the face of competitive entrance examinations, without which larger dreams would be rendered unachievable. Although their prospects to succeed in these examinations and in the professional lives that follow are heavily shaped by inequalities (of economic status, caste, language), their efforts make no reference to such differences and actively hail their equality in the face of their quests ahead.

The new and the established middle classes

In accounting for the Indian middle class as a heterogeneous and internally differentiated social formation, anthropologists have frequently, for the purposes of sociocultural analysis, used two overarching categories: the 'new' and the 'established' middle classes. The established middle classes usually refer to groups and individuals of higher-caste origin, who can benefit from a variety of inherited material, social and cultural capital. It also refers to groups who have participated for various generations in middle-class culture, descending from the colonial middle class who came into being in the late nineteenth and early twentieth centuries through participation in particular projects: the creation of professions, the emergence of modern education, social reform movements and the anti-colonial struggle (see, for example, Joshi 2010). Although much of their privileges derive from a historically beneficial relationship with the states, contemporary established middle classes in present-day India mistrust the state. Historical accounts have revealed to us that the first groups that rearticulated their identities as middle class and entered the new social, cultural and economic roles becoming available in colonial India belong to the upper echelons of society rather than to any sort of middle position. As mentioned before, there continues to be a strong congruency of caste and class status.

On the contrary, the new middle classes' history is shallow: their acquired social and economic position is of recent origin. In the context of rapid social and economic transformations of the last twenty years, much anthropological interest has been especially directed to exploring the experiences and actual practices through which upwardly mobile people who do not possess any form of inherited material, social or symbolic capital (see, for example, De Neve 2011; Saavala 2003), and who normally rank low in caste hierarchies (ex-untouchables, 'tribal' *jaatis* and officially labelled OBCs), forge new class-based strategies and identities. As a result of their often more precarious position – mainly as a result of their lack of capital – they have been described as being most keenly involved in the maintenance of their position within the middle class. They have been described as 'actively engaged in the process of social classification, seeking to draw a clear line between themselves and "the poor" and identify themselves as middle-class people without being able to follow the established cultural code of the middle class to the full' (Saavala 2003: 235). Empirical accounts of new middle-class groups highlight their material constraints and anxieties inherent to their position, but also their creative strategies and agency. For example, recent ethnographic accounts have looked at educated lower middle-class Indian men participating in student politics and youth activism as a means of preventing downward mobility, leveraging status and dealing with the social anxiety associated with their class position (Fernandes and Heller 2006; Jeffrey 2010; Jeffrey *et al.* 2008).

Empirical accounts describe their recent ascension and highlight links to specific social and economic transformations. Many of them derive their social and economic position from an advantageous relationship with the state: many have benefited from recent education and job reservations, while others in rural areas benefited from green revolution policies that led to the growth of a rural middle class (Jeffery *et al.* 2011). In Kerala, and other parts of India, migration to work in Persian Gulf countries after the 1970s oil boom has been a central factor allowing families of various less-privileged communities to access middle-class lifestyles and escape local unemployment (Kanna 2010; Osella and Osella 2000; Vora 2008, 2013). These and other phenomena have provided the ground for a broadening and transformation of the notion of middle classness, allowing upwardly mobile communities, new practices and values to enter the middle-class social field (Donner 2011).

Many of the empirical accounts on the middle classes of the last twenty years have focused on the influx of consumer goods, the growing rhetoric of consumerist Indians and emergent patterns of consumption, relating them to the formation of new cultural identities and orientations towards modernity (Liechty 2003; Lukose 2009). With the rising purchasing power and changing patterns of consumption amongst some segments of the population, the new middle classes have become most visible through the consumer-oriented lifestyles that have dramatically appeared in cities across South Asia. Mark Liechty (2003) documents how since Nepal's opening in the 1950, when a popular democratic movement put an end to a century of isolationist rule in Nepal, a new urban population of bureaucrats, service personnel, small business owners and others has worked to create a space between Kathmandu's old and still-privileged elites, and the poor population. He looks at the cultural practices of this new middle class, especially around the consumption of goods and media, and argues that consumption and the narratives and performances around consumer goods and media are amongst the most important cultural processes through which this emerging middle class creates itself as a sociocultural entity. Liechty and others (for example, Donner and De Neve 2011: 11) stress that this does not signal the adoption of new values and practices (for instance, global capitalist consumerism) and the rejection of the old. Middle classness is produced at the confluence of earlier affiliations, values and narratives (for example, narratives of honour and propriety) and new practices and logics (for example, progress and individual achievement). The old and the new are braided into a particular local middle-class cultural life.

Moving beyond the narrow emphasis on consumption, other ethnographies of the middle classes have sought to examine other practices and sites where middle classness is produced, such as the workplace, educational institutions, the urban space and the home (De Neve 2011; Dickey 2000; Donner 2005, 2008a; Fernandes 2006; Fuller and Narasimhan 2006; Jeffrey *et al.* 2008). For example, De Neve (2011) shows how a previously rural business community of now-affluent entrepreneurs in Tiruppur, Tamil Nadu, articulates gender-specific education, employment and marriage strategies that inspire both practices and projects that are commonly seen as typically middle class, and simultaneously values (for example, respectability) and moralities that are caste based and more rural in origin. Similarly, the account of Jeffery *et al.* (2011) traces the strategies deployed by rich Jats to overcome the tension between living in a rural context without the amenities that support middle-class lifestyles and their desire to inhabit an urban, middle-class world. Jats become very active in their quest: moving out of agriculture into white-collar work, giving large dowries to marry their daughters into urban, 'professional' families, and seeking education in urban centres. Based on extensive fieldwork in Calcutta, Henrike Donner's (Donner 2008b) book, *Domestic Goddesses*, also provides an ethnography of new middle classes but from a domestic perspective. Donner shows that in the wake of globalisation and the integration of employment markets into worldwide discourses of skills and mobility, middle-class mothering has been reoriented towards supporting children throughout their education and towards turning children into future white-collared workers for a global economy. Through practices such as sending children from a very early age to English-medium nurseries, speaking English at home – what she called the 'pedagogising' of the home – mothers attempt to enhance the marketable skills acquired in educational institutions (Donner 2006).

These accounts show that a simple look at contemporary India reveals communities and individuals described as middle class differ widely, not just in term of economic position and consumption practices, but also in terms of status and values (Donner 2011: 3). Moreover, they show that over the last few decades there has been a growth in size[11] and a widening[12] of the sort of individuals, families and communities of a moderately prosperous stratum who have gained access to the material lifestyles, the 'objective conditions' (Joshi 2010: xix) that make 'middle classness' possible (Donner and De Neve 2011). The result is that what makes middle classness and who can claim it has become a broader and strongly contested field.

Class, production and education

A central contention in this book is that education is a central cultural dynamic in middle-class cultural life. Since the 1990s, fiscal crisis, the reduction of state expenditure and more recently the official endorsement of privatisation as the most effective means to deliver education have resulted in an increasingly commercialised education sector. In the context of a progressive expansion of private schooling, parental choice has been given wide scope, at the expense of those whose mundane social, economic and political realities obliterates any possible choices. Individuals and groups across India have been shown to use their rising incomes to buy privilege through private schooling for their children, while public sector schooling has become increasingly 'residual'; the children who continue to attend state-funded schools are increasingly those from families who cannot access private institutions (Jeffery 2005; Subrahmanian 2005). The consumption of private schooling has emerged as a key social terrain on which families realise their class identities.

In relation to Kathmandu, Liechty (2003: 212) argues that commercialised education has emerged as not only one of the key commodities by which class membership is asserted but has also become one of the primary institutions around which new class-based communities are formed. He draws from the work of anthropologists of consumption (Miller 1994; for example, Miller and Miller 2005) who are less concerned with the 'objectness' of commodities and the 'moment' of purchase than with their meaning, social use and how they become centres around which new forms of behaviour and identities form (Liechty 2003: 31). In line with such an approach to consumption, Liechty posits that catering to differentiated economic capabilities, commercialised or private schooling generates sentiments in which consumers of education come to consider themselves in terms of their access to power and financial resources or more simply, in terms of their class.

Liechty's account, like many grounded empirical explorations of the middle class in South Asia since the 1990s, has focused primarily on patterns of consumption, relating them to the formation of cultural identities and orientations towards modernity. A recent study of this kind, for instance, has led to the theorisation of new forms of consumer citizenship (Lukose 2009). I concur with the argument that class and consumption are mutually constitutive: to be part of the middle class in twenty-first-century South Asia, and India in particular, is to express oneself through consumption and to construct one's identity as distinct from those class others below through a set of cultural markers that announce one's 'good taste' (Schein 1999). In India, with rising incomes, expanding global links, and the influx of new consumer goods since the opening up of the economy since the late 1980s, the middle class has become most visible through consumer-oriented lifestyles that have dramatically sprouted in Indian cities. The landscapes of cities, such as Bangalore and Hyderabad, have been radically altered by the sudden emergence of apartment buildings and gated communities, lavish shopping malls with multiplex theatres, upscale restaurants and coffee shops, luxury cars and a variety of leisure opportunities catering to the global lifestyles of the 'new rich'; all testifying to the enhanced buying power and the consumerist drive of some segments of the population (Upadhya 2011: 167). The forms of commercialised education with which this book engages are indeed a prime currency of middle-class life. The consumer practices around private schools and entrance coaching centres are amongst the most important cultural processes through which the Kochi middle class is constituted.

In this new context, representations of the middle class in the media as well as those produced by many scholars have been led to overemphasise 'new' consumerist practices as the trope through which all other relationships, including those of the middle class with themselves, with the poor, with the state and globalisation, are discussed and understood (Donner 2011: 9). Consumption has therefore been theorised as the primary mode of cultural production of the middle class, and middle-class practices seem inescapably consumer practice. While paying due attention to the importance of a successful engagement with the economy to the production of middle-class culture – through processes of consumption – this literature has failed to acknowledge the equally important role played by the processes of *production*. To be middle class is as much about expressing oneself through consumption as it is to successfully engage (or aspire to engage) with particular productive roles, turning oneself into particular kinds of producers. It is middle-class people's deep orientation towards the economy as producers that attracts the bulk of my attention in this book.

Seen historically, the longstanding, mutually constitutive relationship between class and production becomes clear. As many scholars have noted, and as I do in Chapter 2, the emergence and consolidation of the middle class can be traced back to the colonial period; a class that established pre-eminence under the post-Independence Nehruvian developmental regime (Fernandes 2000, 2006). The social construction of the 'old' middle class, as it is usually referred to in literature, was fundamentally bound to the 'concrete' base of government and public-sector employment, enabled by English-medium education. Following the liberalisation of the Indian economy, the 'new' middle class locates itself and is dependent on the rapidly expanding private sector and the globalising economy (Upadhya 2011: 168). As Fernandes (2006) argues, this 'new' middle class – not to be mistaken with the new middle classes discussed earlier – is not really new, but is a new image of the middle class as leading the nation under conditions of globalisation. They are an upper section of the middle classes, usually belonging to what I described as the established middle class, consisting primarily of managerial, professional or entrepreneur urban elites that have most benefited from liberalisation (Ganguly-Scrase and Scrase 2001). Ideologically, the 'new' middle class is imbued with the ideal of leading India to become a global economic player, while reinvigorating politics by bringing efficiency and eradicating corruption. The 'old' middle class was imbued with principles of national economic development. Their hegemony has, now and then, performed a wider ideological role: the desire to be middle-class and belong properly to this social group is a powerful aspiration amongst more and more social groups, just as becoming a public servant was a driving desire amongst individuals, social groups and reform movements at the start of the twentieth century. That is, the social and economic base, as well as the ideological and cultural orientations of the middle class have undergone profound transformations to the extent that the middle classes share a common orientation to the economy as producers, and to the extent that becoming a certain kind of producer becomes a primary mode of production, middle class practice is inescapably producer practice. The middle class are those who constantly cultivate and market their 'skills', 'competences' and 'accomplishments' in the capitalist economy and aspire to access the productive roles deemed as garnering greater success, prestige and wealth. As such, middle-class people live in a continuum of different degrees of anxiety/instability or relative certainty depending on their differential access to the economic, social and cultural capital required to access those positions. While social historians have documented the change in social identification that accompanied the emergence of the middle class in western societies as marked by a shift from 'you are what you do' to 'you are what you have', in twenty-first-century South Asia, what one *does* plays a tremendously important role in middle-class life and is a key generative cultural dynamics of middle-class practice.

There are a growing number of studies that examine this dimension of the middle class as doers. An important number of these focus on the 'flagship' industry of India's new economy: the IT industry. The vaunted IT industry has come to be perceived as the quintessential reflection of the 'rise' of India as a global economic player, while the leading IT entrepreneurs have assumed the role of economic, intellectual and ideological leaders amongst the middle classes (Baviskar and Ray 2011; Fuller and Narasimhan 2007; Jeffrey 2010; Upadhya 2011). In turn, the IT industry is perceived as the primordial niche for India's 'new' middle class, depicted as offering opportunities for lucrative employment and rapid social mobility. Simultaneously, the IT industry's marketing depicts itself as a product of middle-class values and enterprise (Gooptu 2013). In this context more and more young people in India, like those in Bangalore described by Nisbett (2013), orient their life and education to secure a place in the IT industry as their ticket to success, inspired by the spectacular global success of a handful of iconic IT individuals and companies. However, most scholars have shown how the industry remains closely tied to pre-existing structures of class and caste: its primary resources are urban, English-educated middle-class, upper-caste youth (see, for example, Fuller and Narasimhan 2006; Upadhya 2011). In addition to contributing to the reproduction of a hegemonic section of the middle class, the IT industry has also been shown to be imbricated in the reconstitution of middle-class culture by contributing to the formation of new kinds of cultural capital. IT companies implement training programmes to mould their workforce into the right shape to function in a global economy by inculcating appropriate cultural styles and global orientation (Upadhya 2008). Recent studies on the middle class, youth, work and media highlight how the Indian middle class relates to economic or productive processes, not primarily as consumers of goods in the market place but as *producers*: professionals (workers) and entrepreneurs.

A focus on education here is crucial, for it places the analysis of middle-class cultural production at the confluence of consumption and production: where consumer practice meets aspirational practice. My aim is to present education as a lens that allows us to open up and historicise our understanding of middle-class cultural practice that provides a more accurate representation of the importance of a successful engagement with the globalised economy, both as consumers and as *producers*. The consumption practices around education are an important means through which families assert and perform their middle-class standing. Most crucially, education is at the centre of particular shared aspirations and strategies of mobility. Middle classness is defined and supported by the success of the family (Béteille 1991) to turn their children into specific kinds of producers, and education is perceived as an alchemy that can produce those results, the single most important factor improving their children's chances for the future. It is an almost mystical commodity that represents the single most important avenue to attaining maximum achiever status.

Youth as sociocultural category, experience and identity

Early anthropological research established adolescence as a topic of anthropological enquiry, as a result of which issues associated with this life stage – rites of passage, courtship and marital costumes and so on – have formed an integral part of anthropological investigation (Bucholtz 2002). Informed by physiological and psychological models of adolescence, as 'not-yet-finished human beings', anthropologists constructed youth primarily *in relation to* adulthood (Nisbett 2007; Schlegel and Barry 1991), emphasising adults' role in guiding young people into full or adult cultural membership (Bucholtz 2002: 529). Building on this early research, subsequent work considered the disruption of traditional socialisation process as a result of globalisation and economic restructuring across the world. The difficulties believed to be endemic to this stage of life, the argument went, became exacerbated in societies undergoing rapid cultural change as fragile young people also faced the tension between tradition and modernity. For example, research on adolescent suicide in the 1980s and 1990s has tended to attribute the high rate of suicide and suicide attempt by young people in some Pacific and Native American societies to cultural changes that disrupt traditional social roles and socialisation processes (Bucholtz 2002: 530). But although recent studies demonstrate that rapid social change need not be experienced as dramatic, unsettling or as a rupture by young people who are as often the agents as well as the experiencers of cultural change (Bucholtz 2002; Jeffrey and McDowell 2004; Skelton and Valentine 1997), the approach to 'adolescence' and 'youth' as a natural and ahistorical life stage, and not a socially constructed category, is still thriving. Going against this grain, this book seeks two objectives: first, to chart the historically specific sociocultural construction of class-based youth and youth culture in post-liberalisation India, and second, to highlight how young people not only experience notions of 'youth', but are also agents contributing to but also contesting their constitution.

Over time, social categories of 'youth' and 'youth culture' have been brought into existence for an array of purposes (see Bucholtz 2002, for examples). As many have noted, the significant political, economic and cultural transformations experienced in India following the reform policies commonly referred to as 'liberalisation', have brought protagonism to 'youth' in ways never seen before. The social category of youth and youth culture has been above any other enlisted to the cause of reconfiguring the way in which the Indian nation in the age of liberalisation and globalisation is imagined. Images of Indian youth as global consumers have been brought to prominence. As work on Mumbai advertising agencies illustrates, with the advent of liberalisation popular representations and media images have placed youth at the heart of 'India's consumerist turn' (Mazzarella 2003). Youth is thought to straightforwardly embody the desire for the globally inflected middle-class consumerist lifestyles and the new forms of labour that enable this consumption (Nisbett 2007: 936). In his analysis of class formation in Nepal, Liechty describes how in capitalist modernity, 'youth' and 'youth culture' have been produced as the vanguard of an emergent middle-class consumer culture. He argues that 'perhaps the most enduring cultural process of youth production has been their constitutions as bearers of middle-class culture' (Liechty 2003: 36).

But more importantly perhaps, media images and campaigns increasingly celebrate youth as the driving force of an emergent, pulsating and 'rising' India, brimming over with optimism and aspirations 'to fly' (Gooptu 2013: 1). Again, a common example used to illustrate this shift has been the highly publicised campaign run by the national daily newspaper *Times of India* in 2007, entitled Lead India (Baviskar and Ray 2011; Gooptu 2013). The aim of the campaign was to rally a particular kind of young Indian to action, to dominate the world, but primarily to direct their talents to the task of public governance, just as they have applied their skills and aptitudes in the private corporate world (Gooptu 2013: 1). Above all, these narratives celebrate the unleashing of new Indians, whose dreams passions and desires are imagined as the drivers of India's economic growth over the last fifteen years, and the redeemers of the corruption-ridden machinery of old India. The protagonist of this new India, it is envisaged, is a particular kind of young person, who is imagined to embody India's newly found confidence and ambition on the global stage (Lukose 2009: 5). An new youthful persona now dominates public imagination, representing ambition, spirit of adventure and individualism, as well as aggressiveness to achieve a desired end; all projected to be fundamental qualities of the new generation of urban youth across India, qualities that makes a direct link between this new generation to economic liberalisation. Chapter 3 examines how this construction of youth gets appropriated by an urban school, while Chapter 4 examines how the narrative of a new Indian youth is brought into being in the domestic realm. Both of these chapters, and the book as a whole, highlight the abysmal gap between the idea of youth presented by the media and the realities and opportunities of most young people in Kochi and India as a whole.

But perhaps more important than charting, the specific sociocultural configuration of youth and youth cultures in any given time and place is to analyse the experiences of young people themselves 'as they navigate the treacherous narrative currents of youth' (Amit-Talai and Wulff 1995; Liechty 2003: 37; Miles 2000; Saldanha 2002). While retaining the concern for the lives of young people in contexts of rapid social and economic change of the anthropology of adolescence, a relatively new and still-small anthropology of youth has emerged that seeks to document how young people forge identities through social and cultural practice, and shape their worlds creatively combining elements of global capitalism, transnationalism and local culture (Bucholtz 2002; Froerer 2009; Gilroy 1991; Hebdige 1979; Nisbett 2009; Rogers 2008). Most of these new anthropologies of young people have been influenced by the work of scholars associated with the Centre for Contemporary Cultural Studies or 'Birmingham School' established at Birmingham University in 1963.

Paul Willis'[13] (1977) *Learning to Labour* has become perhaps the most widely read and most influential critical youth study. Willis (1977) describes how a group of working-class boys, the 'lads', perpetuated their class position in the work arena by taking up an anti-school youth culture. Through cultivating masculine identities that resisted and rejected the distinctively 'middle-class' project of the school, the lads in effect ended up sealing their own fate (Levinson and Holland 1996: 9). However, Willis' contribution lies in how he attributed the eventual reproduction of their working-class position to the lads' everyday practices, their participation in school life (disrupting its smooth functioning) and their creative forging of their own subjectivities. In this way, Willis highlighted the boys' 'cultural production': 'the active and creative use of available symbolic resources in ways shaped by people's structural position' (Jeffrey 2010: 22).

Drawing on the Birmingham School, the new anthropology of youth has sought to engage with youth not as phase of life, but as identity, not in the sense of popular psychological formulations of adolescence as a prolonged 'search for identity', but rather, 'identity as agentive, flexible and ever-changing, but no more for youth than for people of any age' (Bucholtz 2002: 532). Although the study of adolescence in general focuses on how bodies and minds are moulded for adult futures, the study of youth puts emphasis on the 'here-and-now of young people's experience, the social and cultural practices through which they shape their worlds' (Bucholtz 2002: 532).

Lukose (2005, 2009) offers a nuanced analysis of the ways in which youth apprehend globally-inflected consumption practices and discourses. In her article *Consuming Globalization*, Lukose (2005) shows the different relationships that young Kerala men and women have with new globally inflected consumer spaces. She demonstrates how lower-caste/class young men engage with the consumption of new commodities (i.e. motorbikes and jeans) as a site of agency, desire and self-fashioning according to the idea of *chethu*, understood as a masculine, fun-loving, consumer identity. Unlike idealised images of the new Indian youth bursting with ambitions about the future, *chetu* identity is located in the here-and-now and is marked by the explicit rejection of the future, unburdened by a sense of the past (Lukose 2005: 931). In the same way, she outlines how a new middle-class female consumer identity that is aggressively sexual, confident in public and interested in fashion shows, modelling and beauty pageants, sits in tension with the demands on young women to navigate consumption respectably and modestly (Lukose 2005: 931). In other words, she argues that the variety of new consumer identities youth is producing can only be understood in conjunction with long-standing preoccupations/orientations (for example, ideas of modesty) and through a close look at intersecting categories of distinction (such as caste and class). How low-class/caste men refashion themselves through the desire for globally inflected commodities is not simply an index of globalisation but the reflection of a novel consumer identity that reveals the specificity of the location out of which this desire emerges (Lukose 2005: 926).

The contribution of this sort of research that documents the way in which consumption allows youth to forge new identities is crucial for situating globalisation within long-standing histories of the production of notions of modernity[14] around the world, which is in turn crucial to interrogating claims about new-ness, homogenisation and cultural force that the discourse of globalisation itself produces. However, in privileging consumption in the analysis of youth cultures, these works have failed to give enough importance to other crucial dimensions of young people's identities. Their concern for highly visible styles and with symbolic representations of identity, manifested in their emphasis on media images, inevitably enforces the view of youth cultures as heavily dependent on consumption. Current debates within the anthropology of the middle class have begun to question the key role according to practices of consumption within the self-definition of the middle class and 'by implication, the idea of a youth vanguard leading the way in defining middle-class identity through their practices of consumption' (Nisbett 2007: 936). These accounts highlight the deployment of moral narratives as a central practice generative of middle-class youth subjectivities (Nisbett 2007; van Wessel 2004).

Responding to calls for research on how neoliberal social and economic change are transforming the experiences of youth and early adulthoods in many part of the world, an important body of research has emerged and argued that young people's lives in many postcolonial contexts is the progressively uncertain nature of youth transitions into adult life.[15] A time when ideas of fully fledged adulthood strongly linked to economic wealth, consumption, education and white-collar employment have gained in prominence in the projects and aspirations of young people and their parents, and access to formal education has extended to previously marginalised populations (Osella and Osella 1999), has coincided with a rapid decline and deterioration of opportunities for salaried work across social groups and classes (Jeffrey *et al.* 2004). Anthropological research on youth transitions to adult futures has thus focused on the various ways in which youth navigate and manage these terrains of uncertainty with the cultivation of distinctive identities and strategies. Within the Indian context, research has demonstrated how in the face of poor occupational outcomes, educated unemployed or underemployed young men embrace education and construct educated identities 'that provide young people and their families the political purchase in ongoing struggles to critique entrenched social prejudices' (Jeffrey and McDowell 2004: 138). Jeffrey *et al.* (2004) show how Muslim and Dalit young men have reacted to their exclusion from secure white-collar occupations by embracing education as a form of embodied cultural distinction. This cultural production of educated identities is dependent on their capacity to find work (often precarious and temporary) within the informal economy, allowing them to craft and maintain an identity of 'educated people in transition'.[16] Even though education fails to provide opportunities for secure employment, youth and their families' engagement with the cultural production of the educated person in western Uttar Pradesh has become a type of discursive 'scaffold' upon which Muslim and Dalit young men and many of their parents display their ideas about knowledge, comportment, morality and respect (Jeffrey *et al.* 2004). In his recent monograph, *Timepass*, Jeffrey (2010) examines the practices and experiences of unemployed young men engaged in forms of waiting, which despite characterising themselves as being lost in time and their activities as simply aimless 'timepass', offered opportunities to acquire skills, fashion, new cultural styles and mobilise politically, which in turn allowed them to maintain their identity of people in transition. These studies stress the potential of young people to strategise and response inventively to educated unemployment or underemployment and highly uncertain transitions to adulthood, even in the most adverse circumstances. However, they also remain sensitive to the resilient inequalities that shape young people's strategies and trajectories, and receptive to the possibility that these may, at times, be better explained in terms of Bourdieu's ideas of cultural capital, social capital and habitus (Jeffrey *et al.* 2008: 15).

Theorising education and schooled youth

Critical educational or schooling studies have long been characterised by a concern with social difference and inequality (Levinson *et al.* 1996). From its beginnings in the 1970s until today, the durability of class power has remained a central concern as class continues to structure young people's experiences of school, as well as post-school education, and the search for work (Jeffrey and McDowell 2004). In the first wave of critical studies of schooling, which emerged in the 1970s, scholars such as Althusser (1971), Apple (1979) and Young (1971) moved away from accounts that assumed schools to be 'meritocratic springboards for upward mobility' of the previous decades (Levinson and Holland 1996). Instead, their accounts documented the ways in which schools served to reproduce rather than undermine existing structural class inequalities in capitalist economies by responding to the requirements of discipline and conformity demanded by capitalism and the nation-state (Levinson and Holland 1996: 5).

Significantly adding to early theories of social reproduction, subsequent studies, mainly drawing from the work of Pierre Bourdieu and his associates, turned their attention to the cultural basis of class privilege. In his analysis of French schools (as a particular field of play), Bourdieu suggested that educational institutions only recognised as signs of 'intelligence' the particular tastes, bodily comportment and skills possessed by elite classes, and thus automatically gave greater currency and legitimacy to their actions (Bourdieu and Passeron 1990; Levinson and Holland 1996). In turn, 'imbued with the cultural capital recognised, examined and re-warded within schools, and drawing also on their wealth and social contacts, the upper and middle class are typically able to manipulate the education system so as to reproduce their advantage in the next generation' (Jeffrey and McDowell 2004). Thus, for the elites and the middle classes, cultural capital was more easily convert-ible to economic capital through advanced academic credentials, or by helping them face interviews or secure loans.

Consequently, while they may be able to acquire some of the legitimised styles and competences, those of lower social standing, according to Bourdieu, inevitably become targets of a kind of 'symbolic violence'. As their cultural-linguistic resources fail to match those valued, legitimised and rewarded in school, people of lower social standing develop a sense of their social position, and of the relatively debased value of their own cultural resources. As a consequence, non-elite youth also tend to develop 'a sense of their own social limits' (Levinson and Holland 1996). As these limits become habitus, they will also learn to self-censor and self-silence in the company of, and in institutional settings that give value and legitimacy to the cultural resources of, those with greater social standing (Levinson and Holland 1996: 6). On the contrary, people with a habitus attuned to the edu-cational field will know by intuition and navigate the field instantaneously with ease and with the confidence that comes with being able to succeed routinely within it and other spheres of social competition (Jeffrey 2010: 20). That internalised sense of self-confidence, which in India is inevitably caste informed, has been shown to be of high importance when it comes to accessing sought-after salaried jobs (for example, in IT companies), even greater than the educational qualifi-cations themselves (Fuller and Narasimhan 2006). As Jeffrey (2010: 20) notes, Bourdieu also wrote of how a sense of timing is also woven into people's ability, or lack of, to navigate fields of power on an everyday basis. The field of education requires the ability to micro-manage in order to act in a timely way according to daily routines, studying schedules, deadlines, application procedures, examinations and so on.

Although Bourdieuian reproduction theories constitute the foundation of most anthropological research on education carried out today, including this thesis, recent research tends to combine an exploration of schools as an instrument of control with an appreciation for human creativity or change (Jeffrey 2010; Levinson *et al.* 1996).

Since the 1980s, approaches to schooling have sought to grasp the complex relation between processes of social and cultural reproduction and young people's cultural production. Specifically, the focus has shifted towards a concern for the everyday practices through which young people creatively occupy the space of education and schooling, and hence confront the larger societal forces and structures instantiated in them. As with youth cultures studies, with the influence of feminism and race studies scholars have also moved away from an emphasis on class relations as a privilege lens in the critical analysis of schools and as the main/sole social division that structures young people's experiences of school. Instead, they consider the complex intersections of class, gender, caste and age structures (Gilroy 1991). Likewise, since the 1980s, there has been a rapid increase in the number of scholars applying the notions of reproduction and cultural production in postcolonial contexts to the study of schooling and inequalities (Levinson 1999; Oni 1988).

In South Asia, and more specifically in India, the notion of cultural production has only marginally been picked up in recent studies on schooled youth. Explorations of youth within school environments have remained focused, to a large extent, on how educational institutions shape young mind and bodies, most of the time leaving out students' experience and perspectives. Scholars have tended to concentrate on the disciplinary dimension in the daily operation of institutions. They have looked at both the visible (and at times violent) and the more subtle practices by which students' verbal and bodily languages are transformed to comply with the norms of institutions and with particular lifestyles and modes of behaviour seen as more desirable and as garnering greater prestige and opportunity (Caddell 2005: 77). This disciplining entails not just the imbibing of knowledge but also the embodying of social and moral values. MacDougall (2005), for example, shows how the school space and the practices within it attune elite boys in Dehra Doon to the school's ethos of egalitarianism, secularism, rationality and self-discipline, while teaching them to conform to the age hierarchy that enables older boys to exert power over their juniors. By the end of the 1990s, the production of particular types of citizenships/national identities have become the main paradigm for the study of schools and the young people within (Srivastava 1998). A large strand of anthropological research has thus focused on the relationship between education and (Hindu) nationalism, specifically on the role played by schools in nationalist projects as sites for the manufacturing of the 'ideal' citizen for the modern post-colonial state (Benei 2008; Caddell 2005; Crook 1996; Froerer 2007; Kumar and Oesterheld 2007; Srivastava 1998). They have endeavoured to show how schools, more than 'innocent' sites of cultural transmission, are sites geared towards the reproduction of discipline and conformity demanded by the nation-state (Froerer 2007: 1038). Reproduction theory here has been put to work with reference to the nationalist projects wherein schools were thought as serving to 'inculcate the skills, subjectivities and disciplines that underpin the modern nation-state' (Levinson *et al.* 1996: 1). For example, Caddell's work demonstrates how 'national education' in Nepal has endorsed particular visions of the nation state and the 'Nepali citizen' that have benefited a particular group within Nepal, whose culture and lifestyles have become aspirational models for all (Caddell 2005, 2006). Srivastava (1998) has focused on the Indian public school as a central site for the construction of urban post-colonial identity. Specifically he shows how the Doon School has produced generations of post-independence middle-class boys who embody the modernist, all-conquering national character the school transmitted.

However, as Levinson and Holland (1996) note, educational institutions cannot simply be assumed to shape and discipline youth into particular models of the 'ideal' person. This is not to deny that schools are powerful institutions that hegemonic groups (or the state) often utilise to form and promote certain kinds of subjectivities (Levinson and Holland 1996: 24). Indeed 'the historically specific models of the "educated person" encouraged in schools often represent the subjectivities which dominant groups endorse', which then must seem appealing to broader demands (Levinson and Holland 1996: 24). Following Levinson and Holland's framework, schools and other institutions should be understood as 'contradictory resources' (1996: 1) and sites of cultural production in which the practices of various actors may accommodate, undermine or otherwise partially adapt to the dominant school project. Schools should be understood not only as sites of reproduction but also of creativity. In schools, young people and their families may seek to assert influence over others, enhance their status and gain access to new resources (Caddell 2005). Schools are also sites where the young socialise with each other (Merten 1999) and where important social connections/alliances are developed (Jeffrey and McDowell 2004: 139). One must not lose sight of how young people's perception of the school projects they inhabit may render these same projects useless. Peggy Froerer's (2007) article, *Disciplining the Saffron Way*, explores the disciplinary apparatus at a Rashtriya Swayamsevak Sangh (RSS) school, which aims to draw pupils into the project of Hindu nationalism. Froerer's exploration of children's experiences of the school's regime demonstrates how students' views 'hail[ed] the disciplinary enterprise more as an effective vehicle for inculcating success in educational terms than for inculcating a sense of superiority over and hatred of minority communities' (Froerer 2007: 1037).

Accounts more attuned to educational spaces as sites of cultural production recognise that education takes place in multiple, competing arenas (Jeffery 2005; Levinson *et al.* 1996). These offer valuations of knowledge, skills and attitudes alternative to those given in schools, which then work as cultural resources creatively used by young people in any given educational site. The peer group and the home are two such arenas where education takes place (Jeffery 2005). In other words, rather than being shaped by one monolithic educational institution, young people navigate a variety of educational sites that both shape, and are shaped in response, by youth's creative practices and discourses. Sometimes educational sites support each other's priorities and values; sometimes they run counter to each other. Within these, young people's creative agency works both within and against institutional projects.

Two schools, two sites

This study is based on research in and around two schools in two interlinked sites: Kochi, the economic capital of Kerala and the primary location to this study, and Kothad, an islet in the backwaters in the northern outskirts of the city. According to the 2001 census, the urban agglomeration of Kochi has a population of 1,355,972 people. It is the largest urban agglomeration in Kerala and the capital of the district (Ernakulam District[17]) with the highest urban population in Kerala: 68 per cent (Government of Kerala 2010). In Kerala, Kochi is touted as the state's 'symbol of progress and promise of prosperity'. Aspirations to transform Kochi into a hub of global trade and tourism and a rival to established South Indian metros are high (Shaw and Satish 2007). These dreams find anchor in numerous projects aimed at transforming the city, such as the Vallarpadam terminal, Infopark, the Smartcity and the Kochi Metro. The linkages between local notions of prosperity and modernity and Kochi are not new. In the following section I highlight how Kochi has been characterised as a space of modernity and progress.

Mulavukad, Kadamakkudi, Cheranellur, Kumbalangi, Edakochi and Vallarpadam are some of the islands that dot the backwaters surrounding Kochi. These low and swampy islands, formed by the deposit of alluvium brought down by the rivers during the monsoons, have favoured the growth of coconut palms and pokily rice. Over the last five decades the local economy has benefited from the emergence of prawn fishing as a lucrative business. Kothad, the second site of this study, is the main village of the Kadamakkudi *grama panchayat*,[18] with the majority of its 21,000 inhabitants. The population in Kothad belongs mostly to the Latin Catholic (inland) fishing community, with the exception of a few low-caste Hindu fishing families. A number of studies have shown how fishing communities have remained separate from the mainstream population socially and geographically, reproducing inequality and marginalisation of the fisherfolk over time[19] (George and Domi 2002: 16; Hoeppe 2007; Klausen 1968; Ram 1991). In the realm of education, a field that has been the hallmark of dominant accounts of Kerala's social advancement, fishing communities also lag behind as a result of a number of constraints such as family background, income and inadequacy of political mobilisation. Government reports also show how the percentage of the population below the poverty line is higher in the coastal areas, whereas fisherfolk constitute a major share of the population (Government of Kerala 2010). Kothad, laying so close to the state's main economic node, is no exception to these trends. However, as I will show in Chapter 6, these exclusionary trends have been altered as a result of the construction of a bridge linking Kothad to Kochi. Instead of undermining a long history of marginalisation, the bridge has entrenched the feeling of alienation amongst the people of Kothad.

A brief history of the port city

The story of Kochi is best understood as the story of a port city. The emergence of Kochi is attributed to the great floods of the river Periyar in 1341, forming a wide harbour, which by the beginning of the fifteenth century began to be frequented by merchant ships. Throughout the fifteenth century, commercial activities were vibrant, especially between Kochi and China. In 1409 Chinese merchant Ma Huan wrote of ships from Arabia and Persia frequently casting anchor in the port of Kochi (Malekandathil 2001: 32). By the mid-fifteenth century, the port had been incorporated into the exchange systems of South East Asia and had established trade activities with the Persian Gulf and the ports of the Red Sea. Christian and later Jewish merchants also shifted to Kochi. Around the port of Kochi an urban centre developed, which though it raised a serious challenge to the port of Calicut to the north, could not rise up to the level of the Zamorin's port all through the pre-Portuguese phase (Malekandathil 2001: 33).

With the arrival of the Portuguese in the sixteenth century, Kochi acquired a prime position as the economic and political centre of the Malabar Coast, not without continuous clashes with Calicut. This period of Portuguese domination was perhaps the most influential in Kochi's history, shaping to a large extent the character of the city. Kochi was never a territory 'conquered' by the Portuguese, who built a seaborne empire based on inter-dependency with the hinterland and the King of Kochi. At sea, two important features were introduced by the Portuguese. First, the Portuguese introduced the new Euro-Asian trade relations, different from the Asian trade routes dominated by Muslim merchants. The new trade route to Europe required a much larger investment and risk, but procured spectacular profit, which was ruthlessly protected at sea. Second, they introduced a system of permits that controlled the movement of native ships and merchants (Das Gupta 2001: 424). As the system gradually unfolded, trade declined in Calicut (Das Gupta 2001: 426). The Portuguese established control over the pepper trade inland and off the Malabar coast (Das Gupta 2001; Malekandathil 2001; Osella and Osella 2007).

In the hinterlands, this was achieved through an expanding access to an increasing number of cultivators, mainly St Thomas Christians. The Portuguese never actually controlled the hinterlands; these were integrated into the city of Kochi only insofar as they enjoyed some advantages and had their interests protected (Malekandathil 2001: 286). In spite of some clashes between the hinterlands and the Portuguese, the extraction of produce was normally carried out peacefully. There was an equal synergy and reciprocity between the king of Kochi and the Portuguese, as the former had a sense of indebtedness to the Portuguese for freeing them of the Zamorin. In the city, the rising Christian population (as a result of conversions, immigration and the marriages between Portuguese and local women) and the great influence of the various church institutions, gave Kochi a distinctively Christian character, with these institutions acting as cohesive and integrating forces in the city. In the urban society of Kochi, the European clergy took the topmost position, followed by the local clergy. Amongst the 'common' people the social hierarchy was differentiated on the basis of religion (with Christians at the top), profession and the ownership of wealth. Kochi's Christian loyalties and its functioning as an international commercial port (Christian's mercantile and commercial spirit), gave the city its particular orientation to the outside world, very much alive today in the tropes of progress previously described.

Subsequently, the Dutch East India Company began dispatching ships to compete with the mercantile economy of Portugal. Portuguese Kochi was conquered by the Dutch in 1663. The synergic relationship between Kochi's locals and the Portuguese disappeared. After winning their fight, the Dutch tried to keep alive the system of tariffs and the compulsory and exclusive delivery of pepper introduced by the Portuguese. However, by the middle of the eighteenth century, their lack of naval policing and the increasing non-compliance of native merchants resulted in the breaking down of the trade system established by the Portuguese. With the effective establishment of the Dutch, Calicut experienced a revival, only as an export centre for local products and an entry point for goods from West Asia and North India (Das Gupta 2001; Osella and Osella 2007). By the end of the eighteenth century the Dutch had abandoned Malabar, leaving the field to the British East India Company.

Although not in direct rule as in Malabar, the British Resident extended his tutelage over the Kingdom of Kochi and the city's port by the turn of the nineteenth century. However, never before, nor afterwards under the control of European powers, could the city of Kochi regain the commercial importance that it had acquired under the Portuguese (Malekandathil 2001: 283). During the British period, Kochi was reduced to a rather insignificant satellite port city, as the main British interests rested in Madras, Bombay and Calcutta (Lemercinier and Rendel 1983; Malekandathil 2001). It was not until well into the twentieth century that the British saw the need to expand the port. In the 1920s Sir Robert Bristow led the transformation of the port into a modern port with a safe inner harbour. In 1928 the new port was completed, augmenting the value of the city to colonial rule and the value of port and the economic activities associated with it as one of the major economic pillars of the region. These developments also allowed Kochi to become an important military base. Since the 1930s the Southern Naval Command, a major unit of the Royal Indian Navy, has been based in Kochi's Wellington Island, where most of the Indian Navy's training programmes are carried out (Dimesh Mani n.d.).

After Independence the port was taken over by the Government of India. At the heart of the post-independence plans for state-owned and state-controlled economic growth laid stringent policies of import substitution pursued until the mid-1980s. These entailed an elaborate system of tariffs, licenses and other regulations that kept most imports out, hence undermining the already peripheral trade in Kochi. After Independence, the shipbuilding industry received important incentives. In line with Nehru's socialist vision, development and progress were to come from large state-owned industrial complexes: dams, power plants, steel plants and the large, modern cities to accompany them. In 1976 (long after Independence), the central government launched one of India's major public-sector undertakings[20] in the shipbuilding sector: the Cochin Shipyard Limited (CSL). CSL, a landmark in the city, was one of the largest employers in the city and continues to act as a reference point in terms of employment and social mobility amongst various social groups.

The full-blown embrace of liberalisation reforms in the 1990s translated in a complete rethinking of post-Independence Kochi within the economic aspirations of India in the global era. Instead of large public sector industries, transport infrastructure – especially that directly affecting Indian exporters' competitiveness in the global market – became understood as the backbone of the nation's economy and the most critical elements of economic liberalisation strategies of countries throughout the world (Government of Kerala 2010). The Indian government began to accord high priority to investment in sectors such as railways, power, ports and airports. Within this context, there has been an attempt to awaken Kochi from the commercial lethargy of the pre-liberalisation era, and to revive and reimagine the city. Specifically, 1990 saw the gradual development of a project to turn Kochi Port into a major hub in the Indian Ocean region. The new terminal – the Vallarpadam International Container Transhipment Terminal (ICTT) – was built to reduce India's dependence on neighbouring hub ports[21] to haul container cargo. This time, in line with the new neoliberal vision, the state was no longer to take sole responsibility for this transformation. The government signed a public–private partnership (PPP) with Dubai Port World for the execution of the project. After substantial delays, in 2011 Vallarpadam became India's first hub port, raising great expectations about the development of the city.

In addition, the last decade saw the emergence of Kochi as an important tourist destination for international luxury cruises. The port, in all of its dimensions, has become the axis of the post-liberalisation Kerala dream: achieving what is locally referred to as 'international standard'. In 2004, the government's magazine, *Kerala Calling*, wrote 'the possibilities are mind boggling and it suffices to point out the example of Singapore,[22] which thrived to the status of a developed nation thanks mainly to its port'. This desire to 'become like Singapore', has already been used as an aspirational reference in South Indian cities such as Bangalore (Nisbett 2009). Like in Bangalore, middle-class and NRIs[23] are particularly keen in this desire to transform the city and to 'lift' it to 'international standards'. Amongst them, civic action initiatives to achieve this goal, mainly through campaigns aimed, quite literally, at cleaning the streets and taking up 'proper' waste management[24] (for the eyes of the globally connected middle-class and foreign visitors). During fieldwork there was a campaign dubbed 'Green Kochi' aimed at making city dwellers aware of the need to rid the city of rubbish. Even the neighbours of the middle-class residential area where I was staying formed a cooperative to teach residents how to separate home waste so as to recycle it, despite the lack of recycling facilities.

Simultaneously, the state government and the city's development authorities have been keen in trying to keep up with developments in other areas of the economy, especially the IT industry. Since its inception in 2004, Kochi's IT park – Infopark Kerala – has been rapidly growing and has attracted investments from IT companies such as Tata Consultancy Services, Wipro, Affiliated Computer Services, OPI Global, IBS Software Services and US Technology. As Nisbett (2009) notes, contemporary images of Kochi portray it as a serious rival to Bangalore as a place for ITES/BPO (information technology enabled services/

business process outsourcing) services, thanks to its large number of unemployed and highly educated English-speaking graduates. Here too, expectations are flying high. A state government manuscript about the city reads: 'Kochi is poised for a big leap forward in all the sunrise industries such as Information Technology, Bio-Technology and Tourism, and also in areas like Multi Model Transport Linkages, IT Connectivity and Bandwidth Commercial Track Record' (Dimesh Mani n.d.). This demonstrates the extent to which the IT industry dominates Indian ideas of progress, in which not only the phenomenal success of Indian software companies such as Infosys Technologies, but also the everyday lives of the 'new-rich' middle class in urban India, i.e. the 'knowledge professionals', are envisaged as 'the engine that can drive India's take off and transform our country' (Fuller and Narasimhan 2007: 123). Large numbers of young people in Kochi aspire to become employed in the local IT park, but still creeping under the shadow of reputed 'metros' such as Bangalore, Kochi's 'metro' status is still very much a matter of debate.

There is a broader and more mundane dimension to the reimagining of Kochi as Kerala's emergent metro. But if there is footing that grounds local images of Kochi as an emerging 'metro' of 'international standard', it is the growing choice of cafes, restaurants, bars, cinemas, shopping malls, supermarkets and high-rise luxury apartment buildings. As I show throughout the book, private schools also attempt to project international standard. One of the areas that most clearly symbolises the reputation of a fast emerging metro is the neighbourhood where I conducted the core of my research, the residential area that I call Kumar Nagar. The now-crowded area of Kumar Nagar was once barren and muddy land where the first colonies in Kochi were built. In the mid-1970s, some of the earliest residents of the area remember taking their children to school through what they described as a swamp dotted with a few houses. In the late 1970s, Kumar Nagar was a purely residential area consisting of the 'lower-income group' (LIG) colony and the Central Government Quarters (Kochi Shipyard Ltd., BSNL and navy quarters amongst other). These were meant to house the military and the labour force of the city's public sector offices and industries. Soon the area gave way to 'middle- and high-income group' housing colonies (MIG and HIG respectively), meant to accommodate professionals such as doctors, advocates and businessmen. As the city developed, the cost of land and housing rose sharply. Today, an LIG house costs around Rs22 lakh.[25] Most of them are no longer occupied by their original owners and are now owned by high-income professionals; Kumar Nagar is now one of the most expensive neighbourhoods in the city. No longer a residential area alone, the neighbourhood now houses the offices of various private companies, banks, doctors, advocates, consultants, beauty salons, expensive cafes, as well as the regional passport office. In addition, the neighbourhood houses a rapidly increasing number of gated apartment complexes. Many of these are constructed by Kerala's number one building company, Skyline, whose slogan 'the address says it all' appeals to many of the area's growing middle-class population. BVM, the school where I conducted a large portion of the research, is located in the heart of this neighbourhood.

Research methods

A recent paper on the state of education in Kerala suggested that over the last two decades the education system has shifted from an inclusive system to an exclusive one, primarily as a result of the growth of the private schooling sector. The paper described the changes in the schooling landscape as almost tectonic in scale, depicting at one extreme the (righteous) state sponsored system, and at the other, the (immoral) private sector. The authors conclude that this gap would inevitably produce two distinct kinds of youth, which would inevitably lead to the collapse of Kerala's social fabric and values. They argued:

> At the school level, *a new generation of students* who have little knowledge of the local language, literature, culture, history and even geography is emerging in the state. They are *a socially disengaged* lot insulated from the Kerala society. The concept of neighbourhood schools is now at a discount as students are transported over long distances. These students are disconnected from their neighbourhood and lack local community identity and feelings. Two classes of students seem to be emerging in the state and in each locality with very little opportunities for interaction with each other. Most of the students in the unaided [private] schools come from more or less similar socio-economic backgrounds. Without the physical proximity of and social interaction with the under privileged, which were provided by public institutions like government and government aided schools, the middle class in Kerala can never again hope to vocalize the genuine aspirations of the less privileged. They no more are effective participants of public action. Long-term consequences of the recent developments in education on Kerala society have not yet been understood and therefore are not yet part of the political discourse in the state.
>
> (Kumar and George 2009: 15)

This prompted my decision to carry out fieldwork across this 'gap'; research that would attempt to interrogate these alleged transformations. I decided to conduct fieldwork that focused on the lives of two groups of schooled youth: one in an aided school and another in an unaided school.

As previously explained, the research was conducted on two sites. The study, however, was anchored in Kochi, where my wife and I lived in a two-bedroom flat in a middle-class neighbourhood. At each location, I concentrated on the students of two schools. In urban Kochi, I focused on the everyday lives of a group of higher secondary students schooled at BVM in Kumar Nagar, a private school. In Kothad, I concentrated on a similar group of higher secondary pupils schooled at the Higher Secondary School of Jesus (HSS of Jesus), a government-aided school. As frequently happens in fieldwork, I came to this particular site by a mixture of luck and chance, rather than through any rigorous process of selection; I had originally planned to anchor the research on two adjacent schools, but ended up travelling by bus on a weekly basis to the aided school to which I managed to gain access.

My fieldwork was not limited to schools: the sheer complexity of youth's everyday experiences – sometimes attending school, entrance coaching, school tuition classes, hanging out with friends, and spending leisure and studying time at home in a single day –made it quintessential not to limit the project to an 'in-school' ethnography. I sought to explore a comprehensive collection of research sites that more or less captured the intricacy of young people's experiences, with special emphasis on those around education. My work in schools could be thought of as the launch pad, which facilitated my entry into a number of key research locations, and most importantly, enabled me to build lasting relationships and friendships with a number of young people.

Conducting ethnographic research in and around schools is perhaps one of the most delicate tasks an anthropologist can undertake. Managements, families, communities, the state and society at large have so much at stake in the unperturbed running of educational institutions that for an outsider these may seem more like fortresses. I started a round of meetings with various school managements, to present myself, the study and my proposed methodology. Prior to these encounters I also found myself concerned with the ethical dimension of my role within schools: how to conduct research while remaining loyal to the needs of pupils within specific institutional settings and times.[26] Trusting my judgement, conscience and the phronesis (Colnerud 2006: 371) derived from my previous experience in the field of education in South India,[27] I proposed, as my core in-school role, to conduct a series of weekly discussion sessions and workshops that would provide a learning experience for pupils – in the form of weekly meaningful and exciting debates – and an insightful research tool.

As I had foreseen, my participation in the schools' everyday life and inter-action with students, especially the twelfth standards (year 12), became the main issue of concern when I first introduced the project to school officials.[28] However, both BVM and HHS of Jesus were welcoming. The sessions were conducted over the first four months of fieldwork each lasting between forty-five minutes and one and a half hours. At HSS of Jesus the sessions took place in regular classrooms with the assistance of one teacher who helped me communicate in Malayalam when it was necessary. In BVM the sessions started being conducted entirely in English, in a small auditorium that the school used for special events, but were then relocated to regular classrooms. One or two teachers audited the first few sessions, but after that they were held without teachers present. Some of the discussion sessions focused on topics such as preparing for board exam-inations, career choices, overseas studies and English communication. The discussion sessions also served as an arena in which students brought forward other topics of their own interest in order to be discussed. Finally, apart from providing a space for voicing and developing opinions, these sessions turned into a complex research tool, which allowed me to explore peer group dynamics. In both schools, I also audited a few classes and participated in all sorts of festive days, special events and competitions.

As the weeks passed, relationships with a number of youth started to crystallise. This enabled the research to move out of the school and into other spaces of enquiry. Method-wise, the single biggest challenge of this project was to work 'within' a variety of educational institutions, while also working 'around' them in space where young people spend time amongst friends. This entailed a delicate balancing of 'formal' and 'informal' roles, putting myself in an inevitably ambiguous position. In order to establish a more egalitarian connection with the young people involved in the research, I actively tried to dissociate myself from teachers, for example, by asking students to avoid calling me 'Sir' and systematically limiting my interaction with teachers.

As rapport grew with a number of youth they granted me access to out-of-school practices and spaces shared by different groups of peers. The walks home at the end of each school day became, quite literally, a central practice that enabled this access and contributed hugely to bridging the gap between young people and me in the early stage of fieldwork. The walk from BVM actually took me home, whereas in Kothad, the walk led to a bus stand, from which the majority of students and I rode the bus into the city. The walks opened up the door to other spaces such as the local *chaat* centre, tea shops, the cyber cafe, the regional sports centre or simply the streets surrounding the school where my friends and informants spent their limited spare time. In those places, we spoke casually about all sorts of issues, such as school politics, groups in schools, football, bikes and *lines* (love relationships). Contact with students opened up 'non-physical' spaces of enquiry, such as social networking websites (for example, Orkut and Facebook) and mobile text messaging (Leander and McKim 2003). Interweaving enquiry in these multiple locations allowed me to collect the necessary data to draw a more coherent and comprehensive picture of the lives of the youth participating in the study.

Despite the success in connecting with informants on a more equal ground, the ambiguity of my role never fully dissipated. Several months into the research, as I walked out of BVM accompanied by a key informant, Jacob, who gave me an insightful look into the work I had done so far in trying to be 'like a peer' outside institutions and a researcher/teacher inside them. Jacob said:

> You should like, get more interaction with the teachers ... they barely know you ... and to be completely honest with you, to them you are more of an annoyance than a blessing. You should start strengthening those ties. You should start with the English teachers, and then the subject teachers that are not as good in English ... You are not a student, and yet you are more of a student than a teacher [pointing with his finger at us, a group of students and me]. But officially you're officially a teacher. I mean, you are part of the staff now.

I reminded Jacob that I did not want to be thought as a teacher, to which he replied: 'yes definitely, and you have done so well ... otherwise you wouldn't feel so close to us, well' (he pauses) 'you would feel close to us, but we wouldn't feel so close to you ... But you should not miss on that, you should strengthen those bonds with the teachers'. The contradictions teeming in Jacob's advice point to the challenges and limitations of studies of this kind. They also signal one of the pitfalls of this particular project: the lack of depth as far as the teachers' point of view is concerned.

As my relationship with a group of students grew stronger, invitations to visit their homes to meet their families rapidly grew in number. Throughout the last six months of field research I visited more than twenty houses of informants both in Kochi and Kothad. Through these visits I was able to extensively converse with participants' parents, sisters, brothers and sometimes grandparents. In Kothad, I was always accompanied by a research assistant who helped me translate and take notes. Through semi-structured interviews, these encounters helped me collect families' educational and occupational stories as well as parents' opinions on a number of issues that emerged during the conversations, such as campus politics, entrance coaching institutions, the importance of English communication skills, marriage and dowry practices. Rapport with students and the backing of schools and parents also facilitated the opening of other off-school spaces for further enquiry, such as entrance coaching centres and school tuition centres, where I interviewed coaching instructors and managers.

Household visits also allowed me to correct to some degree the marked gender imbalance of the data being gathered. Although my work within schools involved equally boys and girls, the information gathered from spending time amongst students outside educational institutions was turning the project into an ethnographic study of male youth as I was spending time almost always with boys alone. During household visits I was able to converse with female informants unchecked by the institutional setting and peers' presence (although in the presence of parents). Conversations with female informants in the household space did render a different register to that gathered in schools.

In order to give a broader background to the information elicited from particular participants, I conducted two small sociological surveys of the neighbourhood in which they lived. In each location, I surveyed sixty households. For the survey, I developed a questionnaire designed to collect quantitative and qualitative information on four major topics: family/community, education, employment/assets/income and migration. Surveys have helped me locate my informants within a wider sociocultural context. In the family/community section I was particularly interested in tracing changes in family size and composition. The education section of the questionnaire was designed to collect the educational backgrounds of families across three generations. This has been key in tracing changes and continuities of practices and ideas of education through time. This section also gathered data on school choices across gender. The employment/assets/income section of the survey gathered information about families' occupational backgrounds in the last three generations. It collected data on various socioeconomic indicators such as reported monthly income, consumer assets, house ownership and ownership of other properties. Similarly, this section gathered information on household expenditure on education in the form of school or college fees, school or college 'donations', entrance coaching fees and school tuition charges. Finally, in the migration section of the questionnaire I collected data on periods of migration of household members.

Notes

1　For an overview of the patters and implications of private supplementary tutoring, see Bray (2006).
2　I also draw inspiration from Upadhya (1997), who examined the social and cultural aspects of class formation in coastal Andhra Pradesh.
3　For a recent article written in this language, see Alves *et al.* (1991).
4　For a review of urban anthropology see Sanjek (1990).
5　Since the 1990s, a deep fiscal crisis in Kerala has meant that the share of expenditure is under strain; the component of aided schools consumes all funds available.
6　Belonging to higher Hindu castes.
7　Nairs were the sudras in the caste hierarchy (Mathew 1989). They were comprised of the warriors, landed gentry and yeomen of pre-British Kerala (Jeffrey 1976).
8　Not belonging to the *varna* division.
9　For Bourdieu, a person's habitus does not determine his or her actions and thoughts. Operating as 'a system of lasting, transposable dispositions, which integrat[e] past experiences', habitus 'functions at every moment as a matrix of perceptions, appreciations, and actions' (Bourdieu 1977: 82), thus giving people a 'practical sense' of how to act, which itself embodies a social or class habitus.
10　This politics of exclusion and inclusion performed by the 'middle class' as a social construct is not new. Historical accounts of the middle class have shown how the elites refashioned themselves as the embodiment of a colonial and later post-colonial middle class, while rallying among various other social groups' ideas of social mobility, with them as representations of what could be attained through education and employment in the public sector (Joshi 2010: xxi; Lemercinier and Rendel 1983).
11　On the contrary, Jeffrey (2010) shows how, under condition of liberalisation, the reduced supplies of government jobs and undermined state services such as educational and health facilities have threatened the strategies of the lower middle classes.
12　Others, such as Fernandes (2006), argue that there is not a widening of the number of people joining the ranks of the middle class but only a reconstruction of the political and social identity of the previously existing middle classes, now rearticulated as a social group that operates as a proponent of economic liberalisation.
13　He is perhaps the most prominent figure produced by the Centre for Contemporary Cultural Studies or 'Birmingham School', the birthplace of youth culture studies.
14　Here I refer to modernity not as corresponding to the meta-category of analysis of classical theories (taking off from Marx, Weber, Durkheim), which are embedded in 'a teleology that sets the premises and promises of [a single] modernity as a yardstick for envisaging possible futures and for hierarchically ordering the somewhat "lacking" present of others' (Osella and Osella 2006: 585). Instead, I refer to historically and ethnographically specific concepts, ideas and practices of something called 'modernity', central to our lives and to the lives of those with whom we work (Ferguson 1999).
15　See Jeffrey and McDowell (2004) for a comparative overview of this field not just in postcolonial settings but also in Euro-American context.
16　Contrary to these accounts, much recent evidence suggests that unemployment or underemployed young people in postcolonial contexts are particularly likely to embrace identities construed as 'traditional' or 'indigenous' in their attempts to maintain their status (for example, Levinson 1996; Oni 1988). Similarly, Levinson (1996) demonstrates that many educated young people in the Mexican city of San Pablo had begun to distance themselves from educated identities. Against a background of pervasive

economic insecurity, young people in Levinson's study frequently sought out work perceived as 'traditional', while also criticising ideas of education as progress.

17   As per the 2001 census, Hindus are the largest religious group in the district (1,444,994 people), followed by Christians (1,204,471 people) and Muslims (451,764).

18   This is a local self-government unit at the village or small town level. Kadamakkudi *panchayath* is in itself divided into three residential villages, or *karas*, which are also three islets: Moolampalli, Pizhala and Kothad (Klausen 1968: 69). *Grama panchayats* constitute larger bloc *panchayats*. Multiple bloc *panchayats* in turn form district *panchayats*. The Kadamakkudi, Cheranalloor and the Trikkakara *grama panchayats* constitute the Edappalli bloc *panchayat*.

19   In *Learning to Leave: the irony of schooling in a coastal community*, Michel Corbett (2008) observes how similar marginalisation patterns affect a fishing community in Nova Scotia, Canada.

20   The Industrial Policy Resolution of 1948 gave the government the right to start new enterprises in key sectors. Along with the CSL, other major public sector industries, such as Fertilisers and Chemicals Travancore Limited and Kochi Refineries Limited, developed around the border townships of Kochi city. Other major industries established in and around Kochi in the post-Independence era were the Travancore Kochi Chemicals, Indian Aluminium Co., Hindustan Organics Ltd., Appollo Tyres, Binani Zinc Limited, Hindustan Machine Tools and Indian Rare Earths Ltd. While centred in Kochi more than other cities in Kerala, industrialisation in the state has still been slow when compared to other states in the country. In spite of this, these public sector industries have played a major role in the city's development and an important source for employment. In addition to being the industrial centre of the state, Kochi has also been an important military hub.

21   To date, India has relied on the hub port in Colombo, Sri Lanka. India's exporters and importers incur extra costs of at least Rs1,000 crore a year on trans-shipment of containers through ports outside the country, according to the shipping ministry. In fact, India's traders pay an additional Rs600 crore every year to ship their containers through Colombo alone (www.livemint.com/2011/05/23215132/Restrictive-law-inadequate-de.html).

22   The attempt to reimagine Kochi with reference to Singapore, and not Dubai, for example, is an important element to consider. Even though Christians are not the majority, Kochi is considered to be the Christian capital of Kerala. There has been an attempt to downplay its historical link to native Muslims as well as its connections with Muslim merchants from overseas.

23   In legal terms, NRI refers only to the tax status of an Indian citizen who, as per section 6 of the Income Tax Act of 1961, has not resided in India for a specified period for the purposes of the Income Tax Act. In everyday practices, as in this chapter, NRI refers to a citizen of India who has temporarily emigrated to another country, generally for work, and who stays abroad under circumstances indicating an intention for an uncertain duration of stay abroad.

24   Baviskar (2003) discusses how the middle class in Delhi imbue urban space with particular kinds of meaning that ultimately exclude all others.

25   A lakh is a unit in the South Asian numbering system equal to 100,000. In 2014, a lakh is approximately GB££1,000.

26   See Colnerud (2006) for a thorough discussion of the ethical dimension of the teaching profession.

27   As a volunteer project officer in a Spanish non-government organisation.

28   In fact, I failed to get access to another school because of this issue.

Bibliography

Aiyappan, A. 1965. *Social Revolution in a Kerala Village: A Study of Culture Change.* (1st edition). Asia Publishing House.

Althusser, L. 1971. Ideology and ideological state apparatuses. In *Lenin and Philosophy and Other Essays*, (ed.) L. Althusser, 121–173. Monthly Review Press.

Alves, M. H. M., S. Amin, P. Patnaik and C. M. Vilas 1991. Four Comments on Kerala. *Monthly Review* **42**, 24.

Amit-Talai, V. and H. Wulff (eds) 1995. *Youth Cultures: A Cross-Cultural Perspective.* Routledge.

Apple, M. W. 1979. *Ideology and Curriculum.* Routledge and Kegan Paul.

Arnold, D. and S. H. Blackburn 2004. *Telling Lives in India: Biography, Autobiography, and Life History.* Indiana University Press.

Baviskar, A. 2003. Between violence and desire: Space, power, and identity in the making of metropolitan Delhi. *International Social Science Journal* **55**, 89–98.

Baviskar, A. and R. Ray 2011. *Elite and Everyman: The Cultural Politics of the Indian Middle Classes.* (1st edition). Routledge.

Benei, V. 2008. *Schooling Passions: Nation, History, and Language in Contemporary Western India.* Stanford University Press.

Béteille, A. 1991. The reproduction of inequality: Occupation, caste and family. *Contributions to Indian Sociology* **25**, 3–28.

Bloch, F., V. Rao and S. Desai 2004. Wedding celebrations as conspicuous consumption: Signaling social status in rural India. *The Journal of Human Resources* **39**, 675–695.

Bourdieu, P. 1977. *Outline of a Theory of Practice* (ed. J. Goody; trans R. Nice). Cambridge University Press.

Bourdieu, P. 1984. *Distinction: A Social Critique of the Judgement of Taste.* Harvard University Press.

Bourdieu, P. 1986. The forms of capital. In *Handbook of Theory and Research for the Sociology of Education* (ed.) J. G. Richardson, 241–258. Greenwood Press.

Bourdieu, P. 1992. *An Invitation to Reflexive Sociology.* (1st edition). University of Chicago Press.

Bourdieu, P. and J.-C. Passeron 1990. *Reproduction in Education, Society and Culture.* Sage.

Bray, M. 2006. Private supplementary tutoring: comparative perspectives on patterns and implications. *Compare* **36**, 515–530.

Bucholtz, M. 2002. Youth and cultural practice. *Annual Review of Anthropology* **31**, 525–552.

Caddell, M. 2005. 'Discipline makes the nation great': Visioning development and the Nepali nation-state through schools. In *Manufacturing Citizenship: Education and Nationalism in Europe, South Asia and China* (ed.) V. Benei, 76–103. Routledge.

Caddell, M. 2006. Private schools as battlefields: Contested visions of learning and livelihood in Nepal. Compare: *A Journal of Comparative and International Education* **36**, 463–479.

Colnerud, G. 2006. Teacher ethics as a research problem: Syntheses achieved and new issues. *Teachers and Teaching* **12**, 365–385.

Corbett, M. 2008. *Learning to Leave: The Irony of Schooling in a Coastal Community.* Fernwood Publishing Co Ltd.

Crook, N. (ed.) 1996. *The Transmission of Knowledge in South Asia: Essays on Education, Religion, History, and Politics.* School of Oriental and African Studies.

Das Gupta, A. 2001. *The World of the Indian Ocean Merchant, 1500 1800. Collected Essays of Ashin Das Gupta.* OUP India.

De Neve, G. 2011. 'Keeping it in the family': Work, education and gender hierarchies among Tiruppur's industrial capitalists. In *Being Middle-Class in India: A Way of Life* (ed.) H. Donner, 73–99. Routledge.

Deshpande, S. 2003. *Contemporary India: A Sociological View*. Penguin Books India.

Deshpande, S. 2006. Exclusive inequalities: Merit, caste and discrimination in Indian higher education today. *Economic and Political Weekly* **41**, 2438–2444.

Deshpande, S. and Y. Yadav 2006. Redesigning affirmative action: Castes and benefits in higher education. *Economic and Political Weekly* **41**, 2419–2424.

Dickey, S. 2000. Permeable homes: Domestic service, household space, and the vulnerability of class boundaries in urban India. *American Ethnologist* **27**, 462–489.

Dickey, S. 2013. Apprehensions: On gaining recognition as middle class in Madurai. *Contributions to Indian Sociology* **47**, 217–243.

Dimesh Mani C. M. n.d. Cochin (A monograph) (available online: *www.corporationof-cochin.net/Cochin.pdf*).

Dirks, N. B. 2003. *Castes of Mind: Colonialism and the Making of Modern India*. Permanent Black.

Donner, H. 2005. Children are capital, grandchildren are interest: Changing educational strategies and parenting in Calcutta's middle-class families. In *Globalizing India : Perspectives from Below* (eds) J. Assayag and C. J. Fuller, 119–139. Anthem Press.

Donner, H. 2006. Committed mothers and well-adjusted children: Privatisation, early-years education and motherhood in Calcutta. *Modern Asian Studies* **40**, 371–395.

Donner, H. 2008a. New vegetarianism: Food, gender and neo-liberal regimes in Bengali middle-class families. *South Asia: Journal of South Asian Studies* **31**, 143–169.

Donner, H. 2008b. *Domestic Goddesses: Maternity, Globalization and Middle-class Identity in Contemporary India*. Ashgate.

Donner, H. (ed.) 2011. *Being Middle-class in India: A Way of Life*. (1st edition). Routledge.

Donner, H. and G. De Neve 2011. Introduction. In *Being Middle-class in India: A Way of Life*, (ed.) H. Donner, 1–22. Routledge.

Ferguson, J. 1999. *Expectations of Modernity: Myths and Meanings of Urban Life on the Zambian Copperbelt*. University of California Press.

Fernandes, L. 2000. Nationalizing 'the global': Media images, cultural politics and the middle class in India. *Media, Culture & Society* **22**, 611–628.

Fernandes, L. 2006. *India's New Middle Class: Democratic Politics in an Era of Economic Reform*. University of Minnesota Press.

Fernandes, L. and P. Heller 2006. Hegemonic aspirations: New middle class politics and India's democracy in comparative perspective. *Critical Asian Studies* **38**, 495.

Froerer, P. 2007. Disciplining the saffron way: Moral education and the Hindu Rashtra. *Modern Asian Studies* **41**, 1033–1071.

Froerer, P. 2009. Ethnographies of childhood and childrearing. *Reviews in Anthropology* **38**, 3–27.

Fuller, C. J. 1976. Kerala Christians and the caste system. *Man* **11**, 53–70.

Fuller, C. J. and H. Narasimhan 2006. Engineering colleges, 'exposure' and information technology professionals in Tamil Nadu. *Economic and Political Weekly* **3**, 258–262.

Fuller, C. J. and H. Narasimhan 2007. Information technology professionals and the new-rich middle class in Chennai (Madras). *Modern Asian Studies* **41**, 121–150.

Ganguly Scrase, R. and T. J. Scrase 2001. Who wins? Who loses? And who even knows? Responses to economic liberalisation and cultural globalisation in India. *South Asia: Journal of South Asian Studies* **24**, 141–158.

George, K. K., G. Zachariah and N. A. Kumar 2002. *Grant in Aid Policies and Practices towards Secondary Education in Kerala*. Centre for Socio-Economic and Environmental Studies (available online: *http://artsonline.monash.edu.au/mai/files/2012/07/dan autanu.pdf* accessed 2 September 2013).

George, M. K. and J. Domi 2002. *Residual Literacy in a Coastal Village: Poovar village of Thiruvananthapuram district*. (KRPLLD Discussion Paper No. 45). CDS.

Gilroy, P. 1991. *'There Ain't no Black in the Union Jack': The Cultural Politics of Race and Nation*. (Reprint). University of Chicago Press.

Gooptu, N. (ed.) 2013. *Enterprise Culture in Neoliberal India: Studies in Youth, Class, Work and Media*. Routledge.

Government of Kerala 2010. *Economic Review*. Kerala State Planning Board.

Hayden, M. 2011. Transnational spaces of education: The growth of the international school sector. *Globalisation, Societies and Education* **9**, 211–224.

Hebdige, D. 1979. *Subculture: The Meaning of Style*. (1st edition). Routledge.

Hoeppe, G. 2007. *Conversations on the Beach: Fishermen's Knowledge, Metaphor and Environmental Change in South India*. Berghahn Books.

Jeffrey, C. 2010. *Timepass: Youth, Class, and the Politics of Waiting in India*. Stanford University Press.

Jeffrey, C. and L. McDowell 2004. Youth in a comparative perspective. *Youth & Society* **36**, 131–142.

Jeffrey, C., P. Jeffery and R. Jeffery 2004. 'A useless thing!' or 'nectar of the gods?' The cultural production of education and young men's struggles for respect in liberalizing North India. *Annals of the Association of American Geographers* **94**, 961–981.

Jeffrey, C., P. Jeffery and R. Jeffery 2008. *Degrees Without Freedom?: Education, Masculinities, and Unemployment in North India*. Stanford University Press.

Jeffery, P. 2005. Introduction: Hearts, minds, and pockets. In *Educational Regimes in Contemporary India* (eds) R. Chopra and P. Jeffery, 13–38. Sage.

Jeffrey, R. 1976. *The Decline of Nair Dominance: Society and Politics in Tranvancore, 1847–1908*. Vikas Publishing House.

Jeffrey, R., P. Jeffrey and C. Jeffrey 2005. Social inequalitites and the privatisation of secondary schooling in North India. In *Educational Regimes in Contemporary India* (eds) R. Chopra and P. Jeffery, 41–61. Sage.

Jeffery, R., P. Jeffery and C. Jeffrey 2011. 'Are rich rural Jats middle-class?'. In *Elite and Everyman: The Cultural Politics of the Indian Middle Classes* (eds) A. Baviskar and R. Ray, 140–163. Routledge.

Joshi, S. 2010. *The Middle Class in Colonial India*. Oxford University Press.

Kanna, A. 2010. Flexible citizenship in Dubai: Neoliberal subjectivity in the emerging 'city-corporation'. *Cultural Anthropology* **25**, 100–129.

Klausen, A. M. 1968. *Kerala Fishermen and the Indo-Norwegian Pilot Project*. Scandinavian University Books.

Kumar, K. and J. Oesterheldeds (eds) 2007. *Education and Social Change in South Asia*. Orient Longman.

Kumar, N. 2011. The middle-class child: Ruminations on failure. In *Elite and Everyman: The Cultural Politics of the Indian Middle Classes* (eds) A. Baviskar and R. Ray, 220–245. Routledge.

Kumar, N. A. and K. K. George 2009. *Kerala's Education System: From Inclusion to Exclusion?* Working paper no. 22. Centre for Socio-economic & Environmental Studies.

Leander, K. M. and K. K. McKim 2003. Tracing the everyday 'sitings' of adolescents on the internet: A strategic adaptation of ethnography across online and offline spaces. *Education, Communication & Information* **3**, 211–240.

Lemercinier, G. and Y. Rendel 1983. *Religion and Ideology in Kerala*. D. K. Agencies.

Levinson, B. A. (1996). Social difference and schooled identity in a Mexican secundria. In *The Cultural Production of the Educated Person: Critical ethnographies of schooling and local practice* (eds) B. A. Levinson, D. E. Foley and D. C. Holland, 1–56. State University of New York Press.

Levinson, B. A. 1999. ' Una etapa siempre dificil': Concepts of adolescence and secondary education in Mexico. *Comparative Education Review* **43**, 129–161.

Levinson, B. A. and D. Holland 1996. The cultural production of the educated person: An introduction. In *The Cultural Production of the Educated Person: Critical Ethnographies of Schooling and Local Practice*, (eds) B. A. Levinson, D. E. Foley and D. C. Holland, 1–54. State University of New York Press.

Levinson, B. A., D. E. Foley and D. C. Holland 1996. *The Cultural Production of the Educated Person: Critical Ethnographies of Schooling and Local Practice*. State University of New York Press.

Liechty, M. 2003. *Suitably Modern: Making Middle-Class Culture in a New Consumer Society*. Princeton University Press.

Lukose, R. 2005. Consuming globalization: Youth and gender in Kerala, India. *Journal of Social History* **38**, 915–935.

Lukose, R. A. 2009. *Liberalization's Children: Gender, youth, and consumer citizenship in globalizing India*. Duke University Press Books.

MacDougall, D. 2005. Doon School aesthetics. In *Educational Regimes in Contemporary India* (eds) R. Chopra and P. Jeffery, 121–140. Sage.

Malekandathil, P. 2001. *Portuguese Cochin and the Maritime Trade of India 1500–1663*. Manohar Publishers and Distributors.

Mathew, G. 1989. *Communal Road To A Secular Kerala*. Concept Publishing Company.

Mazzarella, W. 2003. 'Very Bombay': Contending with the global in an Indian advertising agency. *Cultural Anthropology* **18**, 33–71.

Merten, D. E. 1999. Enculturation into secrecy among junior high school girls. *Journal of Contemporary Ethnography* **28**, 107–137.

Miles, A. 2000. Poor adolescent girls and social transformations in Cuenca, Ecuador. *Ethos* **28**, 54–74.

Miller, D. 1994. *Modernity: An Ethnographic Approach: Dualism and Mass Consumption in Trinidad*. (1st edition). Bloomsbury Academic.

Miller, D. and D. Miller 2005. *Acknowledging Consumption*. Routledge.

Narasimhan, H. (2009). 'Unfinishing schools': Learning 'computer' in Mofussil Tamil Nadu. Mofussil India, London School of Economics, 6–7 July.

Nigam, A. 2004. Imagining the global nation. *Economic and Political Weekly* (available online: www.epw.in/special-articles/imagining-global-nation.html).

Nisbett, N. 2007. Friendship, consumption, morality: Practising identity, negotiating hierarchy in middle-class Bangalore. *Journal of the Royal Anthropological Institute* **13**, 935–950.

Nisbett, N. 2009. *Growing up in the Knowledge Society: Living the IT Dream in Bangalore*. (1st edition). Routledge India.

Nisbett, N. 2013. Youth and the practice of IT enterprise: Narratives of the knowledge society and the creation of new subjectivities amongst Bangalore's IT aspirants. In *Enterprise Culture in Neoliberal India: Studies in youth, class, work and media* (ed.) N. Gooptu, 175–189. Routledge.

Oni, B. 1988. Education and alternative avenues of mobility: A Nigerian study. *Comparative Education Review* **32**, 87–99.

Osella, C. and F. Osella 2006. Once upon a time in the West? Stories of migration and modernity from Kerala, South India. *Journal of the Royal Anthropological Institute* **12**, 569–588.

Osella, F. and C. Osella 1999. From transience to immanence: Consumption, life-cycle and social mobility in Kerala, South India. *Modern Asian Studies* **33**, 989–1020.

Osella, F. and C. Osella 2000. *Social Mobility in Kerala: Modernity and identity in conflict.* Pluto Press.

Osella, F. and C. Osella 2007. 'I am Gulf': The production of cosmopolitanism in Kozhikode, Kerala, India. In Struggling with History: Islam and Cosmopolitanism in the Western Indian Ocean (eds) E. Simpson and K. Kress, 323–355. C. Hurst & Co Publishers Ltd.

Qureshi, K. and F. Osella 2013. Transnational schooling in Punjab, India: designer migrants and cultural politics. In *Refugees, Immigrants, and Education in the Global South: Lives in Motion* (eds) L. Bartlett and A. Ghaffar-Kucher, 99–115. Routledge.

Rajagopal, A. 2001. Thinking about the new Indian middle classes: Gender, advertising and politics in an age of globalisation. In *Signposts: Gender Issues in Post-independence India* (ed.) R. S. Rajan, 57–99. Rutgers University Press.

Ram, K. 1991. *Mukkuvar Women: Gender, hegemony and capitalist transformation in a south Indian fishing community.* Zed Books.

Rogers, M. 2008. Modernity, 'authenticity', and ambivalence: Subaltern masculinities on a South Indian college campus. *Journal of the Royal Anthropological Institute* **14**, 79–95.

Saavala, M. 2003. Auspicious Hindu houses. The new middle classes in Hyderabad, India. *Social Anthropology* **11**, 231–247.

Saldanha, A. 2002. Music, space, identity: Geographies of youth culture in Bangalore. *Cultural Studies* **16**, 337–350.

Sanjek, R. 1990. Urban anthropology in the 1980s: A world view. *Annual Review of Anthropology* **19**, 151–186.

Schein, L. 1999. Performing modernity. *Cultural Anthropology* **14**, 361–395.

Schlegel, A. and H. Barry 1991. *Adolescence: An Anthropological Inquiry.* Free Press.

Shaw, A. and M. K. Satish 2007. Metropolitan restructuring in post-liberalized India: Separating the global and the local. *Cities* **24**, 148–163.

Short, P. J. R. 2006. *Urban Theory: A Critical Assessment.* Palgrave Macmillan.

Skelton, T. and G. Valentine (eds) 1997. *Cool Places: Geographies of Youth Cultures.* (1st edition). Routledge.

Srivastava, S. 1998. *Constructing 'Post-Colonial' India: National Character and the Doon School.* (1st edition). Routledge.

Subrahmanian, R. 2005. Education exclusion and the developmental state. In *Educational Regimes in Contemporary India* (eds) R. Chopra and P. Jeffery, 62–82. Sage.

Upadhya, C. 1997. Social and cultural strategies of class formation in coastal Andhra Pradesh. *Contributions to Indian Sociology* **31**, 169–193.

Upadhya, C. 2008. Management of culture and management through culture in the Indian software outsorcing industry. In *In an Outpost of the Global Economy: Work and Workers in India's Information Technology Industry* (eds) C. Upadhya and A. R. Vasavi, 101–135. Routledge.

Upadhya, C. 2011. Software and the 'new' middle class in the 'new India'. In *Elite and Everyman: The Cultural Politics of the Indian Middle Classes* (eds) A. Baviskar and R. Ray, 167–192. Routledge.

Vora, N. 2008. Producing diasporas and globalization: Indian middle-class migrants in Dubai. *Anthropological Quarterly* **81**, 377–406.

Vora, N. 2011. From golden frontier to global city: Shifting forms of belonging, 'freedom,' and governance among Indian businessmen in Dubai. *American Anthropologist* **113**, 306–318.

Vora, N. 2013. *Impossible Citizens: Dubai's Indian Diaspora*. Duke University Press.

Weber, M. and A. M. Henderson 2012. *The Theory of Social and Economic Organization* (ed.) T. Parsons. Martino Fine Books.

Van Wessel, M. 2004. Talking about consumption: How an Indian middle class dissociates from middle-class life. *Cultural Dynamics* **16**, 93–116.

Willis, P. 1977. *Learning to Labour: How working class kids get working class jobs*. Ashgate Publishing Limited.

Wilson, C. 2011. The social transformation of the medical profession in urban Kerala. In *Being Middle-Class in India: A Way of Life* (ed.) H. Donner, 139–161. Routledge.

Young, M. F. D. 1971. *Knowledge and Control: New directions for the sociology of education*. Collier-Macmillan.

2 Education and the rise of a middle-class dream

Within and outside India, Kerala is known for its total literacy and the historical penchant for the education of its population. Its renowned position in educational development is the result of the work of a variety of agents – western missionaries, local churches, community organisations, social reformers and the state – who, over the last two centuries have supported the cause of education and taken diverse initiatives in starting and maintaining educational institutions of different kinds. In what follows, I briefly sketch the growth of school education in the two princely states of Travancore and Cochin, what constitutes central and southern Kerala today.[1]

This chapter examines the social processes that went into making Kerala the most literate state in the Indian Union. Central to this development, this chapter shows that with education, Kerala saw the emergence of the idea of the middle class, which entailed the crafting of a social space in which the ascribed criteria of caste lost currency as basis of social hierarchy (Joshi 2010: xix) with reference to the privileging of achieved criteria: primarily education and employment as markers of power and status. By uncovering the uneven experiences and outcomes of education and middle classness along the axes of caste and religion, this chapter shows that rather than displacing caste hierarchies, education and the middle-class idea have become complicated, yet allow for the continuation of differences amongst social groups. In short, caste and class continue to be intertwined in contemporary Kerala. By uncovering this long and uneven history of education and its link to the middle class, this chapter builds a case against discontinuity represented by local critics of privatisation[2] who argue that with liberalisation (from the 1990s onwards) there has been a new clean break in the provision of education from an inclusive state-sponsored education to an exclusive system. Going against the grain of the dominant rhetoric on Kerala, the chapter portrays schooling as the site of continuous struggle, fragmentation and hierarchy.

Early modern education in Travancore and Cochin

Modern school education in Kerala dates back to the beginning of the nineteenth century.[3] Throughout the first half of the century, it was mainly spearheaded by Christian missionaries, who built the first schools attached to their churches. One of such early institutions was an English school opened by Reverend Tobias

Ringeltaube, a London Mission Society (LMS) missionary in Nagercoil, southern Travancore. Soon after, the governments of Travancore and Cochin – under the tutelage of their British Residents – made initial efforts in school education.[4] Several government schools were opened following the Royal Rescript of 1817, which acknowledge the Travancore state's responsibility in meeting the cost of education and running schools (George *et al.* 2002: 3). In 1818, the Cochin government established thirty-three vernacular schools following a Royal Proclamation at the instance of the British Resident. In 1835, six more schools, one in each taluk, were established. However, although these decrees ordered the creation of primary schools in all villages, and the obligation of attendance of all children from five to ten years of age (Lemercinier and Rendel 1983: 172), the few government schools, many of which closed for want of pupils, were strictly for children of the upper castes (Mathew 1989: 35). Missionary schools welcomed children of the lower castes but many faced problems recruiting children from such groups as a result of ideas of pollution, which forbade any sort of contact between children of lower and upper castes (Lemercinier and Rendel 1983).

The second half of the nineteenth century saw a more rapid growth of the number of schools and enrolment of pupils as a result of the expansion of the colonial administration – mostly an urban phenomenon – and the development of the colonial agrarian economy in rural areas (George *et al.* 2002: 3). As the judiciary, revenue, police and public works expanded, local personnel were needed in an increasing number of government jobs, to which access depended on education (Lemercinier and Rendel 1983; Tharakan 1984). In urban areas, there was a rising glamour surrounding government jobs, which slowly became a prominent source of power and status. Even beyond cities, lower posts, such as that of *pravarthikar* (village revenue officer) were increasingly coveted (Mathew 1989: 40). Similarly, the commercialisation of agriculture and establishment of plantation industries increasingly demanded a new kind of workforce able to handle commercial contracts and accounts. In this changing context, schools were envisaged as means to make 'better subjects and public servants, and to advance the reputation of the state' (excerpt from the 1817 decree in Tharakan 1984: 1917). In cities, the value of education gradually gained momentum amongst the sectors in the population aspiring for civil service.

In the decades leading into the twentieth century, Travancore and Cochin experienced further growth, with Christian churches playing a pivotal role. Through a system of 'a school along with every church', Christian missionaries and local churches were able to extend access to school education, pioneering English education and the formal schooling of girls. Growth was also bolstered by state support to vernacular education and the introduction – in 1865 (Travancore) and 1889 (Cochin) – of a system of grants-in-aid[5] to facilitate the opening and maintenance of private schools. Cochin also witnessed the opening of vocational schools where carpentry and tailoring, amongst other subjects, were taught. In Travancore and Cochin, private schools outnumber government schools by a big margin. In Travancore, the state was very successful in bringing private schools into the purview of state funding and monitoring. However, in Cochin, the bulk of the private schooling sector continued to operate independently. In 1901 there were 181 government and aided schools and 1108 private schools catering for the population. As a result of these developments, literacy in Travancore and Cochin, above 11 per cent, surpassed that of the Indian level, 5.8 per cent (George *et al.* 2002: 5).

What is significant in these developments is that in the nineteenth century we witness the emergence of education and the labour market as new focal points of local identities. Throughout the nineteenth century, a section of society came to see themselves not only as members of a religious or caste group but increasingly in terms of their education and employment, as members of an economic class. For the first time, people's relationship with the labour market, determined to a large extent by people's engagement with education, increasingly became a powerful factor in communicating who they were and who they were not. This entailed a move away from ascribed (caste-based) criteria of power and status to the privileging of achieved criteria, primarily education and employment. The 'self' became something one aspired to self-consciously craft: a fundamentally middle-class idea (Joshi 2010).

As Joshi notes, the middle class in colonial India was not a social group that could be classified as occupying a median position in terms of standard of sociological indicators such as occupation, income or status (Joshi 2010: xviii). There is no doubt that they were from the upper echelons of society. Most of them were male, upper-caste Hindus, or other such high-status groups. In Kerala, Tamil Brahmins quickly entered and monopolised[6] the new kinds of social, economic and political roles being opened up in British Travancore and Cochin. Influenced by the progressive role attributed to the middle class in British history, Tamil Brahmins in Kerala were the first group who accessed the English education and employment that allowed them to consciously rearticulate themselves as 'middle class', effectively transforming the basis for social hierarchy (Joshi 2010: xxi; Lemercinier and Rendel 1983: 172). They became the producers and products of a new cultural politics that allowed them to articulate of a new set of values, beliefs, practices and modes of politics that distinguished them from the upper and lower order of society and to put forward a moral superiority above both (Joshi 2010: xviii).

One's engagement with the labour market and a particular desire for education came to stand for a new form of identity, not based on religion or caste membership. What is significant here is that education began to signal one's position in a new social hierarchy. Education was not only essential to the emergence of this new form of identity, as a requisite to access the new roles made available, but was also in itself a conveyor of new ideas and a space for the critical appraisal of local society and its entrenched hierarchies (Devika 2007). In practice, these new cultural logic operated only amongst upper castes who had access to English education and government employment (Jeffrey 1976). But for the first time, the belief in social mobility through the newly introduced idea of competence (largely the product of one's education and engagement with the labour market), and no longer on social group membership, began to be circulated.

Rising demand for education

What had begun as experiments with foreign-style education mainly by the elites, at the turn of the twentieth century became an obsession of more and more sections of society. Access to education and government offices, increasingly seen as means to achieve status and power, became the focal point of struggles for more and more educated young men of privileged religious and caste communities. In 1891, Travancore saw a political agitation on the question of sharing government jobs. As Mathew (1989) notes, the central theme in urban Travancore and Cochin in the final decades of the nineteenth century and early twentieth century was one of competing demands for education and larger representation in government office.

The start of the twentieth century saw the emergence of social reform movements and the formation of strong caste organisation that endeavoured to improve the influence and circumstance of their respective castes (Mathew 1989). This included the Sree Narayana Dharma Paripalana (SNDP), established in 1903 to work for the benefit of the Ezhava caste, and the Sadhujana Paripalana Sangham (SJPS), established in 1907 by social reformer Ayyankali to campaign for education for Scheduled castes. Although there were some individuals within these communities who had achieved good economic standing as a result of early access to English education and their engagement in trade – many of whom became community leaders – the majority remained virtually excluded from government jobs and admission to village and district schools. Even in 1920, 3,800 out of 4,000 officials of the revenue department of Travancore were Caste Hindus (Lemercinier and Rendel 1983: 195). Discrimination was the result of material disadvantage and overwhelmingly negative caste stereotypes. The work of these movements was underpinned by a vision of society as constituted by various independent and tendentially equal 'communities' competing for power and wealth (Osella and Osella 2000: 235). Access to English education and employment were the central concerns of these movements, who had the construction of schools and colleges at the top of their priorities. Nevertheless, community efforts concentrated on the removal of pollution codes and symbols of social inferiority (Mathew 1989; Osella and Osella 2000), which operated as an impediment to the fulfilment of their ultimate objectives.

Privileged groups such as Nairs, who found their status had eroded in a rapidly changing society, also sought to defend their position and power, which led to the formation in 1914 of the Nair Service Society (NSS) to advance the welfare, education and employment of their caste. In the second half of the nineteenth century, the power of the Nair community was in decline as a result of number of factors, including the increasing trading monopoly of the East India Company (EIC), and the new rigid legal interpretation of previously flexible land custom that resulted in Nairs losing hold of land to prosperous Syrian Christians[7] (Jeffrey 1976). Meanwhile, the prominence of Syrian Christians, who occupied a high social position roughly on par with the Nairs (Mathew 1989: 29) was on the rise. As a result of their early access to missionary schools – by reason of religious allegiance – they became successful at finding employment and doing business with British companies (Osella and Osella 2000: 140). In this context, Nairs increasingly sought to overcome the lost ground by following Christians into English-medium education and challenging Tamil Brahmins' control of key posts in government. That is, they attempted to boost their class status through education and other 'Christianised' practices, such as entering technical and professional occupations, migration and high consumption (Osella and Osella 2000: 244).

What is crucial here is that these associations created more demand for education, as a primary avenue for social mobility and social status, and established many new schools on their own. Demands were articulated in terms of different religious/caste struggles. Such struggles were vastly different: from the Nair's scramble for English-medium education and their efforts to challenge the prominence of Tamil Brahmins and Christians in key government posts, to the struggle of Ezhavas and Pulayas to get basic access to schooling. These very different initiatives and struggles spurred the growth of education through the twentieth century. As a result, education became not only instrumental to the use of ethnic identity in organisations and politics, and to people's tendency to see themselves as members of ethnic blocs (Jeffrey 1992: 63), but also brought with it new gaps and inequalities.

Access to education and especially to English education and the concomitant capacity to turn those qualifications into real employments varied widely across communities. The transition of Nairs and Christians to the new kinds of social, economic and political roles that emerged in colonial Kerala were, to a large extent, smooth. Christians and Nairs have found good employment opportunities outside the state and later outside India, sealing in these communities' collective imagination the middle-class idea of power and status through education and economic success (Osella and Osella 2000). At present, Nairs and Christians are perceived as unequivocally middle class and in possession of prestige and wealth.

For less-privileged communities (Ezhavas, Latin Catholics or Muslims), the outcomes have been different. Many who had received a systematic education became upwardly mobile individuals or families; many of them have gained access to the amenities of modern middle-class life, coming elbow to elbow with their high-status Christians and Nair neighbours. Yet as groups, they continue to be constrained as a result of their overall material situation, the resource available to them and the 'inadequate' qualities attributed to the group. For them the promises of the middle-class ideal (for example, that education leads to employment, which in turn leads to economic success) continue to yield contradictory material outcomes.

Considered jointly, the work of Christian missionaries and caste-based organisations helped the people of Kerala seal in a particular penchant for education as the key means through which individuals of more or less commensurate communities can achieve and consolidate social mobility. This has in turn fuelled an expansion of schooling and literacy like in no other Indian state. Here it is important to note the role played by the governments of Travancore and Cochin, which responded positively to private educational initiatives and sought to expand education amongst the population of Kerala, mainly through supporting private schools rather than starting schools on their own (George *et al.* 2002). The government's efforts to support private education have always had the dual purpose of implementing stricter regulations regarding fees, rules of admission and curricula and teachers' salary and appointment, and hence curbing the power and influence that private providers and community organisations may exert through education.

The governments of Travancore and Cochin have been particularly responsive to initiatives and the rapidly growing demand for education amongst the less-privileged sections of society. Throughout the twentieth century they took important actions to extend education to such groups: mainly the opening of government schools and the expansion of grant-in-aid systems. In 1904 the state of Travancore established free primary education for lower castes (Aiya 1906: 495), and in 1909 it granted lower castes admission to government schools (Oomen 2007). In Cochin, fees were abolished for girls and scholarships and stipends were made available to children of the backward castes in secondary schools (Jeffrey 1992: 61). Spurred by the growing demand for education, both the Travancore and Cochin governments turned to vernacular (Malayalam) primary schooling as the primary means for the 'instruction of the masses' (Aiya 1906: 478). Many private schools became aided schools,[8] through which vernacular education rapidly penetrated the bulk of the population. The Travancore government recognised a de facto dual education system constituted by English education for a minority and vernacular primary and 'a system of technical or industrial education for the masses, for whom 'it is desirable that at least the elements of education should be made familiar to them' (Aiya 1906: 478).

By the 1940s most families had at least one child at school and the number of schools continued to grow. This is directly linked to the context of social reform movements, which fuel a high demand for schools, leading to the proliferation of schools and massive pupil enrolment. Since 1910, there had been a big jump in Travancore and Cochin in the proportion of government educational expenditure to total government expenditure.

Education in modern Kerala and the emergence of 'the model' discourse

In the second half of the twentieth century, the expansion of literacy, schooling and the rise in demand for education in Kerala continued. The literacy level for Kerala rose from 40.47 per cent in 1951, to 56.85 per cent in 1961, to 60.42 per cent in 1971. The corresponding figures for all of India were 16.67 per cent, 24.02 per cent and 29.45 per cent (George *et al.* 2002).

An important feature of this period was that schooling came to be largely subsidised by the government. In the early 1950s, private schools continued to attract large numbers of students. By 1951, private (unaided) schools accounted for 39.9 per cent of the total number of higher schools and 29.7 per cent of upper primary schools (see Table 2.1). Many school managements and community organisations continue to view governments' grants-in-aid schemes as infringements on their rights and freedom to run schools. Following the formation of the Travancore-Cochin state in July 1949, the government sought to expand its grants system and subsidise more and more private schools. In 1950, the Private Secondary School Scheme (PSS) was introduced offering better payment and services to teachers to attract more private schools. Expenditure rose from an average 16 per cent in the first half of the twentieth century to 26 per cent in 1955 (Abdul Salim and Gopinathan Nair 2002).

Following the formation of the modern Kerala State in 1956, the government's continuous efforts to augment its clout through bringing private schools into its grants system clashed with the increasing power of private educational and communal lobbies. The latter had become progressively more influential in coalition politics in the state as they were backed by one or more political parties in the coalition governments defending their interests. In 1957, the Kerala Education Bill was enacted, introducing the direct payment of salaries of teachers in all aided schools, as well as other provisions that sought to restrict the rights of managements to appointing teachers. Communal opposition from the Catholic Church in Kerala, the Nair Service Society and the Indian Union Muslim League, as well as pressure from the political coalition led by the Indian National Congress Party (UDF), against these educational policies and the Land Reform Ordinance[9] developed into an open struggle and state-wide violence against the government. These events finally culminated in the intervention of the central government of India and the dismissal of the state government in 1959. Giving in to communal pressures, the education bill was subsequently amended by the new government giving back private managements the freedom to appoint teaching staff.

With the salaries of teaching and non-teaching staff being paid directly by government, the 1960s to 1980s saw a rapid increase in the proportion private schools being drawn into the grant-in-aid system: the private schools in the state dropped from 39.9 per cent in 1951 to 3.9 per cent in 1981. Education became largely subsidised through the grant-in-aid scheme; aided schools gained a pre-eminent position amongst Kerala schools. Religious and community organisations – the main driver of educational development in the state – increasingly sought to secure funding from the state in order to attend to the educational demands of their communities. However, as I will discuss later, the last few decades have witnessed a gradual resurgence of private schooling.

Table 2.1 Management of the distribution of high schools in Kerala (%)

Year	High schools			
	Government	Aided	Unaided	Total
1950–51	21.0	39.1	39.9	100.0
1980–81	39.9	56.8	3.3	100.0
1985–86	38.6	57.0	4.5	100.0
1990–91	39.2	56.3	4.5	100.0
1995–96	37.9	54.2	7.9	100.0
2000–01	37.7	53.8	8.5	100.0
2010–11	37.1	49.7	13.2	100.0

Source: Recognised Unaided Schools in Kerala Report 2010

By 1981 the literacy level in Kerala had reached 70.42 per cent, nearly doubling the national average of 36.03 per cent. In Ernakulam, a district pioneering in the field of education largely due to the work of the Christian community, this figure was even higher: 76.8 per cent. Efforts towards augmenting literacy continued after the 1980s, focusing on residual pockets of illiterate populations. The National Literacy Mission was launched in the Ernakulam district in 1981 as a pilot project, which later became a 'model' for the Total Literacy Campaign in many districts in Kerala and across India (Tharakan 2004: 48). In February 1990, Ernakulam was touted as the first district in the state and the nation to claim total literacy[10] (Tharakan 2004). Literacy in present-day Ernakulam is estimated at 95.68 per cent, slightly higher than Kerala's at 93.91 per cent (Government of Kerala 2010). As most Indian state governments failed to provide education and literacy for all, Kerala's reputation as 'a model' grew; a vision that continues to animate much of what it is written and thought about it (Devika 2007: 11).

The dominant accounts of Kerala's development – the mainstream literature known as the 'Kerala Model'[11] (Baby and Sukumara Pillai 2008; Chakraborty 2005; Franke and Chasin 1994; Kumar and George 2009) – have tended to glorify education in Kerala as 'inclusive' and 'liberating'. Accounts of the glorious achievement of an inclusive, highly subsidised, state-led education system are deployed to explain the broad scenario of total literacy, marginal rural–urban and gender difference in literacy, low drop-out rates and easy access to educational institutions in what used to be a somewhat poor state (Kumar and George 2009). These accounts tend to hype the role played by the allegedly 'enlightened' governments of Travancore and Cochin, and subsequently by Kerala (Baby and Sukumara Pillai 2008). They tend to underplay the fact that it was primarily the efforts of religious and community-based leaders and organisations that led to the widespread desire for education as a key means to achieve and consolidate social mobility amongst Keralites, which has in turn driven the expansion of schooling and the ever-increasing levels of pupil enrolment.

The model literature also veers away from critical engagements with the gaps and inequalities created by the vertiginous expansion of schooling in Kerala. Through the historical processes previously described, education emerged as an avenue to social mobility and as a key site for the maintenance of social difference with a shift from direct to 'mediated' reproduction (Jeffery *et al.* 2007: 444). In Kerala, most graduates and professionals are Nair or Christian, as are most of those who can speak English, the prestige language, confidently (Osella and Osella 2000). Despite the laudatory expansion of schooling, different types of schools (for example, English- or Malayalam-medium, government-aided or private) facilitate the production of very different kinds of aspirations and trajectories, which continue to make education an overwhelmingly positive resource for privileged groups and a contradictory resource for less-privileged ones. In spite of high levels of literacy, the failure rate at the secondary school leaving stage is around 50 per cent and the performance of students from government and aided schools at the all-India competitive examinations for admissions to higher education institutions lags significantly behind when compared with private schools (George *et al.* 2002: 57). In addition, high levels of education have failed to translate in the promised rewards, as unemployment[12] in the state ranks amongst the highest in India.

This point has recently been made by Scaria (2014), who reminds us that although no one refutes the significance of literacy, universal enrolment and the number of educational institutions in the state, remarkable indicators alone do not guarantee equal opportunities. His study stresses that in Kerala educational opportunities are very much embedded within the social structure organised along the lines of caste and class. Although old forms of inequalities are being challenged by the educational policies of the state, 'old forms of inequalities are being replaced by new forms of inequalities in education' (Scaria 2014: 157). His study demonstrates the glaring inequalities in the educational attainments of the population, and especially how Scheduled castes (SC) still stand at the bottom of the rankings in educational attainments and continue to show relatively low levels of enrolment in higher education as compared to other communities. For SCs, the unequal access to economic resources, including land and remittances, plays a major role in defining and determining access to education.

A number of other local studies (see, for example, George and Domi 2002) show how state achievements in education have failed to benefit three sections of Malayali society: the tribesfolk, the fisherfolk and the floating Tamil population. In the fishing communities, this is manifest in the high dropout and low achievement levels amongst their children. In Poovar, the village where George and Domi (2002) conducted their study, dropout rates were 41.44 and 36.95 per cent for girls and boys respectively, while the state figures approached 1 per cent (Government of Kerala 2010). Moreover, as Chapter 6 further elaborates, while many Latin Catholics in the city have managed to improve their position through education and employment, entering the rising middle classes, the Latin Catholic backwater fishing community at the city's fringes continued to be excluded. In late-nineteenth-century Kochi, the Latin Catholic Archdiocese, which is supposed to cater to the needs of the community, opened two major schools: St Teresa's (girls) School (est. 1887) and St Albert's (boys) School (est. 1892). These institutions developed into reputed colleges. The schools open by the Archdiocese in Kothad were poorly served and developed at a very slow pace when compared to their urban counterparts. In addition, the Archdiocese failed to provide the fishing community room for its members to emerge as socio-political leaders (George and Domi 2002: 12).

The development of education in the state has not entailed a clean break from the social order of 'old' Kerala. Rather than being an all-inclusive system and the pillar of a new modern, class-based society, education in Kerala has been a primordial site for the (re)production of caste/religious hierarchies and its entanglement with class (Béteille 1991; Osella and Osella 2000).

The (re)emergence of private schooling

Since the 1980s, and more markedly since the 1990s, there has been a gradual yet important emergence of a new private English-medium sector of schools. While private secondary schools accounted for 4.5 per cent of the total number of schools in 1991, in 2011, this proportion rose to 13.2 per cent. The number of annual entrants in unaided schools has been increasing steadily since the early 1980s, while there is a steady decrease in the number of overall entrants, largely a result of a decrease in the number of children due to low birth rates[13] (Nambuthiri 2004). In 2011, higher secondary schools[14] comprised a quarter of the schools available in the state. Table 2.2 indicates the growth in the number of recognised unaided schools vis-à-vis government and aided schools in Kerala during the period of 1990–1991 to 2009–2010. This growth can be put down to three reasons: a rising middle class, a decrease in government's capacity and willingness to subsidise education, and India's wider endorsement of privatisation in education.

Kerala's per capita state domestic product in the 1960s, 1970s and 1980s ranked low amongst Indian states. In the late 1980s, however, the economy has seen steady recovery and household income has been on the rise. Some of this income has been originated within the state as a result of gradually expanding job markets. Many benefited from the state's long history of widespread education, and acquired jobs and levels of income and consumption that are typically thought as middle class (De Neve 2011). In Kochi, many secured jobs in public sector industries such as the Cochin Shipyard Limited, which in 1976 received important incentives from the central government.[15] Since then, CSL has been one of the largest employers in the city. But in spite of the development of a local job market, rising educational level in Kerala have been accompanied by a stagnant opportunities for salaried employment (Jeffrey *et al.* 2008) largely a result of low industrial and economic development.

To a larger extent, however, the increasing income in Kerala is a result of the flow of remittances received from migrants within or outside India, crucially in the Persian Gulf countries. The number of Keralites working and residing abroad (non-resident Keralites) increased from 2.1 million in 1998, to 2.7 million in 2003 and 3.4 million in 2008. For a total population of 33.7 million in Kerala in 2008, it is estimated that one quarter of Kerala households have at least one member working abroad. Remittances have in turn increased from Rs136,520 million (£2,037 million) in 1999 (Kumar and George 2009) to Rs432,880 million (£5,033) in 2008 (Zachariah and Rajan 2010), accounting for as much as a third of Kerala's state domestic product in 2008. At the level of households, remittances have contributed substantially to their annual income. In addition to the reduction in household size as a result of a decrease in the number of children, remittance has enabled families of various communities to opt out of the government and aided schooling system and meet the increasing costs of private education (Osella and Osella 2000).

Since the 1990s, Kerala is no longer a relatively poor state. The context is one of economic recovery and growing per capita income due to the increasing inflow of remittances and the expansion of private job markets (Chakraborty 2005; Kumar and George 2009). At the turn of twenty-first century, the proportion of Kerala households owning luxury commodity items was larger than in the country as a whole (Kumar and George 2009: 11).

Despite the large volume of external remittances to the state, and despite the recovery of its economy in the 1990s, the state government has been facing recurrent fiscal crises (Kumar and George 2009: 10). Rather than seeking to raise additional resources, the state has turned to compressing public expenditure on sectors such as education as a way to reduce its deficit. The share of education in its total expenditure came down from 27.4 per cent in 1982 to 18.6 per cent in 2007 (Kumar and George 2009: 10). This reduction in state expenditure has prevented the government from expanding the capacity and maintaining the standard of government-owned and government-aided institutions when educational demand was on the rise across all social groups. The vacuum created has increasingly been filled by self-financing (private) institutions.

This trend is not exclusive to Kerala. The liberalisation of the Indian economy has led to a wider transformation in education policy and practice over the last two decades, made possible through the growing privatisation and commercialisation of the education sector and the involvement of private multinational companies in it (Chakravarti 2013; Qureshi and Osella 2013; Sharma 2005). These changes have underscored the need for competitiveness in the global market.

Much of the success of the liberalisation project in India seems to rest on the nation's ability to become a 'knowledge economy', a term now used widely in state education policy statements as a kind of aspirational horizon. 'As India enters the global economy, what it is needed are more English-educated, technically trained personnel for its expanding IT and IT enabled service industries' (Chakravarti 2013: 42). The life and professional success of young Indians is increasingly tied to their capacity to acquire IT certificates and degrees, and competitive knowledge and skills, to be sold in the global labour market. Chakravarti (2013) points out that the National Knowledge Commission (NKC) Report (Government of India 2009) openly stresses the need to gear Indian education policies towards making India a 'knowledge economy' with a focus on creating IT proficiency, efficiency; all of which is thought to be most effectively achieved through the private market. Never before has the Indian government endorsed privatisation as it does now.

In the context of increasing middle-class purchasing power and the overall endorsement of private education, the value of education as a precious economic resource has grown too. Private managements increasingly resort to the wallets of middle-class families as a source of funding rather than the state coffers. In Kochi, the management of some of the oldest running aided schools have recently open self-financing institutions, sometimes right next to their original, government-funded campuses.

These changes have opened up new educational possibilities for the middle classes and elites. In turn, private schooling has become one of the primary commodities by which class membership is asserted (Liechty 2003: 213). Invest-ing in English-medium private schooling has emerged as a ubiquitous practice amongst not only what anthropologist have called the 'established' middle classes – who have for several generations enjoyed maximum-achiever status and inherited privilege from their upper-caste and urban forebearers – but also amongst the new middle-class families of less-privileged backgrounds who have more recently gained access to consumerist lifestyles, wealth and power (Saavala 2003). In addition to its value as a prestige commodity, parental desire for such schools derives from their comparatively better results in all-India competitive examinations for admission to higher education when compared with the weak performance of Kerala government and aided schools (George *et al.* 2002: 57). Their attraction towards such schools is also an indicator of the strong orientation towards English-medium, which has, since colonial times, being linked to greater prestige and opportunities for gainful employment. In Kerala and elsewhere in India, this shift has been bolstered by the growing disdain towards government schools (Jeffery *et al.* 2005, 2007). Discourses about the lack accountability, sloth, corruption and rigidity of such schools and their dependence on orthodox, rote learning, increasingly dominate the public imagination (Chakravarti 2013: 52).

Although this growth has quickly been read by supporters of the 'Model' as a drastic shift in Kerala's education system from an inclusive and state-led one to an exclusive and commercialised one (Kumar and George 2009), this is not a new trend. The proportion of private schools was very high in the early 1950s, which only came down as a result of private management's decision to seek government resources between the 1960s and 1980s. Before aided schools attained their pre-eminent position, fees and resources to maintain and start schools and colleges were mobilised from families and within communities (Kumar and George 2009: 13). In addition, in Travancore and Cochin there has been a historic willingness of parents to pay for their children's education. In 1904, the British Resident did not seem fully convinced by the free primary education policy being introduced in Travancore when he wrote that 'judging from its past history, Travancoreans are willing to pay for the education of their children, at least of their sons, and I do not see why primary education should now be given free' (Aiya 1906: 444). These changes signal not only families' capacity to meet the private cost of education, but also that the orientation towards specific forms of education continues to be at the centre of middle-class aspirations and strategies of social mobility. In Kerala it has not been the emphasis on education that distinguishes the middle classes from the poorer sections of society, but their penchant for particular or exclusive forms of education that are thought to facilitate the access to the more profitable and prestigious employment opportunities available in the job market at a particular moment in time.

The private schooling landscape in Kochi

The schooling sector in the city of Kochi is increasingly divided into a mass of underfunded[16] government schools catering for poor families, aided schools fragmented according to the identity projects of diverse religious/caste communities and a growing number of private schools catering for the widening middle classes and elites. The last of these is also fragmented in terms of religious and caste orientations and stratified according to a wide range of economic capabilities.[17]

Table 2.2 Number of government-aided and private schools in Kerala, 1990–1991 and 2009–2010

Category	1990–91			2009–10		
	Government	Private aided	Recognised unaided	Government	Private aided	Recognised unaided
High school	961	1380	111	1006	1429	379
Upper primary school	960	1883	72	953	1870	217
Lower primary school	2565	4068	134	2542	3979	267
Total	4486	7331	317	4501	7278	863

Source: Recognised Unaided Schools in Kerala Report 2010

Like private schooling in the first half of the twentieth century, the initiative for establishing new private schools has often come from local churches and community organisations, as well as from educational entrepreneurs. In a Christian-dominated city, many schools are affiliated to local Christian communities. Other schools have been established by Hindu trusts, some of which impart an openly Hindu education while others are advertised as 'pan-Indian' and claim to offer an education moored in 'Indian' values and traditions. In the early 2000s, Kochi saw the opening of its first Muslim private school. In addition, there are also a number of schools marketed as secular, which try to appeal to a 'modern' constituency by incorporating the words 'Public School' into their names (Jeffery *et al.* 2005: 54).

As elsewhere in South Asia, private schools are distinguished by their reputation for higher academic standards and above all their emphasis on the English language as a medium of instruction. Most private schools are affiliated to the Central Board of Secondary Education (CBSE) or Indian Council of Secondary Education (ICSE). CBSE and ICSE curricula are perceived as offering better academic standards and better quality of English instruction than the Kerala state curriculum. However, there is also the view amongst parents that the quality of English teaching varies widely from one private school to another, and that the higher the tuition fee the better the quality of English instruction, an opinion also found by Liechty in Kathmandu (2003: 213).

In terms of cost, the new private sector is nothing but heterogeneous. Many schools charge affordable fees at around Rs15,000 (£153) per year. Others charge fees many times that amount, catering for the upper social strata. The new private schooling sector responds to and in turn reinforces sentiments in which individuals and groups are defined in terms of highly uneven financial capabilities. The peer groups in such schools are increasingly likely to be class groups rather than groups based on religion or caste (Liechty 2003: 213).

It is important to note that apart from the cost of unaided schools, there has been a much broader increase in the private cost[18] of education since the 1990s. Local studies have demonstrated how even within the aided and government sector, where students do not have to pay fees, students have to incur cost of various types such as 'special fees', examination fees, cost of reading and writing materials, clothing, travelling, study tours and donations to parent–teacher associations (PTAs) (Nambuthiri 2004). Moreover, the proportion of household spending in extra coaching and private tuitions has been on the rise. There has been a rapid growth of self-financing colleges, institutions in the higher education and the technical education sector. Most of the highly sought-after job-oriented courses such a engineering, medicine, nursing and management are now in the self-financing sector (Kumar and George 2009).

At the higher end of the private education sector, Kochi has seen the recent emergence of a new kind of private institutions advertised as 'international' schools,[19] such as the Choice School or Global Public School (known locally as GPS). These schools have been established by entrepreneurs who have benefited from the long history of migration and have seen in education a highly profitable field, a phenomenon described in other out-migratory states in present day India (see, for example, Qureshi and Osella 2013). They are modelled on 'western' educational institutions, but adapted to the cultural requirements of the Indian market through offering curricula moored in 'Indian' cultural values. They charge fees unaffordable to the vast majority and offer foreign or international curricula, such the Cambridge Certificate or the International Baccalaureate, promising parents and students favourable access to higher education overseas. Although they are certainly the realm of the elite – a new arena, which has provided the most privileged with new opportunities to assert and impose their status – they are producing wider effects in local demand and the private schooling sector as a whole.

These schools seemed to have fuelled an overall demand for an education attuned to global standards, driving private schools catering for the urban middle classes to (re)design their curricula and pedagogies to embrace an 'international' or 'cosmopolitan' flavour (ethos, practices and orientations), seeking to provide students with 'exposure to global culture' (Fuller and Narasimhan 2006; Narasimhan 2009). Brahmacharya Vidya Mandir is one such school that has sought to transform their educational project in an attempt to 'keep up' with the alleged contemporary demands for cutting-edge internationalised forms of education. In aiming to capture this growing market, these middle-class schools in turn help seal in the minds of middle-class families the desire for 'international' schools as a new prestigious commodity, and the idea that they offer a superior quality of education than would be experienced in local schools. These schools are imbricate in the fact that increasing numbers of middle-class parents in India, and elsewhere (Hayden 2011), aspire for their children to benefit from schools thought to offer the English-medium education, personalities, skills and credentials that will allow them to become socially and geographically mobile (Qureshi and Osella 2013).

BVM, the unaided school where I conducted the core of my in-school fieldwork, is reflective of many of these points. It was the creation of the 'Brahmacharya',[20] an educational trust founded in Mumbai in 1939. Contrary to what the 'Model' literature would have us believe, some early unaided schools, such as BVM, were opened as a result of the collaboration between private agents and public sector industries (that is, with direct involvement of the state). BVM was established in 1977 in the neighbourhood known as Kumar Nagar, as a result of the collaboration of two major public sector industries: the Fertilisers & Chemicals Travancore and CSL. The latter provided the land for the construction of the school – 1.72 acres on a thirty-year lease – in exchange for a reduction of admission fees to the children of shipyard employees. Shipyard workers of all levels and social groups thus became more attracted to sending their children to the English-medium school, which grew rapidly into the popular school it is today.

Like any other private school it has always been an institution that catered to families with some economic standing, but its fees have, until recently, been relatively low when compared to more recently open private schools. In addition, the privileges offered to CSL children have resulted in a student population of diverse social and economic background. However, the school has recently implemented a marked increase in fees in an effort to stay in tune with the exigencies of the increasingly better-off families to which the school aspires to cater. This is linked to the transformation of the area of Kumar Nagar where many of these families now live and has noticeably impinged upon less-privileged CSL workers' capacity to school their children at BVM. Over the school's three decades of existence, BVM parents have shifted from being government and public sector employees at large, to being professionals, business people and private sector entrepreneurs. Now, with 1,738 students and 101 staff members, BVM is one of the most highly reputed schools in Kochi.

Conclusion

This chapter has examined the long history of educational demand and provision in the state of Kerala. It does not deny that Kerala is a land of extraordinary educational achievements. Rather, I have sought to delve underneath remarkable educational indicators and explore the social processes that lead to the widespread penchant for education. What emerges from this chapter is an uneven history of education. Formal, western-style education began as an elite experiment, which allowed that elite to articulate itself as members of an economic class and as the maximum exponents of achieved status. Thereafter, diverse, community-based struggles for education emerged, becoming, later on, a crucial dimension of various social reform movements. With the support of the state policies, community-based educational struggles helped spread the middle-class imaginary of education as a key means to achieve and consolidate social mobility across all sections of society. Underneath this middle-class ideology of education, a complexly stratified schooling landscape emerged, replacing old forms of inequalities with new forms of inequalities in education. Recent changes in the private schooling sector have provided the elite new spaces to reinstate their power through education.

Notes

1   Kerala's penchant for education and its widespread schooling are the legacy of social and economic dynamics that emerged in these two princely states. For the most part Malabar, present day northern Kerala, is left out of this chapter's discussion and is only incorporated into this book's accounts after the formation of the modern Kerala State in 1956. The reason for this is that Malabar's position as an outpost of the Madras presidency, and the absence of key social processes, such as the emergence of social reform movements in the early twentieth century, resulted in a markedly different history of educational development.

2   Discussion of the relative merits of private/state schools continues to be mostly based on quantitative, yet partial, markers of efficiency and effectiveness. There are few accounts that take a critical and politically engaged approach to understanding the contribution of private schooling to learning and livelihoods. This book and Caddell (2006) are exceptions.

3   The kingdom of Cochin, in modern-day central Kerala, saw the first 'western'-style educational institutions established in the sixteenth and seventeenth centuries. At that time importance was only given to the improvement of seminary education with a view to producing better priests (Malekandathil 2001: 87). In 1558, the city of Cochin's first college, Madre de Deu College, had 300 seminarists aspiring for priesthood (Malekandathil 2001: 87).

4   This entailed a departure from earlier educational policy by which royal or governmental support for education was primarily for centres of higher learning education and not for primary schools (Tharakan 1984: 1918).

5   This was a system by which private schools would receive financial aid if they met the state criteria on teachers' qualifications, curriculum and books used. It sought to standardise schooling in the state.

6   In nineteenth-century Travancore they held most posts in government service (Mathew 1989: 24). At the turn of the twentieth century there were numerous Nair government officials and petty officials; Tamil Brahmins held most key posts (Jeffrey 1976; Mathew 1989).

7   Syrian Christians involved themselves in large-scale agricultural and commercial projects through which they acquired more power than the Nairs and their small-landholding joint families (Jeffrey 1976; Lemercinier and Rendel 1983).

8   These are government-funded schools with private management.

9   This law was aimed at ending the old feudal relations by legitimising the right of real peasants to own the land they cultivate.

10   In Kerala more than 90 per cent literacy is considered total literacy (Tharakan 2004: 48).

11   The Kerala Model literature represents Kerala as an alternative model of development, that emphasises the equitable distribution of resources rather than the growth of capitalist production; a place where, despite low per capita income, the state has achieved significant improvements in the material conditions of living. The Model literature usually draws upon indicators such low levels of infant mortality and population growth, and high levels of literacy and life expectancy in order to support its claims (see, for example, Sen *et al.* 1991).

12   Kerala's ever-growing unemployment is the highest in the country. 'It is not only about educational unemployment of the general category but it is also unemployment of skilled, professional, semi skilled and unskilled workers. One important feature of the Kerala economy is the out-migration of the labour force, particularly to Gulf region, and inflow of huge remittances into the State' (Government of Kerala 2010).

13 In 2008–2009, 45.46 lakh students were enrolled in schools in the state. In 2010–2011 this was reduced to 43.51 lakh students (Government of Kerala 2010).

14 Education after the first ten years was a part of the higher education system for many decades. Higher secondary courses were introduced in the state during 1990–1991 to reorganise the secondary level of education in accordance with National Education Policy. There were 1,907 higher secondary schools in 2011 in the state. Out of these, 760 (39.86 per cent) were government schools, 686 (35.97 per cent) were aided schools and the remaining 461 (24.17 per cent) were unaided schools (George *et al.* 2002).

15 Along with the CSL, other major public sector industries, such as Fertilisers and Chemicals Travancore Limited and Cochin Refineries Limited, developed around the border townships of Ernakulam/Kochi city. Other major industries established in and around Ernakulam/Kochi in the post-Independence era were the Travancore Cochin Chemicals, Indian Aluminium Co., Hindustan Organics Ltd, Appollo Tyres, Binani Zinc Limited, Hindustan Machine Tools and Indian Rare Earths Ltd. Although centred in Ernakulam, industrialisation in the state has still been slow when compared to other states in the country. In spite of this, these public sector industries have played a major role in the city's development and an important source for employment. In addition to being the industrial centre of the state, Ernakulam/Kochi has also been an important military hub.

16 Since the 1990s, a deep fiscal crisis in Kerala has meant that the share of expenditure is under strain, the component of aided schools consumes all funds available.

17 For an extensive discussion about the diverse nature of the private schooling sector in South Asia, see Caddell and Ashley (2006). This discussion is an extension of a prior debate about the decentralisation of education (Dyer and Rose 2005).

18 This is the part of the investment in education that is either made by the student or the parent, or both (Nambuthiri 2004).

19 The growth of this type of school has inevitably been skewed in out-migratory states with economies substantially dependent on remittances, such as the case of Kerala (Zachariah and Rajan 2010). As Dale and Robertson rightly note, one of the key effects of globalisation on education has been the 'shift away from a predominantly national education system to a more fragmented, multi-scale and multi-sectoral distribution of activity that now involves new players, new ways of thinking about knowledge production and distribution, and new challenges in terms of ensuring the distribution of opportunities for access and social mobility' (Robertson and Dale 2008: 20).

20 Pseudonym.

Bibliography

Abdul Salim, A. and P. R. Gopinathan Nair 2002. *Educational Development in India: The Kerala experience since 1800.* Anmol.

Aiya, V. N. 1906. *The Travancore State Manual.* (3 vols). Indian Educational Services.

Baby, A. A. and K. G. Sukumara Pillai 2008. *Recognised Unaided Schools in Kerala.* Government of Kerala.

Béteille, A. 1991. The reproduction of inequality: Occupation, caste and family. *Contributions to Indian Sociology* **25**, 3–28.

Caddell, M. 2006. Private schools as battlefields: Contested visions of learning and livelihood in Nepal. *Compare: A Journal of Comparative and International Education* **36**, 463–479.

Caddell, M. and L. D. Ashley 2006. Blurring boundaries: Towards a reconceptualisation of the private sector in education. *Compare: A Journal of Comparative and International Education* **36**, 411–419.

Chakraborty, A. 2005. Kerala's changing development narratives. *Economic and Political Weekly* **40**, 541–547.

Chakravarti, P. 2013. Fantasies of transformation: Education neoliberal self-making, and Bollywood. In *Enterprise Culture in Neoliberal India: Studies in Youth, Class, Work and Media* (ed.) N. Gooptu, 42–56. Routledge.

De Neve, G. 2011. 'Keeping it in the family': Work, education and gender hierarchies among Tiruppur's industrial capitalists. In *Being Middle-Class in India: A Way of Life* (ed.) H. Donner, 73–99. Routledge.

Devika, J. 2007. *En-gendering Individuals: The Language of Re-forming in Early Twentieth Century Keralam*. Orient Longman.

Dyer, C. and P. Rose 2005. Decentralisation for educational development? An editorial introduction. *Compare: A Journal of Comparative and International Education* **35**, 105–113.

Franke, R. W. and B. H. Chasin 1994. *Kerala: Development Through Radical Reform*. (Auflage: 2 Sub). Bibliophile South Asia.

Fuller, C. J. and H. Narasimhan 2006. Engineering colleges, 'exposure' and information technology professionals in Tamil Nadu. *Economic and Political Weekly* **3**, 258–262.

George, M. K. and J. Domi 2002. *Residual Literacy in a Coastal Village: Poovar Village of Thiruvananthapuram District*. (KRPLLD Discussion Paper No. 45). CDS.

George, K. K., G. Zachariah and N. A. Kumar 2002. *Grant in Aid Policies and Practices Towards Secondary Education in Kerala*. Centre for Socio-Economic and Environmental Studies.

Government of Kerala 2010. *Economic Review*. Kerala State Planning Board.

Government of India 2009. *The National Knowledge Commission Report 2006–2009*. Government of India.

Hayden, M. 2011. Transnational spaces of education: The growth of the international school sector. *Globalisation, Societies and Education* **9**, 211–224.

Jeffrey, C., P. Jeffery and R. Jeffery 2008. *Degrees Without Freedom?: Education, Masculinities, and Unemployment in North India*. Stanford University Press.

Jeffrey, R. 1976. *The Decline of Nair Dominance: Society and Politics in Tranvancore, 1847–1908*. Vikas Publishing House.

Jeffrey, R. 1992. *Politics, Women and Well-being: How Kerala Became 'a Model'*. Macmillan.

Jeffery, R., P. Jeffery and C. Jeffrey 2005. Social inequalitites and the privatisation of secondary schooling in North India. In *Educational Regimes in Contemporary India* (eds) R. Chopra and P. Jeffery, 41–61. Sage.

Jeffery, R., P. Jeffery and C. Jeffrey 2007. The privatisation of secondary schooling in Bijnor: A crumbling welfare state? In *Education and Social Change in South Asia* (eds) K. Kumar and J. Oesterheld, 442–474. Orient Longman.

Joshi, S. 2010. *The Middle Class in Colonial India*. Oxford University Press.

Kumar, N. A. and K. K. George 2009. *Kerala's Education System: From Inclusion to Exclusion?*. Working paper no. 22. Centre for Socio-economic & Environmental Studies.

Lemercinier, G. and Y. Rendel 1983. *Religion and Ideology in Kerala*. New Delhi.

Liechty, M. 2003. *Suitably Modern: Making middle-class culture in a new consumer society*. Princeton University Press.

Malekandathil, P. 2001. *Portuguese Cochin and the Maritime Trade of India 1500–1663*. Manohar Publishers and Distributors.

Mathew, G. 1989. *Communal Road To A Secular Kerala*. Concept Publishing Company.

Nambuthiri, S. 2004. *Cost of Schooling in Kerala: A Study of Private and Institutional Cost under Different Types of Management*. (KRPLLD Discussion Paper). CDS.

Narasimhan, H. (2009). 'Unfinishing schools': Learning 'computer' in Mofussil Tamil Nadu. Mofussil India, London School of Economics, 6–7 July.

Oomen, G. 2007. Education, self-perception, and identity: The experience of the Pulaya Christians of Kerala (1860–1930). In *Education and Social Change in South Asia* (eds) K. Kumar and J. Oesterheld, 101–127. Orient Longman.

Osella, F. and C. Osella 2000. *Social Mobility in Kerala: Modernity and Identity in Conflict*. Pluto Press.

Qureshi, K. and F. Osella 2013. Transnational schooling in Punjab, India: Designer migrants and cultural politics. In *Refugees, Immigrants, and Education in the Global South: Lives in Motion* (eds) L. Bartlett and A. Ghaffar-Kucher, 99–115. Routledge.

Robertson, S. and R. Dale 2008. Researching education in a globalising era: Beyond methodological nationalism, methodological statism, methodological educationism and spatial fetishism. In *The Production of Educational Knowledge in the Global Era* (ed.) J. Resnik, 19–32. Sense.

Saavala, M. 2003. Auspicious Hindu houses. The new middle classes in Hyderabad, India. *Social Anthropology* **11**, 231–247.

Scaria, S. 2014. Do caste and class define inequality? Revisiting education in a Kerala village. *Contemporary Education Dialogue* **11**, 153–177.

Sen, B. H. C. and R. W. F., reply by Amartya 1991. The Kerala difference. *The New York Review of Books*, 24 October (available online: www.nybooks.com/articles/archives/1991/oct/24/the-kerala-difference/).

Sharma, V. 2005. Commercialisation of Higher Education in India. *Social Scientist* **33**, 65–74.

Tharakan, P. K. 2004. Ernakulam revisited: A study of literacy in the first totally literate district in India. In *Paradigms of Learning: The Total Literacy Campaign in India* (ed.) M. Karlekar, 48–92. Sage.

Tharakan, P. K. M. 1984. Socio-economic factors in educational development: Case of nineteenth century Travancore. *Economic and Political Weekly* **19**, 1913–1928.

Zachariah, K. C. and S. I. Rajan 2010. *Migration Monitoring Study, 2008: Emigration and Remittances in the Context of Surge in Oil Prices*. (Working Paper). CDS.

3   Aspirational regimes

Mainstream Indian media is now dominated by a new youthful urban persona: hardworking, independent individuals who are endowed with overflowing ambition and aspirations, and whose determination to achieve their dreams was apparently lacking in the previous generation. Echoing this notion of youth, Priti's father once explained to me that:

> Today, a girl studying in eighth standard can talk about what she wants to be. She would say I want to be a doctor, an engineer. The modern generation has got awareness and lots of opportunities and lots of avenue too. Those days [when he was an eighth-standard student] it wasn't like that; simply, you studied.

This account exemplifies parents' deep sense of optimism about the lives and professional prospects of their sons and daughters in the current economic climate. Parents whom I interviewed imagined an abundant terrain of employment opportunities in India and abroad, which was in turn envisioned as offering especially high rewards to individual creativity, innovation, leadership and hard work. Many repeated the phrase 'the sky is the limit' when talking about their children's prospects, projecting a sense of confidence similar to the 'culture of magical belief' surrounding the IT industry that Peter van der Veer (2005) describes. This vision was often supported by narratives of the past as a time when employment opportunities were very scarce, and young people supposedly lacked the level of ambition of contemporary youth.

In this chapter I explore the data collected from middle-class parents and high-school students in urban Kochi, which led me to question this public imaginary of the aspirational young Indian in a time of opportunity, and to explore to what extent it reflects the lives of higher secondary students' and their families'[1] everyday experiences. In particular, this chapter highlights how parents actively reproduce this language of aspiration and individual enterprise as part of their strategies to lead their sons and daughters into specific careers and professions. It focuses on households of markedly different socioeconomic positions within the middle social spectrum who send their children to the same private school, the highly reputed English-medium BVM. I will argue that, despite their differences, parents come together in similar authoritarian educational practices directed at ensuring their children's educational success and entrance into specific professions, perceived as secure and as garnering desired lifestyles. In particular I examine three common-alities: the choice of school, investment in entrance coaching (EC) and decisions regarding career options.

More importantly, I show how parental authority in shaping young people's educational careers is imposed and disguised through shared middle-class dis-courses about modern Indian parents as being 'detached', and new Indian youth as the embodiment of the aspirational and enterprising citizen: one who is not only fiercely ambitious, but also self-disciplined and driven by individual initiative. The articulation of parents' authoritarian projects through a neoliberal discourse that celebrates individual youthful independent drive to 'success' is what I describe as parental 'aspirational regimes'. Finally, the chapter reveals how these shared regimes not only mask their authoritarian character behind a facade of freedom, but also conceal varying degrees of uncertainty and anxiety experienced across households, thus serving to reproduce social inequalities while helping to cement tropes of the enterprising Indian young self.

In what follows, I draw ethnographic portraits of a number of families in order to exemplify the diversity of students attending the school. Next, I examine parents' educational narratives and practices relating to schooling, EC and career prefer-ences. I draw primarily on two sources: in-depth interviews with parents whose sons or daughters attended BVM and a survey carried out in the neighbourhoods surrounding the school.

Ethnographic portraits

Balraj, a seventeen-year-old Hindu Nair in Class 12, played football inside and outside school whenever the hectic routine of the final year allowed it. He dreamed of being able to play football professionally, but more realistically liked the idea of pursuing a degree in hotel management and becoming a chef in a hotel. Half-way through his Class 12, his parents allowed him to nurture that interest by not 'going deep into it' (i.e. by avoiding the matter). Balraj's father (BSc physics), who runs a small business selling medical equipment, claimed to have entered a 'confused stage' about Balraj's future after school. His problem was that Balraj's marks were not very high, 'they are not that encouraging'. As the end of the final year approached, Balraj's parents became more anxious. Decisions at this stage were seen as vital in determining a person's future. As his parents put it: 'There will be no return; it will be a one-way path'. They felt unsure about the appropriateness of a career in hotel management. They saw it as limiting the 'opportunities of growth' through a lifetime that they wished to pass on to him. 'We are putting pressure on him to improve his performance in the exams', his parents said towards the end of the academic year. Although Balraj's future seemed puzzling for his parents, his older sister's trajectory, at the time doing a BSc in medical technology at a private college in Pune, fell more in line with their parents' business and aspirations. In the end, Balraj joined a hotel management degree programme in

Mumbai, while his sister graduated and returned to Kochi to work in the family business.

Priti, a Tamil Brahmin, was at the time of fieldwork aged sixteen and a pupil in Class 11. She was enrolled in one of the two computer/mathematics batches available in school.[2] This was the most sought-after, and hence competitive, higher secondary division. It was understood to lead to the most coveted professional degrees, namely IT-related engineering courses. Priti aspired to gain admission to an Indian Institute of Technology (IIT), and was without a doubt one of the most hard-working students in the batch. At weekends she attended one of the main providers of EC in the city. Even when at school, she devoted every spare moment to keeping up with the demanding EC assignments. Priti acknowledged the advantage of being exposed to EC and valued wholeheartedly the financial effort that her parents made in order to pay Rs35,000 (£356) for the two-year course. Although she found the institute's methods to be harsh at times, Priti valued 'the advantage of knowing the kinds of questions they give at the IIT entrance exam'.

Priti and her family lived in a small house near the school. Priti's mother, a mathematics and education graduate, was a housewife. Her father (BCom) was retired from Godrej (one of India's largest conglomerates) as a finance manager. After he had completed his pre-university course in Madurai, his parents (Priti's grandparents) pressured him to quit studying and work in the family's small business. With eleven siblings, most of them younger than him, he was expected to contribute to the family's income. While helping in the family's business, he took courses in shorthand and typewriting, as well as a course in wireless operation/ Morse code, aiming to find clerical employment or a job on board a merchant ship. After holding several small clerical posts, Priti's father returned to college, completed a degree in commerce, and secured a more stable job in Godrej. He always dreamed, he explained, of being able to say he was a university graduate.

Ajit, in the eleventh standard, was a fresher at BVM. He grew up in a Bengali family settled in Mysore, in the southern Indian state of Karnataka. Ajit, his parents and younger sister were relocated to Kochi in May 2009 because of his father's job as a planner for Hindustan Unilever. Upon arrival, Ajit's parents relied on the advice of local acquaintances to shortlist the best possible schools. Ajit was placed in the same EC as Priti, as they had heard of its professed high success rates in helping students to succeed in competitive examinations leading to the professions. However, Ajit's father told me:

> In today's scenario whatever he requires, he has to pick it up himself ... parents are far behind the present generation's knowledge; we are not in touch with the day-to-day knowledge; we are always busy with our existence in the office. So, what we are doing? We are only spending money and trying to put him in the right place, and it is up to him how far he can grow ... they are on their own.

Throughout the academic year, Ajit struggled to pass term exams in most subjects. Not knowing Malayalam, the local language,[3] and not having enough time and energy to study after attending EC, his academic performance was seriously undermined. Towards the end of the academic year, Ajit's parents pulled him out of EC in an attempt to help him pass the eleventh-standard examinations. But a few weeks later, Ajit was once again attending EC. He seemed disillusioned, yet resigned to his parents' decision and acknowledged that otherwise it would entail a 'waste of money'. Ajit failed Class 11.

Parvathi was one of the few freshers in eleventh standard. She was a Tamil Brahmin, born in Kochi. Until her tenth standard, she studied at another English-medium school, Central Board of Secondary Education (CBSE), where, at the time of my fieldwork, her younger brother continued to go. Her parents' decision to attempt the transfer to a more reputable and expensive school was supported by Parvathi's outstanding score – more than 90 per cent – in the CBSE Class 10 Board examination. 'Everybody was telling us that she should try getting into a school with better coaching so that she can write entrance exams'.

Parvathi's father worked in a local newspaper, while her mother was a housewife. Her parents had what they called 'a normal [school] education'; that is, they attended Malayalam-medium, government schools. Later her father completed a BCom followed by an MCom. With three successfully completed graduate degrees – a Bed,[4] a BA in political science, and another BA in social studies – Parvathi's mother was over qualified, yet she never held any formal employment. After getting married, they pondered over the option of finding her a job as a teacher, but the bribe they had to give for such a job deterred them from it. Her father worked as a clerk in Saudi Arabia for nine years between 1983 and 1992. Life in the Gulf was 'like a prison', he recalled. But at the time jobs in the Gulf were seen as 'something like a money mining job' that inspired him to dream of saving enough money to eventually return to Kerala and start a business of his own. Those ambitions faded away, and he settled with a white collar position at the newspaper.

Parvathi's results in the boards not only entailed an immediate reorientation of her schooling career, it conditioned much of what her parents expected from her in the long and short term. 'I want her to be better than us', the father confessed. He went on talking about computer engineering, the need for an MBA and jobs at the nearest IT park – Infopark – as the opportunities to which she should aspire after school. Her father went even further saying that if she got one such jobs 'she could earn from 40,000 to 50,000, with this 90 per cent mark she could study and get this engineering job. Now I am earning almost 10,000, so she could make five times more if she studies'. In accordance with this, Parvathi's parents placed her at the same entrance coaching institution as Priti, intending that she secured a merit seat at a Kerala engineering college. Her parents enforced a strict studying routine at home. They were pressured from her head teacher, who reportedly called home to urge them to make sure she devoted more time to studying. They complained about the fact that Parvathi spent too much time watching TV.

For Parvathi, the changes that derived from her successful performance in the board exams were mostly a source of distress. Repeatedly she spoke of feeling tense and narrowed her aspirations down to wishing to complete Classes 11 and 12, putting off her father's expectations. For Parvathi, sitting in front a computer –

which she imagined she would have to do if she were to study computer engineering – seemed unhealthy, while attending entrance coaching was simply 'a waste of time'. The social struggle that resulted from changing school mattered a lot to her. Making friends in the new school turned out to be difficult, as 'there were gangs of friends already'. 'I was trying to mingle but they don't want to make friends'. This 'tension' was exacerbated by a heightened sense of competition, or at least a more demanding schooling environment, amongst her new peers. 'It's a very different situation over here ... everybody is brilliant or something'. Parvathi thought these factors contributed to her getting a low mark in her first term examination at BVM.

Vijay is one of the few students at BVM who participated in the school's student exchange programme, which is said to cost Rs1.5 lakh (£1,500) per student. A Class 12 Nair student, he belonged to what some of his peers called the 'English-speaking gang', those who communicate in English amongst peers (and most of the time at home as well). He was an asset to the school for his English public-speaking skills, which he had developed at a young age when his parents put him in English oratory classes. His sharp and eloquent use of the English language was at the school's disposal for all sort events and interschool competitions and as such he was one of a few youth who served as the public face of the institution. These activities, he confessed, worked as an excuse for his not so great academic performance, which Vijay simply saw a result of sloth. 'But you can't say you are lazy'. When I asked him about the future, Vijay said that he would be content with studying any business-related degree and then look after his parent's business. However, his parents convinced him that he should 'learn science' now and subsequently acquire a *professional* (engineering) degree, and then get an MBA to finally work at expanding the family business. In 2011, Vijay completed his first year of an engineering degree programme at VIT, Tamil Nadu.

Vijay, his younger brother and parents (and a Labrador retriever) lived in a sumptuous flat near the school. His parents, in their mid-forties, held multiple postgraduate degrees, which they acquired in New Delhi, Tamil Nadu and Kerala. His father, the son of Ayurvedic doctors, and his mother, the daughter of a navy official, were successful business people. They owned an advertising company that managed billboards across Kerala and a rice mill. Unlike Parvathi's parents, Vijay's mother believed BVM was seriously falling into disfavour. Years back she valued the school's Hindu-oriented (or non-Christian) education, its lower fees (and the fact that it was not a government-aided school) and its physical proximity. She complained that the school had become so 'commercialised' that 'the quality of students they are taking now is almost equivalent to government schools'. Moreover, the facilities of the recently inaugurated top-end schools, such as Global Public School (GPS), were, from her point of view, undermining the school's competitiveness.

Kochi middle classes

As these examples show, schools such as BVM are social nodes in which the various so-called middle-class tiers coexist (Fernandes and Heller 2006). They unite families from established middle-class backgrounds, who have for various generations enjoyed maximum achiever status and who have inherited privilege from their upper caste and urban forbearers.[5] They also attract families who have more recently gained access to the material lifestyles understood to be middle class. Having attained this economic base through education or migration, they now set out to reconvert their economic capital into higher forms of educational capital, which they will aspire to reconvert once more into greater prestige and economic gain. Through education, these families attempt to (re)produce wealth and prestige that can be transmitted to the next generation. Despite their disparate class positions, their expectations of their children were not discernibly different from those of more-established middle-class families.

However, the families of BVM pupils differ from each other in many ways. In terms of employment, BVM parents constitute a pool of skilled, educated and employed people at various levels. A large proportion of my informants' fathers worked in public industries, in positions ranging from semi-skilled labour-intensive posts, for example, as a welder at the CSL, to managerial positions. Another group of informants' parents worked in the private sector, either as entrepreneurs or as salaried employees. Amongst the entrepreneurs, most ventures were small to medium sized. Another cohort of fathers[6] consisted of former Gulf migrants. Being skilled or professionally qualified, unlike the majority of migrants to the Gulf,[7] they had managed to maintain long-term contracts and visas. Having spent considerable periods of time in the Gulf, some of them with more than twenty years abroad, they had amassed considerable wealth, which was regularly remitted to their families in Kochi. Most of these Gulf migrants were high-status Christians or high-caste Hindu Nairs who, thanks to their privileged economic and educational backgrounds, had access to overseas jobs and could afford the considerable amount of capital needed in the initial stages of migration (Osella and Osella 2000: 79). A final cohort of families was that of the most affluent and established upper-middle-class households, characterised by parents in the most coveted professions (engineers, medical doctors and lawyers) and entrepreneurs. Most of the families oriented their children's education towards acquiring the sort of prestige and wealth that this last cohort of families stood for. As a rule of thumb, parents who held semi-skilled jobs rarely spoke English and often had migrated to Kochi fairly recently. On the contrary, parents who held graduate and postgraduate degrees generally spoke English fluently, although most of them attended Malayalam-medium schools.

The choice of school

For middle-class families, the choice of formal education for their children is amongst the most important factors in improving their children's prospects for the future (Kumar 2011). Having consolidated wealth in previous generations, the families described were in pursuit of 'maximal achiever status' (Osella and Osella 2000). In Kerala, since the expansion of the colonial administration in the nineteenth century, English-medium education has been central to attaining this status, not only as a primary marker but also as the means to attain highly coveted forms of employment, which throughout most of the twentieth century meant jobs in public administration. These created the economic and cultural basis for groups of higher-caste and urban dwellers to rearticulate their privilege as successful members of the middle class (Kumar 2011: 224). Today, employment in public administration is losing its glamour vis-à-vis positions in the private sector, especially within the field of engineering. The attainment of maximal middle-class status is supported by the child's success or destroyed by the child's failure to acquire the necessary skills and credentials. As elsewhere in India, parents live in hope that their sons and daughters will somehow (re)produce that position in the employment hierarchy, and they realise with increasing urgency that to do so they must ensure the right education for their children (Parry 2005: 297).

For the majority of parents who participated in this research, the reputation of a school is primarily based on its ability to produce excellent academic results in board examinations and in the subsequent entrance examinations leading to professional degrees. In choosing a school for their children, parents try to maximise the children's chances of success in terms of their future professional careers. This is not to say that the school's academic results are the only criteria for choosing a school: others such as distance, facilities or religious affiliation are also important, but these are secondary by far, compared with academic results, and even more so as sons and daughters approach college age.

Parents and students keep track of schools' performance in board examinations; the news of top performers or IIT entrants quickly becomes public knowledge. In 2009, BVM received an extraordinary number of applications after a student, whom I call Rajan, came second in the nationwide CBSE Class 10 examination. Such information circulates so rapidly in Kochi that even before I met Rajan or gained access to BVM, I had already heard of his achievement from students of other schools. In choosing schools according to results, parents typically incur high expenses, often reported to be beyond the means of the family. As a rule of thumb, the higher a school's success at producing high-ranking students, the higher the fees charged to parents. A mother put it this way: 'If the results are not good, the school will lose that student; every management tries to improve results, and they take different fees according to performance'.

Families make many sacrifices in order to support their children through their education. Apart from fees, they have to pay for books, stationery, uniforms and other supplies, tuition and leisure activities. There are also the spatial and nutritional needs of students, which are imagined to be more crucial than the needs of young people engaged in non-academic activities (Kumar 2011: 230). A great portion of the family's functioning and routine is designed around giving the child time and support. Parents often wait for their children to come home to supervise their homework. Priti's mother described how she provided Priti with every single item of food that she asked for, as soon as she could, and she laughed at the fact that Priti did not know how to cook anything.[8]

Such reports were often accompanied by a parental discourse of inadequacy. Many parents portrayed themselves as being comparatively uneducated in today's subject fields, and therefore unable to help their children to succeed in school.

They increasingly relied on filling their children's agendas with coaching and extra-school tuition to improve their prospects in competitive examinations (Kumar 2011). Ajit's father painted himself as only being able to spend money as a way to ensure his son's success.

Simultaneously, parents actively sought to instil in their children a 'sacred responsibility' to succeed (Kumar 2011). In Classes 11 and 12, this mission became extraordinarily relevant. Priti's father explained how they had encouraged her daughter to understand studying as her work, and good marks as her pay, aiming in other words to teach her to be self-motivated and to take responsibility for her own success. Other parents talked about putting their sons and daughters under 'house arrest', which meant that access to a mobile phone, internet connection and TV was suspended for the duration of the final year. Most young people cooperated with their 'house arrest' and internalised the mission to succeed because of the successful combination of discipline, aspiration and sometimes blackmail deployed by parents (Kumar 2011: 222). At the end of the year some even talked about putting themselves under house arrest. In this sense, Kumar (2011) notes that the middle-class child is educated twice, not only in the content imparted at various educational institutions, but also into a particular disposition to seek success.

The result was that amongst many parents and their children there emerged a discourse and experience of the 'self-sacrificing parent' and the 'dutiful progeny': a middle-class discourse (Kumar 2011). In the context of Kerala, Devika suggests that this idea of productivity, 'of obedient, useful, productive subjects', as 'the norm by which the quality of domestic life was evaluated' (Devika 2007: 57), is not new. This understanding of modern domesticity is indeed linked to the making of a Malayalee middle class since the late nineteenth and early twentieth centuries, a process by which the labour of women in the domestic domain was tied to the production of modern subjects. Although the idea of the dutiful progeny is not completely new, what is new is how this discourse has been oriented towards the globalised economy, and in particular to the belief amongst parents that there is no limit to what their children can achieve. In contemporary Kolkata, Donner (2006) has revealed similar mothering practices amongst middle-class families. She shows that in the wake of globalisation and the integration of employment markets into worldwide discourses of skills and mobility, middle-class mothering has been reoriented towards supporting children throughout their educational career, and hence towards producing future white-collar workers for a global economy (Donner 2006: 378).

Entrance coaching

As students approached the crucial examinations at the end of their final year, parental anxieties and their efforts to assist their children's success intensified. The rising numbers of aspiring middle-class families (Donner and De Neve 2011) and the limited openings in the most sought-after colleges have resulted in a swelling demand for entrance coaching centres. Enrolling one's children in these centres has in turn become a marker of middle classness. Apart from investing in expensive private schooling, parents increasingly rely on EC that is specifically geared towards preparing young people to face entrance examinations for competitive professional degree courses.

The vast majority of the students I worked with attended at least one entrance coaching course in institutes in Kochi or beyond. In the EC lessons I audited there were more than fifty students crammed in a classroom, while I heard of lessons with up to 100 students in other centres. With yearly fees ranging from Rs30,000 to Rs60,000 (£300 to £600), parents chose EC for their children on the basis of criteria similar to those used for choosing schools: primarily the institute's ability to produce successful exam takers. There were some students who attended coaching centres in Kottayam, a city 65km south of Kochi, just for the sake of attending a centre with the best record in a particular examination. The format and content of tutorials vary widely and are adapted to the capabilities and desires of individual families. Centres offer courses at the primary, secondary or higher secondary levels, a choice of weekday and weekend courses and 'crash courses' immediately before entrance examinations. EC centres set frequent mock examinations, after which marks and feedback are given and revision classes are scheduled. In Kochi these centres have rapidly increased in numbers and visibility: its roads are lined with EC publicity, which often includes photographs of their most successful students.

Although the majority of parents I interviewed thought of EC education as an important complement to their children's school education, some saw EC as more crucial than school education. These parents endorsed the notion of better education as 'better coaching' to do well in specific examinations, and attributed the growth of the EC industry to what they saw as a 'lack of support' from schools, which they accused of failing to prepare young people effectively for the sorts of questions formulated in competitive entrance examinations. Their children often concurred, and considered coaching centres as crucial to their life and professional futures. Most pupils argued that school is about cramming facts or 'mugging up', while they described EC centres as teaching them how to solve 'HOT' (high order of thinking) questions, which were said to be 'application-level' questions that made them think and apply concepts to real-world problems. Like Priti, these young people devoted the majority of their time to studying and completing the assignments given to them by the coaching tutors, and they devoted less energy to school work.

Many BVM parents also valued entrance coaching positively for the level of discipline that they believed it instilled in students; something that they felt was being undermined in school. They viewed with scepticism some of the changes taking place in formal schooling, such as the introduction of 'child-friendly' approaches or holistic evaluation schemes.[9] Balraj's father, for example, spoke of 'expecting much more' from the level of discipline enforced in the school. 'They don't impose much on students; there is no pressure given'. He recalled the 'gap' that existed between students and teachers in the past, whereas now 'that relationship [of friendship between students and teachers] is spoiling the discipline of the school'. By exposing their children to the stricter regime of coaching centres, parents sought not only to educate their children in the contents of the course but also to inculcate in them self-discipline and respect for hierarchy, as well as teaching them how to manage 'pressure', generated not just by the burden of a heavier work-load but also by the competition amongst peers that is encouraged in these centres.

Others, however, were ambivalent about the need to burden children with EC lessons, yet they felt the pressure to conform to what has become a norm. Sending children to coaching centres was not a matter of desire but one of necessity in order to maintain their social standing. In this sense, middle-class status demands practices and levels of consumption that are in tune with 'the times', meaning that one must maintain the higher standard of living that upward mobility and the availability of new consumer goods have made 'normal' (van Wessel 2004: 97). An important reason for why EC has become a 'requirement' is the fact that competition for social status demands possession of consumer goods. A number of the parents I interviewed illustrated this point by using the Malayalam expression *nadodumbol naduve odanam*. Often translated as 'when people are running, you should run in the middle', the proverb makes the point that one should always strive to assimilate to the norm. Although some parents criticised the educational workload imposed on children, they nonetheless reproduced it, for it was as if their children's competi-tiveness was always hanging by the slenderest threat (Parry 2005: 290).

'We are only spending money' and the self-reliant youthful persona

Both the domestic practices related to education, and the choices of school and EC, which constitute a great deal of what Donner (2006) terms the 'pedagogising' of the home, are the main means through which parents exert a kind of 'intensive parenting' (Davies 2004). Davies (2004: 239) argues: 'Parents who hire or desire tutors are not overly busy but may in fact be more intensely involved with their children's education. Tutoring may be purchased by parents who are actually more closely involved with their children's homework schooling'. Entrance coaching and 'systematic' studying at home are for parents an alchemy that produces maximum achiever status. Through these, it is thought, 'the sky is the limit'.

Even though the lives of most BVM pupils were governed by their parents' educational expectations and by their efforts to develop self-motivated, self-disciplined, self-reliant and competitive characters, parents deployed narratives of contemporary youth as 'being on their own', which aimed at disguising their intensive parenting. As Ajit's father said, 'it is up to him how far he can grow'. These narratives depict an idealised past in which members of the family provided the necessary support to children's school careers. As Priti's father said, the family 'would never allow anyone to go astray'. It was claimed that elder siblings, cousins or aunts had always made sure that children studied every lesson, while now youth are said to have to fend for themselves. Parents in my study portrayed themselves as powerless, their only means of putting their children 'in the right place' being their ability to 'make money' and 'spend money'. Throughout my fieldwork in Kochi, teachers, parents and students alike contributed to an omnipresent view that in this generation it is up to the individual to work, learn, aspire and achieve.

Teachers and school staff reproduced this discourse and claimed that the mushrooming of coaching centres was a response to the lack of family support for pupils' everyday study needs. The popularity of EC is seen as evidence of the stereotype that modern parents are overworked and thus have no time or energy to look after their children. This ran into the fact that for the most part, mothers were at home as housewives and readily available to facilitate studying. This belief, however, is the most recurrent basis for schools' critique of contemporary parenting. In my interview with BVM's director, he blamed many parents for failing to cooperate in the education of their children. Parents are said not to convey moral values, but to leave children exposed without limits to valueless TV channels. He portrayed parents as neglecting family life and excessively focused on their professional lives, thus echoing negative stereotypes attributed to the modern family across India (Fuller and Narasimhan 2007). But if we examine parental engagement with their children's education, we see that, while parents are indeed busy, young people are far from being left 'on their own'. Moreover, as Priti's father's educational trajectory shows, extended families were not always supportive of children's education. As has been shown elsewhere in India, in extended families it is typical that only the youngest sibling is encouraged to continue their studies, while others are made to stop studying and start working or look after younger siblings, many of whom are left alone from a very young age (De Neve 2011; Parry 2005).

By disguising intensive parenting practices behind narratives of making and spending money, parents in effect helped to craft a pervasive, idealised image of contemporary youth as self-reliant, self-motivated and highly ambitious individuals; characteristics said to be lacking in the previous generation. By discursively placing the responsibility for 'growth' on their children, they sought to shape and educate them into the now normative subjectivity of the youthful enterprising Indian person. Parents helped to cement this notion by juxtaposing it with idealised memories of their own school and college years. Their generation was often characterised as being 'relaxed', 'enjoying' and concerned with 'playing only', while their children's generation was said to be obsessed with studying and innately ambitious. Ambition, to which I now turn, was always marked by the quest for professional careers.

Career choices

As with practices relating to school education and entrance coaching, decisions concerning higher education were also a site of parents' aspirational regimes. Parents' preferences for higher education were driven by a desire to guide their sons and daughters into careers with 'opportunities for growth'.[10] Having benefited from higher education and having accumulated wealth, BVM families now aspired to achieve (or maintain) the locally coveted professional status. This meant that parents almost unanimously expected their children to pursue professional degrees (engineering, medicine, chartered accountancy or law), locally seen as the sources of wealth and status *par excellence*. In addition, a large number of parents agreed that an engineering degree should ideally be followed by an MBA. A twelfth-standard female student put it succinctly:

> Now those who get BSc physics don't get jobs; now a BTech (engineering degree) is actually the minimum qualification, then you have to add an MBA. You should start from the BTech, the basic degree, that's what my parents tell me.

For parents, professional qualifications constituted the apex of a hierarchy of degrees interlinked with local class hierarchies. University degrees in the arts and sciences, which most parents had themselves acquired, were marked as conferring less status and fewer opportunities for economic gain. Parents who, for example, got a degree in commerce from St Albert's College, one of the oldest and most prestigious colleges in Kochi, regarded the college as a place with little status. One parent explained that today only 'local *mallus*'[11] attend that college. Those people, he said, 'still have that mindset; they want education for the sake of it'. These 'local' colleges are now 'secondary', he continued, 'for lower middle-class people'. Diametrically opposed to these degrees and colleges, professional degrees are seen as markers of middle-class status, and more importantly as signalling a sense of 'awareness' that characterises the modern middle-class person. 'Awareness' referred to a sense of goal-oriented ambition and competitiveness that shapes one's educational aspirations and leads one to prefer avenues offering 'real' growth (not just education for the sake of it); such aspirations are unaffordable to the bulk of the middle classes, let alone society at large.

The majority of parents I interviewed sought to instil in their children a desire for professional degrees. However, parents always spoke of career choice as being a decision left entirely up to their sons and daughters. Similar to the narratives of 'being on their own', statements such as 'whatever they choose to study, they will study' immediately came up during interviews with parents. These modern idioms of individual ambition and freedom to choose effectively concealed parental authority and the limited list of degrees endorsed by parents. Ajit's father, for example, explained that as a commerce graduate he could not have really informed Ajit's aspiration to pursue a medical career, although he had put pressure on his son to attend a year-long EC course geared towards medical-college entrance examinations. This in turn portrayed his son in terms of the most pervasive stereotype of Indian youth today: the belief that this generation is one of overflowing ambition and determination, personified in Lukose's concept of 'Zippies' (Lukose 2009: 4).

While parents steered children towards very specific and apparently secure higher-education degrees, those understood locally as conferring status and real growth, they often spoke of the current economic context as providing a multitude of 'avenues' and opportunities for growth. Priti's father explained that with India's integration into the global economy there has been:

> [a] great change in opportunities, now there is no stoppage! Earlier, in our days, what it used to happen was after graduation you went off to get a

government clerk job. You learned some typing so that you can do some letters and correspondence and all that, and join a government organization as a typist. Then you get a promotion and become a senior clerk. Like that it was the ambition. Those days we used to think like that, now it is not so. Now there is no limitation; if one student wants to do anything, he can go up to that goal. If he really wants, he can go wherever he wants. 'The sky is the limit'.

As with Priti's father, there was an almost pervasive belief amongst parents that in neoliberal India young people's talents and aspirations can be unleashed, for there is no limit to what they can achieve.

On 'success' and 'failure'

In the final stages of the final year, the majority of young people did, to a large extent, embrace the study regimes, career aspirations and stereotypes of ambitious youth that were circulating in urban Kochi. However, their cooperation with aspirational regimes was far from straightforward. While some embraced them almost without any problems, others struggled to exercise the degree of determination expected of them. Well into the twelfth standard, Vijay, for example, explained that he saw no point in being ambitious, competitive and studying hard in order to gain access to a computing/mathematics batch. He felt that if he could start again he 'would have taken commerce in a heartbeat', for courses in commerce are considered to be much easier than science streams. He felt that his future was secure within the family venture, and believed there was not really a need to struggle with science subjects and rigorous, daily entrance-examination training, which he described as 'hellish'. Vijay said:

> My dad is having a good business, but he told me that there is more than making money. I would be fine just running his business, making lots of money taking my son on trips. He told me I have to achieve more. He told me to better get over the suffering part as soon as possible, learn science now and not when I'm a grown up, it'll make things easier then. Then an MBA is pretty easy compare to this.

For Vijay's parents, parenting was about nurturing enterprising selves, inspiring hard work, learning and ambition through a regime that made youth embody those very same values. In the end, Vijay continued to attend EC and got admission to a reputed engineering college.

For others, the struggle to personify the vision and ambition expected of them was a source of anguish. Parvathi tried to disassociating herself from the professional ambitions that her father envisaged during our interviews. She refused to embody the farsighted determination expected of her, thinking of degrees, careers and possible substantial salaries. She limited herself to talking about short-term objectives such as passing Class 11. Murali, a Class 12 Nair boy, recalled how, since his childhood, his parents, uncles and aunts had posed the question: 'What are you going to become, an engineer or a doctor?'. He spoke of the anxiety that this question had always produced in him. Murali, like many others, wished he could pursuit a career in music, but he resigned himself to doing an engineering degree.

What happened to students who did not conform or internalise the values of ambition, self-motivation and responsibility for their own success? As Kumar (2011) and Fuller and Narasimhan (2006) point out, 'failure' in competitive entrance exams and subsequent job applications is more frequent than 'success'. In India, failure is interpreted through what Kumar terms the dual discourse of the child and childhood (Kumar 2011: 237), which, as I hope to have shown, inflicts a kind of symbolic violence on young people in two respects: 'At the one level, childhood is unmarked and undifferentiated, and children are theoretically the same in that they are malleable and formable' (Kumar 2011: 237). They are a stone to be sculpted, and private schooling and coaching are indeed parents' sculpting tools. Education is understood as being capable of changing a person 'intellectually, psychologically, socially, and emotionally' (Kumar 2011: 237). Conversely, the discourse is one of the individual youth as essentially unyielding to being taught. Failure here comes to be interpreted as a reflection on the individual youth, rather than on the family. Ajit and Balraj illustrate the violence at both ends of the discourse.

A fresher at BVM and new arrival in Kochi, Ajit was struggling to cope with school and entrance coaching. By mid-term it was clear that EC, which took up most of the afternoon, was undermining his ability to pass school examinations. He failed all but one of the mid-term evaluations, which he attributed to the fact that entrance coaching drained all of his energy. He explained that by the time he got home at 7pm he could not get himself to concentrate on studying. In the middle of the term Ajit's father made him stop attending EC. Instead, 'my dad is asking me to come up with a concrete plan of what I want to do in the future and a concrete plan of studies for each day', Ajit told me. But three weeks later, Ajit's father changed his mind and insisted on the inclusion of EC in his son's daily routine once again. Ajit's father insisted that through systematic studying and time management he could succeed in school and at the coaching centre. Sending him to EC was also a way for Ajit's parents to monitor his efforts, for they felt that Ajit might not be 'mature' enough to study in an unsupervised manner at home. In the end Ajit failed the eleventh standard.

Unlike Ajit, other young people who did not achieve high marks were not subjected to parental authority in the same way. For example, pupils who failed to gain entrance to a science group (and hence ended up in the stigmatised commerce group), or who performed poorly at school, were often marked as essentially lacking intelligence, what was locally referred to as not being 'bright' (the English word was used). 'Bright-ness', the main manifestation of which was high marks in tests, was often talked about by parents as a sort of intrinsic quality, which individual young people either lacked or possessed innately. Balraj's parents saw him as not being bright, which they saw reflected in his 'not that encouraging' marks. Until the last stages of the twelfth standard they showed a lack of concern and effort to mould Balraj into a competitive student. Balraj had already been labelled as a failure. Parents such as his still tried to inspire their sons and daughters to get higher marks, but they put much less pressure on them than they exerted on 'bright' youth. Balraj and his elder sister illustrate this point. Their parents expected much less of Balraj, who showed signs of slackness, than of his elder sister, who attended EC, got a professional degree in north India, and now worked in her parents' business. In short, parents adjust the intensity of their expectations according to what they perceive to be their children's individual qualities and eagerness (or lack of it) to embrace the exigencies that come with the competition to succeed.

Confidence and uncertainty

Recent works on contemporary middle classes in India have argued, in quite opposing ways, the degrees to which anxiety or confidence constitute a substantive feature of being middle class (Fuller and Narasimhan 2006; Liechty 2003). BVM parents tell stories at both ends of the spectrum, however, their almost seamless aspirational regimes concealed their differences. Amongst the households that participated in my research were some families, like Vijay's, who belonged to the most privileged fraction of the middle classes. They easily matched the income, housing, consumption and confidence levels of the most idealised images of the Indian middle class. The ways in which Vijay inhabited his own body, dressed in branded Bermuda trousers, flip-flops and t-shirts, rambling along the street waiting for his Labrador dog to sniff the kerb, embodied a sense of upper middle-class security (Fuller and Narasimhan 2007; Tarlo 1996). The way in which he, in perfect English, spoke of his already laid-out educational trajectory, ending in a job in his parents' enterprise, transmitted a sense of confidence and security about the future, which was unthreatened by the imminence of highly competitive entrance exams. Vijay's confidence derived from having a habitus attuned to the multiple spheres of social competition, which in turn allowed him to succeed routinely within these spheres, thus giving him even more confidence (Jeffrey 2010: 20). This confidence emanated largely from his family's economic capital, which could easily get him access to the desired professional degrees in the event that he failed to attain access on merit.

Despite facing the future with such confidence, having to take very little risk, and not being particularly preoccupied by the costs of professional degree courses, parents like Vijay's still invested heavily in schooling and EC. Sending children to these institutes is seen as a key instance through which responsible parenting is established, as well as a sound investment in further prestige. The possibility of gaining the prestige derived from securing a merit-based place in one of India's top institutes of technology is always taken seriously.

At the other end of the spectrum, less-privileged families experienced more anxiety concerning their children's educational and professional prospects. Amongst these families there was much more at stake in their sons' and daughters' performance in board and entrance examinations at the end of the academic year, by which they would attempt to secure one of the few merit-based places available in the fields of engineering, medicine, chartered accountancy or law. Anxiety in the domestic sphere surfaced in many of my interviews. Securing their families' respectable professional status was more dependent on the young people's performance than in the case of wealthier families. In the case of failure, these families would have to either relinquish their aspirations or struggle harder to raise the money and somehow afford their children's professional education. For their parents, the investment dimension of costly private education and EC was obviously more significant than the socially conspicuous element of it. At home, parents demanded more hard work and systematic studying and repeatedly strove to impress upon their sons and daughters the degree of financial struggle implicated in sending them to BVM and EC. This worked as a way of making them aware of their share of responsibility for their family's strategy of upward mobility. Many young people, like Priti, embraced this anxiety, while others refused to partake in this responsibility and just concentrated in their personal struggle to complete school. In short, the aspirational regimes described here were sites for the making of middle classness, bringing together families who safely inhabited this social position and others who were anxiously in the process of constructing and securing their middle-class status.

Conclusion

In this chapter I have examined the domestic politics of education amongst a group of middle-class families in urban Kochi. In particular, I have presented a set of common parenting practices with respect to school education, entrance coaching and higher education, which show that far from being detached and 'only spending money', contemporary middle-class parents actively attempt to govern the lives of their sons and daughters according to their own educational expectations. These practices, combined with a series of discourses depicting Indian youth as being self-reliant and ambitious, constitute what I have described as parental aspirational regimes. More importantly, this chapter demonstrates how an enterprise-focused imaginary is invoked to justify parental regimes of authoritarian control over children's educational training and choices. These regimes, far from contributing to the creation of independent-minded, self-reliant individuals, paradoxically seek to create conformity, discipline and risk-averse life trajectories, which, even if emphasising a competitive and performance-oriented mentality, are ultimately geared towards ensuring middle-class status aspirations. Finally, this chapter has shown how middle-class educational regimes paradoxically help to conceal and hence reproduce inequalities within the socioeconomic spectrum of the middle class: from the comfortably rich, who envisaged the future with confidence, to the struggling and aspirational families, for whom uncertainty loomed ahead.

Notes

1   I follow Béteille (1992) in my concern with families as a crucial site for the production of middle classness.
2   There were two computer/mathematic groups, one biology/mathematics group – seen as linked to the medical profession – and one commerce group. The latter carried negative connotations. Commerce students were seen as failures, as the majority of students in this batch had failed to get a place in a science batch.

3   Although BVM was an English-medium school, substantial parts of lessons were often delivered in Malayalam.
4   Bachelor's degree in education.
5   For detailed literature on the upper-caste stature of the new educated classes of the nineteenth century, see Joshi (2010) and Misra (1961).
6   This was almost exclusively a male phenomenon.
7   These have been described as semi-skilled or unskilled migrants who are male, typically under the age of 35, unmarried and with an education at or below Secondary School Leaving Certificate (Osella and Osella 2000: 78).
8   As a way to support children through their educational careers, their domestic labour was remarkably underutilised, as observed by Parry in the context of Chhattisgarh (2005: 287).
9   The dominant discourse from educationists in India and central-government education organisations at the time of fieldwork was to reduce the levels of stress and anxiety experienced by students' exposure to external examinations.
10   The aspirational regimes described here were to a large extent ungendered, involving similar practices, rhetoric and expectations for boys and girls. There were, however, some nuanced differences, which I examine elsewhere (Sancho 2012).
11   This is a derogatory term for Malayalees.

Bibliography

Béteille, A. 1992. Caste and family: In representations of Indian society. *Anthropology Today* **8**, 13.
Davies, S. 2004. School choice by default? Understanding the demand for private tutoring in Canada. *American Journal of Education* **110**, 233–255.
De Neve, G. 2011. 'Keeping it in the family': Work, education and gender hierarchies among Tiruppur's industrial capitalists. In *Being Middle-class in India: A Way of Life* (ed.) H. Donner, 73–99. Routledge.
Devika, J. 2007. *En-gendering Individuals: The Language of Re-forming in Early Twentieth Century Keralam*. Orient Longman.
Donner, H. 2006. Committed mothers and well-adjusted children: Privatisation, early-years education and motherhood in Calcutta. *Modern Asian Studies* **40**, 371–395.
Donner, H. and G. De Neve 2011. Introduction. In *Being Middle-class in India: A Way of Life* (ed.) H. Donner, 1–22. Routledge.
Fernandes, L. and P. Heller 2006. Hegemonic aspirations: New middle class politics and India's democracy in comparative perspective. *Critical Asian Studies* **38**, 495.
Fuller, C. J. and H. Narasimhan 2006. Engineering colleges, 'exposure' and information technology professionals in Tamil Nadu. *Economic and Political Weekly* **3**, 258–262.
Fuller, C. J. and H. Narasimhan 2007. Information technology professionals and the new-rich middle class in Chennai (Madras). *Modern Asian Studies* **41**, 121–150.
Jeffrey, C. 2010. *Timepass: Youth, Class, and the Politics of Waiting in India*. Stanford University Press.
Joshi, S. 2010. *The Middle Class in Colonial India*. Oxford University Press.
Kumar, N. 2011. The middle-class child: Ruminations on failure. In *Elite and Everyman: The Cultural Politics of the Indian Middle Classes* (eds) A. Baviskar and R. Ray, 220–245. Routledge.
Liechty, M. 2003. *Suitably Modern: Making Middle-Class Culture In a New Consumer Society*. Princeton University Press.

Lukose, R. A. 2009. *Liberalization's Children: Gender, youth, and consumer citizenship in globalizing India*. Duke University Press Books.

Misra, B. B. 1961. *The Indian Middle Classes: Their growth in modern times*. Oxford University Press.

Osella, F. and C. Osella 2000. *Social Mobility in Kerala: Modernity and identity in conflict*. Pluto Press.

Parry, J. 2005. Changing childhoods in industrial Chhattisgarh. In *Educational Regimes in Contemporary India* (eds) R. Chopra and P. Jeffery, 276–298. Sage.

Sancho, D. 2012. 'The year that can break or make you': The politics of secondary schooling, youth and class in urban Kerala, South India. Doctoral thesis, University of Sussex (available online: http://sro.sussex.ac.uk/43282/).

Tarlo, E. 1996. *Clothing Matters: Dress and Identity in India*. C Hurst & Co Publishers Ltd.

Van der Veer, P. 2005. Virtual India: Indian IT labor and the nation-state. In *Sovereign Bodies: Citizens, Migrants, and States in the Postcolonial World* (eds) T. Blom Hansen and F. Stepputat, 276–290. Princeton University Press.

Van Wessel, M. 2004. Talking about consumption: How an Indian middle class dissociates from middle-class life. *Cultural Dynamics* **16**, 93–116.

4 'Keeping up with the times'

Rebranding education in globalising India

In her seminal paper about the growth of the international school sector worldwide, Mary Hayden (2011: 215) signals the emergence of a striking difference in the body of international schools from the time when the 'traditional' international schools[1] were established as a response to the needs of globally mobile elite expatriate families. Hayden (2011: 218) argues that a new form of international school has been rapidly growing in size and influence across the world that caters not to the expatriate but to elite host-country families (i.e. elite nationals). This phenomenon, which has attracted great interest from researchers concerned with international school-level education (for example, Bunnell 2008; Dolby and Rahman 2008; Qureshi and Osella 2013; Yamato and Bray 2006), is, as Hayden herself notes, only one of the multiple ways in which school-level education worldwide is becoming steadily internationalised.

The city of Kochi has recently witnessed the emergence of 'international' schools that fit the criteria set out by Hayden. Two exclusive schools in particular have been established that seek to cater for, and in turn strengthen, elite parents' desire that their children will develop the personalities, skills and credentials required to lead successful lives and careers overseas. These new schools, which are marketed as international, modern and secular, but adapted to the cultural requirements of India, offer national and internationally recognised curriculum and credentials, such the Cambridge Certificate or the International Baccalaureate, promising upper-class parents and students favourable access to higher education overseas. Their fees are unaffordable to the vast majority; as a result, they have provided a new arena for the wealthiest to reinstate their class privileges and distinguish themselves from the expanding middle classes. They have been established by local entrepreneurs with drawn-out migration trajectories (mostly to Persian Gulf countries such as the United Arab Emirates), through which they have experienced schooling modelled on 'western' educational institutions.

More broadly, and beyond the realm of elite schools, many reputed and long-established private schools catering to the middle classes have come to increasingly promote internationalised curricula and concepts such as global citizenship, and to seek support for teachers and students through initiatives run by international organisations, including the British Council and the Rotary Club. This has led to a highly influential group of private schools becoming more obviously internationalised. The last decade has seen an urge amongst these schools to transform their curricula and pedagogies in order to embrace an 'international' flavour seeking to provide students with 'exposure to global culture' (Fuller and Narasimhan 2006; Qureshi and Osella 2013) and the skills to work in a global economy. The private schools that embarked on this process of rebranding their institutional identity in an effort to 'keep up with the times', which I call 'internationalised' schools for the purpose of analysis, constitutes the focus of this chapter. I show how schools such as BVM attempt to reshape themselves as spaces, not only of cutting-edge education, but also of modern propriety; where the 'local' mediates the 'global', seizing its promises while rejecting its evil influences.

This chapter investigates the emergence of 'international' schools and pseudo-internationalism as a form of aspiration and class status in the city of Kochi, India. In particular, the chapter has three aims. First is to provide a detailed ethnographic account as to how a particular school, BVM, has rebranded itself as an internationalised school. This has involved the embedding of new activities into its curriculum, participating in educational programmes of global scale, yet most crucially BVM's turn has concerned the repackaging of old practices and discourses. I pay particular attention to the school's Annual Day celebration as a special instance in which the institution gives concrete expression to its educational project in front of families and guests. Second, I examine the concerns and pressures underpinning the school's refashioning. I attempt to demonstrate how the school's international turn does not simply entail a response to global pressures to 'be international' (Dolby and Rahman 2008: 676), but rather responds to a number of national and local, as well as global, pressures and concerns, including the desire to remain competitive in the city's changing private schooling sector. Finally, I reflect on the implications of the steady internationalisation of private schooling in Kochi. To this regard, Levinson and Holland's (1996) notion of the 'cultural production of the educated person' is important in helping us to think about educational sites as spaces where new demands and understandings of what constitutes a 'good' education are produced. Drawing on my ethnographic insights I seek to complement recent literature on the growth of a new kind of international school, catering for elite host-country nationals (Hayden 2011), with an account that shows how private schools are actively engaged in extending the aspiration for internationalised education amongst the city's middle classes. I argue that by promoting internationalised education as a middle-class aspiration and a marker of status, private schools are ultimately giving greater currency to the lives and dreams of elite or upper middle-class students and their understanding of education as a means to acquiring global competences.

Brahmacharya Vidya Mandir

Since it was founded in 1977, BVM has sought to provide an education that expands beyond its academic curriculum, through encouraging student involvement in a wide range of extra-academic activities and fostering value-based education. Turning pupils into 'all rounders' or what they also referred to as 'wholesome personalities' has been a fundamental objective of the school's project since it began. A student with wide-ranging skills is described as:

> [Someone] at the forefront everywhere: good in academics, good at sports, proficient in co-curricular activities and always in the midst of action. He has to protect the school's image by acquiring various skills: be an excellent debater, have staggering knowledge of current affairs, paint excellent pictures, play games with skill and above all, be a well–balanced, well-behaved person.
>
> (Editorial of the school magazine, 1985)

The school gave, and continues to give (mainly in the early classes), great importance to the arts and sports: teaching various forms of Indian dance, music, yoga and *kalari* (a local form of martial art). From its beginning, the school supported students' clubs and hosted sports events, youth festivals and art competitions. Today the essays, stories, poems, painting and drawings of young students feature prominently in the school's yearly magazine, for which I volunteered as editor in 2009. Emphasis was given to the holistic development of students through 'provid[ing] pupils with participation in the widest possible way' to various non-scholastic events and competitions (school magazine 1982–1983). They prided themselves as being a model of education that emphasised students' participation in cultural and educational activities.

Since inception, the school has also sought to provide an education that radiates the 'values and cultural inheritance unique to India'. This mission has been articulated as fundamental in reconciling 'modern science' (Prakash 1999) with India's traditions, allowing India to 'live under Gandhiji's principles while staying abreast of advances in sciences and technologies' (school magazine 1996–1997). This concern to put to rights 'modernity' and 'tradition' has inspired the most visible proponents of *Hindutva*, the Rashtriya Swayamsevak Sangh (RSS), which, since then, has aimed to redress this problem through an openly Hindu nationalist value education (Corbridge 2013; Hansen 1999). Coding itself as secular, BVM's founding trust (established after Independence), sought to emphasise the inculcation of spirituality, self-discipline and values such as frugality.

> Scientific achievements have made life more and more comfortable. [But] science has glorified the external men. In the process it has denigrated the inner man. This has spurt men and women in a neurotic pursuit of external pleasures (moralising modernity) and generated grisly greed for rights without duties.
>
> (Address by the school's executive secretary, school magazine 1990–1991)

> The capability to control one's own thoughts, words, and actions is the ultimate aim of value based education. This is what we call self-discipline.
>
> (School magazine 1991–1992)

The school also strode to foster national unity through imbuing values of tolerance and appreciation for diversity. This primarily involved the appreciation of religious diversity, reflecting what Srivastava recognises as a particularly Indian understanding of secularism in terms of a multi-religious rather than non-religious stance (1998: 104). This aspect was achieved through, for example, the absence of religious imagery in school and the celebration of Hindu, Muslim and Christian festivals.

Importantly, value education and the quest for all-roundedness amongst its pupils was ultimately a nationalist project:

> Here at BVM, we aim at not merely educating the intellect, but also the mind. We try to create an atmosphere from the student can imbibe certain essential values which will make him a good member of the family and the nation ... an ideal citizen.
>
> (School magazine 1991–1992)

The school aimed not only to 'shap[e] the character of the young minds', but to construct 'worthy Indian citizens', endowed with 'sentiments evoking national integration, solidarity, and unity' (school magazine 1988–1989). The school was created with a commitment to making classrooms 'the citadels of citizenship' (school magazine 1987–1988). As the current school director stated, since early on the emphasis on wholesome personalities was seen as fundamental to 'nurture and build noble citizens who can take over the reins of this country in the years to come', and 'Any school has a syllabus; any school can teach a syllabus. If we fail to provide the students with a set of values, apart from the academic, we fail'. This concern resonates with colonial debates about the 'appropriation' of modern education in India, which were marked by an ambiguous sense of appreciation for western education and a concern for the denationalising heritage that would be left behind by British institutions like public schools (Froerer 2007: 1034; Kumar 2005). As in the case of public schools that resulted from this early debate, such as Doon in North India, education in BVM was actively sought to be made 'consistent with the nationalist project' (Chatterjee 1993: 240).

However, as Qureshi and Osella (2013) show in a Punjabi school, the school life in BVM was embedded in a Hindu framework, in which routinised Hindu practices disguised as Indian values and culture were integrated into the everyday life of the school, giving the school the distinctively 'Hindu flavour' that is associated with it across the city. From the daily repetition of the school motto, 'let noble thoughts come to us from every side', a verse taken from the *Rigveda* (one of the four canonical sacred texts of Hinduism known as the Vedas), to the practices of yoga and vegetarianism, performance of *pujas* and chanting of Sanskrit *slokas*, together with pledges to the nation and singing of the national anthem twice a day, the school inculcated a 'banally Hindu' way of being Indian. Now, let me turn to the school's most contemporary version of its professed project through the school's Annual Day celebration. In particular, I pay attention to the way in which its graduating senior students are imagined through the event.

Rebranding education

The student exchange programme

The school's educational and cultural exchange programme (ECE) has been one of the school's key focal points in its recent efforts to rebrand itself as an internationalised school. The start of the programme marked the beginning of the school's efforts to promote itself in this new light. The ECE consists of a student exchange programme between BVM and a grammar school in the UK. It was established in 1994, when the head teacher of the UK school, accompanied by a member of staff, visited BVM. A reciprocal visit was arranged for the following year. Since 1997, every other year a group of approximately twenty-five BVM students, along with eight teachers, pays a three-week long visit to the partner school in the UK. In alternate years, BVM hosts a similar group of students and staff in India. In either case, students stay with host families. BVM's principal defined the aims of the programme as: 'to impart students with the best academic practices, to study and observe the patterns of the English community, to provide exposure to the lifestyles of English families, and to allow a free exchange of ideas and clarify pre-conceived notions'. The programme was promoted as offering first-hand exposure to 'western' culture and as giving students the opportunity to establish friendships and connections with people in the UK. 'Exposure' and global connections were in turn promoted as desirable components in education, which would better equip the young men and women to live and work in a globalised world, be it overseas or in India.

The ideal modern young person hailed in the Annual Day event was imagined as a transnationally mobile being, confidently and successfully surfing the currents of the global economy. This became most evident in speech delivered by the event's special guest, the development commissioner for the Kochi Special Economic Zone. The speaker directed his speech to the graduating seniors who, as he said, were in the midst of 'stepping out into the real world'; a world that he portrayed as being governed by competition and without 'institutions to protect us'. As girls and boys listened carefully, he spoke of the world as an interconnected place as a result of the 'forces of globalisation'. 'You now form part of the global economic system. You are now world citizens'. As such, he continued:

> Some of you will end up staying in this city. Some will remain within the state. Some of you will even venture outside your state. And many of you will go to other parts of the world. And when you go there, I want you to take three ideas with you. First, it's that of civil respect. You must, when you go to other parts of the world, respect your fellow citizens. Second, you must respect the local laws and cultural traditions of the place that is taking you. The ways they do their things, you must follow them. You have to in order to integrate into that society. And finally, you must never forget your motherland. This is the land of your ancestors and as such you must keep a place in your heart for it. You must come back and bring the fortunes you have made in other lands with you so that your land grows too.

Although the school liked to advertise ECE as a fundamental element in its efforts to produce such ideal youth, the number of students who could actually benefit from it was limited. Only students from the wealthiest families could afford the exchange programme costing: Rs1.5 lakh (almost US$2,800). A school secretary explained the selection process succinctly: 'the rich ones go [to the UK], then there is discipline and behaviour [as other criteria for selection]'. The global exposure, for which the school management praised itself, was far from a shared educational experience. In practice, the programme actually intensified distinctions between wealthier students who could afford it and those whose parents were not able to pay for it; differences I examine in the following chapter.

Despite this, the ECE was promoted as evidence of the school's international turn. One of the instances in which the school gave clear expression to this link was during its Annual Day celebration, which I attended in January 2010. The event was held in a large auditorium and included songs, dances, drama skits, awards and speeches from the school's staff, students and special guests. Towards the end, the students performed a skit that reflected on the ECE programme. This was narrated by a commentator. The voice spoke of how the school's new educational project was simultaneously driven by its founder's 'dreams to impart the youth with the values and cultural inheritance unique to India', and the trust's contemporary desire to 'keep up with the times'. The audience was reassured that the school's project has been transformed so as to uphold India's 'traditions', while embracing a commitment towards 'the true spirit of globalisation and internationalism'. This commitment is most clearly manifested, the voice said, in the school's ECE programme. Following this introduction, a group of students re-enacted a dialogue between a group of BVM students and a visiting UK student, Sam.

Musical instruments in hand, a group of higher secondary girls talked about what song to play at the welcoming event for the UK students. One of the girls suggested they played a Malayalam song (the local language), but she was immediately turned down by the lead singer who argued that it would be better to surprise them by playing one of *their* songs. 'We can sing *their* songs with ease, but can they even dream of singing one of *our* songs?'. After playing an English pop song, Sam came on stage, wearing Bermuda shorts, a polo shirt and spiky hair. Ironically, Sam was played by Kartik, whose English skills were not nearly as fluent as the voice that dubbed him. He was chosen most likely for his fair skin, while his voice was prerecorded by an English-speaking, US-born peer. In a friendly way, one of the girls mocked Sam for his incapability of saying 'Malayalam' properly. Sam tried pronouncing the word again with a heavy accent, which resulted in him being made fun of. Subsequently, a girl asked Sam what he thought of India after having been here for a few days. He effusively praised Indian culture, hospitality, food and the habit of eating with the hand on a plantain leaf. A student playing one of the girl's grandmothers came on stage, while the boy who was accompanying Sam ran to help her sit, after which he touched her feet as a sign of respect. Next, Sam said that he would like them to visit him in England in order to teach them about his culture too. One of the girls replied: 'Western culture? Maybe we could learn something from it, but there's no question of practicing it here'.

The boy turned to Sam and attenuated his peer's remarks: 'we appreciate your commitment to keep public places clean and your willingness to follow rules'. Sam added: 'and our language, you all love English, don't you?'. 'Your language?', the girl said slightly offended. She stressed that if North Americans and Australians claim English as their language, she did not see why Indians could not claim English as theirs too. Finally, the next scene portrayed Sam getting his suitcase ready to fly back to the UK. Before departing, he revered the girl's grandmother by touching her feet: Sam had absorbed some 'Indian-ness'.

The message in the skit can be summarised as follows. At BVM students will not only *acquire* skills (for example, excellence in the English language), connections and the exposure to foreign cultural practices that will make them better prepared to live and work in a globalised world, but will also be able to exclude the 'evil emanations' (Liechty 2003: 251) of modernity; of the 'global'. In this story of modern propriety, being able to *retain* a strong commitment and appreciation for traditions and values identified as 'Indian' is assumed to enable the selective appropriation of modernity. The ideal students imagined in the play were portrayed as extremely fluent in English, and through their first-hand exposure to UK culture they were able to establish global connection and gain an appreciation and mastery for 'benign' or 'practicable' elements in western culture that would ultimately make them better equipped for life and work in the global economy; better citizens. Simultaneously, they were portrayed as fluent in the local language, able to play local music and proud to uphold, respect and adhere to local traditions and values. This ability to do things *their* way as well as *our* way gave them a sense of maturity and superiority that contrasted with the more childish representation of Sam, the UK student. This rhetoric of retaining the 'local', plus selectively adding the 'global', was the framing language the school used to talk about its international turn. This discourse aim to reassure the audience that exposure to 'global', imagined as western culture, would not entail the replacement of local ways with 'modernising' western ideas and values.

It is important to note that while the Annual Day celebration depicted BVM students as being perfectly fluent in English, in reality the level of proficiency amongst the student population varied widely: from fully proficient speakers to students with basic speaking skills and low levels of confidence in English. Again, the high level of competence in English featured in the school play was the exclusive domain of a minority of students whose families already spoke the language proficiently. It was students' relative class positions and caste background that shaped students' proficiency in English rather than the school imbuing its pupils with a standardised and shared level of proficiency in the language. In practice, except the actual English periods, lessons were conducted to a large extent in Malayalam. Indeed, teachers, whose level of English was often equal to that of some students, resorted to the vernacular language to deliver the core of their explanations. The school relied on students who were proficient in English, those who, for example, dubbed the skit presented earlier, to spread its reputation of teaching good English.

Connecting classrooms and the International School Award

The global education programme Connecting Classrooms,[2] designed to enable schools to achieve the International Schools Award (ISA) – both schemes managed by the British Council – has been instrumental to the international turn of reputed private schools in Kochi of the last few years. The overall aim of Connecting Classrooms is to support schools in embedding international learning into their curricula. More specifically, it offers participating schools a platform to establish partnerships with schools in other parts of the world, and a methodology and resources for schools and teachers to embed global themes into their curriculum and the classroom; all giving the school a 'new' ethos and an 'outwardly facing identity' (International School Award n.d.). Students, in turn, are said to benefit by gaining a deep understanding of the world and their rights and responsibilities as global citizens, as well as 'skills needed to work in a global economy and build a fairer, more sustainable world' (Connecting Classrooms n.d.). Finally, participating in Connecting Classrooms gives schools the opportunities to obtain the IAS accreditation, an award said 'to recognise and celebrate schools that are committed to developing international partnerships which enrich the curriculum and help young learners to become global citizens' (International School Award *et al.* n.d.).

In practice, both schemes offered a focal point, institutional anchoring and a source of legitimacy to the claims put forward by top-end private schools about their 'internationalised' educational projects. It was only the most reputed and expensive private schools (excluding the new elite schools offering internationally recognised accreditations) that achieved the award in Kochi. In order to participate, schools were required to develop and implement a portfolio of projects of international relevance on the basis of which they were judged and the ISA was accredited. Such projects included, for example, teaching students about air pollution, global festival, the AIDS epidemic or the role of the UN. Top private schools possessed the resources and connections that allowed them to piece together portfolios that systematically won them the ISA accreditation, gaining the recognition that came with this achievement.

The 2010 Annual Day celebration at BVM was an especially notorious event because the school had managed to obtain the ISA accreditation for the first time; an attainment that featured prominently in the event's programme and speeches by the school staff. Addresses and skits reminded parents in the auditorium that this was a recognition of the school's international dimension, which '[gave] an exposure to every child to experience global culture so as to understand and appreciate the difference between varied cultures'. That year, BVM's global portfolio included a number of activities, such as the celebration of an environmental awareness day, the promotion of international cultural events, such as a Russian film festival, and the school's ECE programme.

Adding further credibility to the school's claims, my presence in the school was also mobilised in the Annual Day event. The event finished with a skit that braided together the achievement of the ISA and my research in the school, boosting the school's tale of modernity. I had been informed by my closest participants of the nature of this final act, in which a student was to play me. 'The international links continue', the narrator said, 'we have advanced in so many ways, to the extent of playing host to many eminent research scholars, scientists, professors, etc. The latest to visit our school is an anthropologist from Spain, David Sancho'. Students clapped. Two students came on stage: one, representing 'Ram', a member of school staff, and the other playing me. The latter wore a blue jacket, a pony tail and a goatee. In addition, he held a notepad and a pen. Ram wore a long white *kurta*. What follows is their conversation:

Anthropologist:	I am indeed happy I reached the perfect place to pursue my research. Ram, how long have you been associated to the Brahmacharya organisation?
Ram:	Nearly a decade. This is our founder [pointing at an image of the school's trust's founder]. Like Swami Vivekananda, [he] has also aimed at the revival of Indian Culture. In a world falling to pieces under the impact of a technological avalanche, Brahmacharya schools try to hold fast to the fundamental values for which our culture stands.
Anthropologist:	Salutations to you, great soul [bowing to the school's trust's founder].
Ram:	[He] aimed not only at cultural revival, but also to the all-round development of a personality that is physical, mental, emotional, intellectual, social and spiritual.
Anthropologist:	I hear that the central government of India is also moving along the same line to bring about a paradigm shift in education.
Ram:	Exactly, the newly introduced continuous and comprehensive evaluation system aimed at testing the multiple intelligences of a child.

Ram and the anthropologist's conversation was suddenly interrupted by a student dressed as one of Vodafone's Zoozoos,[3] the popular human-like characters that star in the latest ads. The character, holding a trophy, ran to the front of the stage reproducing Zoozoo's characteristic hysterical laughter. A second Zoozoo came on stage holding two trophies and ridiculed the first one, laughing even louder. Next, two more Zoozoos come on stage holding a banner, which they open once they reach the front of the stage, physically displacing and over-laughing the previous two characters. The banner read: ISA. At this stage, the anthropologist and Ram continue talking:

Anthropologist:	Who are they?
Ram:	They are symbols of excellence, representing different schools.
Anthropologist:	The ISA?
Ram:	It is the International School Award, accredited by the British Council. Brahmacharya Vidya Mandir is the only

school among all BVM schools to win this highly acclaimed award.

[The audience starts a round of applause]

Anthropologist: Why exactly was the award given?

Ram: The ISA is a global platform that gives an exposure to every child to experience global culture so as to understand and appreciate the difference between varied cultures. It is a scheme that adds an international dimension to the school curriculum.

Anthropologist: Indeed, your country proved that you are still retaining the Indian-ness along with absorbing the international culture.

Ram: Let's have a last dance to international integration.

It is worth mentioning that besides framing its educational mission in the language of international competence, and adopting specific projects of international 'relevance', the school's international turn has also involved a marked increase in fees and the acquisition and introduction of high-tech devices[4] in classrooms. Until recently, the school drew relatively low fees, catering to a wide range of economic capabilities within the middle classes. Now the school was less affordable to families in the lower-middle-class spectrum. Both the fee hike and the introduction of plasma TVs and teaching software in classrooms seem to me an effort to emulate and be seen as somehow commensurate and competitive against the new international schools, to where several upper middle-class families had recently decided to transfer their children.

Global education, local issues

BVM's particular way of rebranding its educational project is linked to two wider pressures that have shaped educational policy and practice in India over the last two decades (Jeffery 2005, 21). One is the pressure to attune education to the exigencies of the global economy; a concern that affects education systems across the world (for example, Tabulawa 2009). In this sense, commercialised private schools increasingly seek to compete on the basis of ensuring the 'marketability' of their students (Jeffery 2005, 20). In the context of changing employment opportunities in the global markets, new exclusive private schools have been established offering international credentials recognised abroad, facilitating the geographical mobility of students. Others schools have stressed the importance of developing English fluency, global awareness and IT skills.

The second pressure is that generated by the fear of cultural loss as a result of globalisation and the increasing exposure to foreign ideas and values; concerns that have been expressed by the Hindu right, many Indian Muslims and many low-caste movements (Jeffery 2005: 22), as well as by sections of the middle classes (van Wessel 2004). Again, in the field of education this concern is not new. Just as there was a concern for the denationalising effect of modern education in post-Independence India, there is a similar unease about 'international' forms of education spreading rapidly across Indian cities. BVM's rebranding as an internationalised school was underpinned by a concern for how to make internationalised education consistent with its (banally Hindu) vision of India. In practice, the introduction of international elements has come hand in hand with a stronger and slightly more open endorsement of Hinduism as a secular and tolerant philosophy embracing all castes and religious communities. Hinduism, a Christian senior student told me, is a 'way of life', the basis for the 'fundamental values' shared by Indians at large. The school has stopped observing Muslim holydays, while India's Vedic culture and Aryan past are openly praised. As Bénéï (2000) argues, the production of 'Indian' culture and the Indian nation as essentially Hindu is not restricted to RSS schools, but has become integrated into the everyday life of many self-defined secular institutions. In the last two decades this understanding of Indian culture has gained more currency. With the opening of India to the global economy in the early 1990s, one of the most salient constructions of the Indian nation and its citizen, vis-à-vis the world outside India, has been the essential 'Hindu-ness' (*Hindutva*) of India (LaDousa 2007: 149). BVM has successfully promoted its project as offering the best of international education – offering exposure to world culture and English language skills – while championing 'true' Indian values and culture. School officials and in turn, students themselves, criticised the recently established elite international schools on the basis of allegedly failing to 'balance' (Sancho 2015) international education with India's 'values and cultural inheritance' (see Qureshi and Osella 2013, for a similar account). BVM's narratives and practices underscore a typically middle-class strategy to distance itself from the elites by perpetually deflecting upon them the curses of modernity.

This strategy to distinguish itself from the new elite international schools through advocating 'value education' is not completely new: it echoed the rhetoric the school had used to differentiate itself from Christian government-aided schools that dominated the educational landscape of Kochi throughout the twentieth century. Kochi has long been one of the most educationally advanced cities in Kerala. The Ernakulam district, of which Kochi is the capital, was the first district to claim total literacy in Kerala and India (Tharakan 2004: 48). This was driven mainly by Christian schools, which, as I described in Chapter 2, since colonial times have led the provisioning of education as well as served as sites for the advancement of new ideas of social mobility, culture, morality and the economy (Devika 2007). Kochi has long been considered the Christian capital of the state, and as such it has been regarded as outward oriented, cosmopolitan and the standard-bearer of values of 'modernisation' and liberalism; qualities locally associated with this particular community.

Since its establishment, school officials at BVM have criticised locally dominant, Christian schools for having a 'narrow' understanding of education, one that is, allegedly, devoid of 'values' and simply concerned with producing academic success through rote learning and the rewarding of those who are ahead in the marks race. They dismissed such approaches for being 'utilitarian' and 'nothing but an information transmission process' leading to 'unhealthy competition' that neglects the 'cultivation of character and the development of noble virtues' (School magazine 2007–2008). In other words, aided schools, the majority run by Christians and catering for lower to middle classes, have too been condemned for lacking in 'values', other than the value of competition. On the contrary, the school has always marketed its commitment to developing 'balanced' personalities through value education, often downplaying the institution's excellent exam records as a reason for their subsequent popularity, something that families across the city valued highly about the school. Instead they professed to deliver education in the 'proper perspective': one that took into account students' individual aptitudes, virtues and temperaments; one that was enjoyable, and inculcated good character both as an individual and as a potential citizen (School magazine 1990–1991 and 2007–2008); one that promoted creativity, active learning and independent and critical thinking; and now one that promoted exposure to global cultures and transmitted skills to live and work in a global economy.

The rhetoric used by the school to promote its educational project sought to clearly distinguish itself from schools above and below the educational ladder, most times on the basis of the (Hinduised) 'value-based education' fostered in school. In doing so, the school sought to capture and in turn create a particular form of international education with Indian values (Qureshi and Osella 2013) as a form of middle-class aspiration and class status.

In practice, however, the school demonstrated a commitment to systematically achieving the best results possible in competitive end of school examinations. As the students progressed towards the final years of school, the imperative to produce excellent results in board examinations overshadowed almost any other educational aim. In Kerala, as in many parts of India (and the world), education has often been understood in very practical and utilitarian terms. Middle-class families have long sought to capture specific professional or technical credentials highly valued as a means to achieve and consolidate social mobility. Today there is an obsession amongst middle-class parents to have their children attain professional degrees; especially IT-related engineering degrees (Nisbett 2009). Obtaining marks in secondary school, allowing access to prestigious engineering (or medical) degree courses, has become a fundamental part of middle-class mobility strategies. As a consequence, schools' reputations have come down to their ability to successfully put their pupils through examination hoops leading to those degrees. Parental demands for results have not only driven a highly competitive exam-oriented school market, wherein fees vary according to schools' success rates, but have also triggered the growth of a (for-profit) parallel education industry geared towards preparing students for competitive entrance examinations, creating new forms of educational inequalities (Sancho 2013).

In practice, schools such as BVM actively tried to maximise the result of their tenth and twelfth STD boards and competitive entrance exams by turning the entire academic year into an exam-oriented training regime. Teachers were pressured to teach the curriculum faster in order to cover it entirely by November (the academic year starts in June). Their performance, and hence their job, depended upon their ability to produce 'toppers' (students with high marks). Thus, their emphasis centred on training students towards specific exam-like questions. The majority of students complained that teachers only cared about results, and hence only taught them how to cram for exams. All of this meant that students often had to attend extra hours on top of their regular schedule or that class periods destined for extracurricular activities were turned into *ad hoc* physics or chemistry lessons. From November onwards, students 'mugged up' the course material in preparation for three rounds of mock examinations. During this intense period, students attended revision sessions held in school with teachers of the various subjects. For students, this was a time of heightened pressure. The majority of them experienced education as a struggle to get marks, or to 'break' the boards and subsequent entrance exams, rather than as being about the development of upright personalities equipped to live and work in the global labour market.

Conclusion

The educational landscape of Kochi, as other parts of India, has been transformed by the emergence of elite international schools bound up with producing 'designer migrants' who are able to circulate in neoliberal labour markets (Qureshi and Osella 2013). In the case of Kochi, these schools have allowed the elite to reinstate privilege and to distinguish itself from the rising middle classes. The emergence of these international schools has been accompanied by what I have described here as the international turn or the increasing 'internationali-sation' of many of the most reputed private schools catering for the middle classes. These have sought to rebrand their educational projects and their identities as providing a school education in tune with the exigencies of the globalising economy and changing employment markets. Unlike their elite counterpart, these schools' rebranding is not a response to a specific middle-class desire for an education oriented towards preparing youth for futures that extend beyond national boundaries and issues. A look at the school's everyday practices reveals that despite the institution's discursive shift towards the need to 'keep up with the times' and make students internationally competent, their everyday activities (with the exception of a few activities of 'international relevance') were most crucially focused on satisfying the core aspirations of the bulk of its middle-class students, centred very much on India and on gaining access to reputed higher education institutions. A similar point was already made by Liechty (2003). He notes that the elite in Kathmandu see education as means of opening avenues to the outside: 'the elites construct their dream around imagined lives in distant global culture/power centres' (Liechty 2003: 215). On the contrary, for the middle classes, he stressed that 'perceptions of the future are still very much centred on Kathmandu'. As I suggested in the previous chapter, a similar argument could be formulated about Kochi's middle classes, amongst whom aspirations seem to be much more short term and focused on higher education prospects in India.

What follows from the discussion and evidence presented in this chapter is a more speculative reflection of the effects of the international rebranding of schools such as BVM. Here is where Levinson and Holland's (1996) notion of the 'cultural production of the educated person' is important in helping us to think about educational sites as spaces where new cultural forms and subjectivities are produced. I aimed to show that BVM's rebranding as an 'internationalised' school did not simply follow a global capitalist pressure to 'be international' or to 'internationalise' education (Dolby and Rahman 2008), but how this particular institution's 'international' turn melded pre-existing concerns and interests, such as their mission to promote a Hindu vision of Indian cultures and traditions, with newer logics of competitiveness on a global scale. These elements were braided together into a particular set of educational practices and rhetorics that tend to the production of – rather than catered for – a particular kind of demand for international education that speaks to certain Hindu, middle-class concerns and anxieties.

But leaving the particularities of specific schools' rebranding aside, top-end private schools may be well producing a wider demand for internationalised forms of education as a form of unifying middle-class aspiration and marker of status, which ultimately summons legitimacy for projects and desires that favours elites (Baviskar and Ray 2011: 7). 'After all "the historically specific models of the 'educated person' encouraged in schools often represent the subjectivities which dominant groups endorse"' (Levinson and Holland 1996: 24). What seems to emerge from the way private schooling is becoming progressively internationalised in Kochi is the influence that the educational demands and practices from the culturally dominant upper-class/caste seems to exert over the private sector, catering for the middle classes. What we may be seeing here is the emergence or the very initial stages of internationalised schooling as a middle-class aspiration and a marker of class status. It will not be long until the international character of these schools becomes a mark of prestige, signalling a 'superior' education to that which would be experienced in local schools. Moreover, these schools will extend a general conviction that internationalised schools will serve children's interests more satisfactorily than schools oriented towards the nation, and potentially produce the notion that exclusive international schools inevitably serve children's interests even better; a view ultimately derived from upper-class/caste parents' views on the relative merits of the schools available.

Notes

1   The diversity to be encountered amongst international school is vast. For an overview of this highly differentiated conglomerate of institutions see Lallo *et al.* (2008).
2   5,200 schools and 936,000 young people across the world are said to have participated in the Connecting Classrooms initiative (Connecting Classrooms n.d.).
3   The Zoozoo ads, which started airing during Indian Premier League (IPL) matches in 2009, have become extraordinarily famous in India.
4   BVM was one of the first schools to introduce plasma TVs and teaching software in Kochi.

Bibliography

Baviskar, A. and R. Ray 2011. *Elite and Everyman: The Cultural Politics of the Indian Middle Classes*. (1st edition). Routledge India.

Bénéï, V. 2000. Teaching nationalism in Maharashtra schools. In *The Everyday State and Society in Modern India* (eds) V. Bénéï and C. J. Fuller, 194–221. Social Science Press.

Bunnell, T. 2008. The exporting and franchising of elite English private schools: the emerging 'second wave'. *Asia Pacific Journal of Education* **28**, 383–393.

Chatterjee, P. (1993). *The Nation and its Fragments*. Princeton University Press.

Connecting Classrooms n.d. (available online: https://schoolsonline.britishcouncil.org/ programmes-and-funding/linking-programmes-worldwide/connecting-classrooms).

Corbridge, S. 2013. *Reinventing India: Liberalization, Hindu Nationalism and Popular Democracy*. (1st edition). Polity.

Devika, J. 2007. *En-gendering Individuals: The Language of Re-forming in Early Twentieth Century Keralam*. Orient Longman.

Dolby, N. and A. Rahman 2008. Research in international education. *Review of Educational Research* **78**, 676–726.

Froerer, P. 2007. Disciplining the saffron way: Moral education and the Hindu Rashtra. *Modern Asian Studies* **41**, 1033–1071.

Fuller, C. J. and H. Narasimhan 2006. Engineering colleges, 'exposure' and information technology professionals in Tamil Nadu. *Economic and Political Weekly* **3**, 258–262.

Hansen, T. B. 1999. *The Saffron Wave: Democracy and Hindu Nationalism in Modern India*. Princeton University Press.

Hayden, M. 2011. Transnational spaces of education: the growth of the international school sector. *Globalisation, Societies and Education* **9**, 211–224.

International School Award n.d. (available on-line: https://schoolsonline.britishcouncil.org/accreditation-and-awards/International-School-Award).

International School Award – Learning, British Council – Connecting Classrooms n.d. (available online: www.britishcouncil.org/learning-connecting-classrooms-international-school-award.htm).

Jeffery, P. 2005. Introduction: Hearts, minds, and pockets. In *Educational Regimes in Contemporary India* (eds) R. Chopra and P. Jeffery, 13–38. Sage.

Kumar, K. 2005. *Political Agenda of Education: A Study of Colonialist and Nationalist Ideas*. (2nd edition). Sage.

LaDousa, C. 2007. Liberalisation, privatisation, modernisation, and schooling in India: An interview with Krishna Kumar. *Globalisation, Societies and Education* **5**, 137–152.

Lallo, O., J. Resnik and J. Resnik 2008. Falafel à la Baguette: Global packaging for local core in international schools. *The Production of Educational Knowledge in the Global era* (ed.) J. Resnitk, 169–183. Sense.

Levinson, B. A. and D. Holland 1996. The cultural production of the educated person: an introduction. In *The Cultural Production of the Educated Person: Critical Ethnographies of Schooling and Local Practice* (eds) B. A. Levinson, D. E. Foley, D. C. Holland and L. Weis, 1–54. State University of New York Press.

Liechty, M. 2003. *Suitably Modern: Making Middle-Class Culture in a New Consumer Society*. Princeton University Press.

Nisbett, N. 2009. *Growing up in the Knowledge Society: Living the IT Dream in Bangalore*. (1st edition). Routledge.

Prakash, G. 1999. *Another Reason: Science and the Imagination of Modern India*. Princeton University Press.

Qureshi, K. and F. Osella 2013. Transnational schooling in Punjab, India: Designer migrants and cultural politics. In *Refugees, Immigrants, and Education in the Global South: Lives in Motion* (eds) L. Bartlett and A. Ghaffar-Kucher, 99–115. Routledge.

Sancho, D. 2013. Aspirational regimes: Parental educational practice and the new Indian youth discourse. In *Enterprise Culture in Neoliberal India: Studies in Youth, Class, Work and Media* (ed.) N. Gooptu, 159–174. Routledge.

Sancho, D. 2015. Ego, balance, and sophistication: Experiences of schooling as self-making strategies in middle-class Kochi. *Contributions to Indian Sociology* **49**, 26–51.

Srivastava, S. 1998. *Constructing 'Post-Colonial' India: National Character and the Doon School.* (1st edition). Routledge.

Tabulawa, R. T. 2009. Education reform in Botswana: Reflections on policy contradictions and paradoxes. *Comparative Education* **45**, 87–107.

Tharakan, P. K. 2004. Ernakulam revisited: A study of literacy in the first totally literate district in India. In *Paradigms of Learning: The Total Literacy Campaign in India* (ed.) M. Karlekar, 48–92. Sage.

Van Wessel, M. 2004. Talking about consumption: How an Indian middle class dissociates from middle-class life. *Cultural Dynamics* **16**, 93–116.

Yamato, Y. and M. Bray 2006. Economic development and the market place for education Dynamics of the international schools sector in Shanghai, China. *Journal of Research in International Education* **5**, 57–82.

5   Experiencing middle-class schooling

As explored in Chapter 2, over the last three decades Kochi has witnessed the rapid expansion of a new private schooling sector. More and more families use a substantial part of their income to send their children to the best possible private school. This chapter examines the quest for prestigious urban schooling, yet not from the perspective of parents, but from that of higher secondary students. In particular, it examines the meaning and value a group of boys give to their experiences of attending Brahmacharya Vidya Mandir in Kochi (Jeffrey *et al.* 2005). I use what they say about their school and the wider schooling sector as a lens to examine the internal politics of the middle-class 'cultural space' (Liechty 2003: 255). I document how, in making sense of their experience of attending a particular school, through narrative, students construct diverse and often antagonistic middle-class subjectivities (Sancho 2015).

I situate the analysis of students' experiences of education within the recent literature about being and becoming middle class in South Asia. I agree with a notions of 'middle classness' as a constantly re-enacted cultural project geared towards the construction of itself in opposition to class others above and below, which is simultaneously a 'domain of internally competing cultural strategies' (Liechty 2003: 15). Over the last few decades, the sociocultural dynamic of competing status claims has been deepened with the widening of social groups who are able to claim middle-class status (Donner 2011). Purchasing English-medium private schooling has surfaced as a fundamental practice in the everyday lives of expanding numbers of social groups and individual families who define themselves as 'middle class'. It has also emerged as key strategy for social mobility amongst those aspiring to become and be recognised as middle class (see, for example, Jeffery *et al.* 2005). The schooling experiences of these 'new-comers' have yet to receive anthropological attention, yet it has been suggested that private schools have become spaces in which young people come to understand themselves less as members of an ethnic or caste community and more as representatives of a particular economic bracket (Liechty 2003: 213). This chapter attempts to delve beneath this rather sweeping understanding and highlight how the process whereby school peers come to imagine themselves in terms of economic class is highly contingent. A closer look at the way in which attending a particular school is appropriated and infused with meaning by students reveals complex and competing social struggles to gain social recognition. These, in turn, respond to diverse attempts to craft oneself as a legitimate middle-class person, as well as struggles over the values and uses of education itself.

The chapter concentrates on the lives and schooling experiences of three higher secondary students whom I came to know well during fieldwork: Vidwath, Jacob and Srijith. I draw inspiration from recent accounts (Arnold and Blackburn 2004) that show how the stories people tell are useful to understand how people cope with society and how individuals and society seek to create their own 'versions of truth' (Arnold and Blackburn 2004: 5), which, importantly, includes creating representations of the self. Stories are particularly useful as they tend to integrate diverse and often contradictory biographical elements into 'a unified narrative of our own identity' (Holliday *et al.* 2004: 152). Crucially, stories always exist in relationship with other people and other times, 'carrying the momentum of the past into the present and into dreams for the future' (Liechty 2003: 25).

The liberalisation of the Indian economy has resulted in major shifts in the education sector, now being reconfigured through growing deregulation and privatisation (Chakravarti 2013; Jeffery 2005). Within this context, the reproduction of social inequality through the purchase of prestigious and exclusive education has become much more far-reaching and transparent than before (Jeffery 2005: 21). But one voice infrequently heard in the literature concerning privatisation and social in/exclusion is that of students themselves. In this chapter, I attempt to contribute to this body of work by providing an ethnographic account and analysis of the differential experiences of schooling, and the social struggle that occurs over the values and uses of education in the context of the progressive expansion of private schooling in post-liberalisation India. What does the highly stratified and fragmented private sector look like from the vantage point of students? This chapter seeks to examine what the recent transformations in the private schooling sector in India look like from the perspective of higher secondary students (Sancho 2015).

While drawing from a notion of schools as sites of social reproduction (for example, Bourdieu and Passeron 1977), I seek to build upon recent works that depict spaces of education as sites of cultural production in which various actors struggle to define what it means to be an educated person in a particular context. I draw particular inspiration from recent papers (for example, Balagopalan 2005; Froerer 2007; Levinson *et al.* 1996) that underscore the need to pay central attention to how young people creatively occupy the space of education and schooling. These suggest that rather than being simply shaped and disciplined according to the kinds of subjectivities promoted within institutions, students are agents who actively put up, challenge or otherwise partially adapt to school projects and the larger societal forces and structures instantiated in them (Levinson *et al.* 1996; Willis 1977).

In the following section, I provide an introduction to education privatisation in India since economic liberalisation. Then I move on to explore the different ways in which three students narrate their experiences of studying at BVM, and the private schooling sector in general, as self-making strategies (Ciotti 2006; Jeffrey *et al.* 2005).

Privatisation of schooling

The decades that followed the independence of India saw increasing public sector involvement in the education sector. This investment was underpinned by a desire to improve India's human capital and expand access to historically excluded sectors of the population through a state-led education system. However, this Nehruvian developmental dream has failed to translate in education and literacy for all. After economic liberalisation, almost all states' education provisioning has become sluggish, with many governments turning a blind eye or encouraging the progressive involvement of private providers of education. State educational rhetoric alternates between the commitments to deliver education for all and the necessity to produce English-educated, technically trained personnel for the nation's expanding IT industries, upon which a great deal of India's economic success is thought to rest (Chakravarti 2013). Crucially, in either end of the discourse the market is increasingly understood to be the most effectively means to delivering education, rather than a bureaucracy-ridden, corrupt, inefficient government system (Chakravarti 2013: 42). This shift has been augmented by the disregard towards government schools and the rising demand for private schooling amongst the expanding middle classes (Jeffery *et al.* 2005). In Kerala, the expansion of private schooling has been rapid in the context of economic recovery and rising per capita incomes of the last two decades (Chakravarti 2013; Kumar and George 2009). In the meantime, government-funded schools come to offer only 'cooling out' functions and 'ghettoisation' for the poorer sections of the population, leading to the reproduction of social and economic inequalities (Chopra and Jeffery 2005; Sancho 2012).

Private education in India has, however, become so widespread that it cannot be linked with any specific class of society (LaDousa 2007), with privatisation advocates arguing for low-cost private schools as a more effective way to school the poor (Sarangapani and Winch 2010; Tooley 2005; Tooley and Dixon 2006). In Kerala, the shift towards private schooling is so strong that even in the context of decreasing numbers of overall school entrants – due to dropping birth rates – the number of annual entrants in private schools has been increasing steadily since the early 1980s (Nambuthiri 2004). As suggested in Chapter 2, a closer look at private schools reveals a highly fragmented and stratified sector with schools catering to very different economic capabilities and to the identity projects of diverse groups (Jeffery *et al.* 2005).

BVM students

BVM's intake consists of students from a wide socioeconomic spectrum: from the comfortably rich to the struggling and aspirational middle contingents (see Chapter 3). The school brings together high-status Christians or Hindu[1] families, whose 'established' (Saavala 2003) middle-class status is a direct result of inherited economic, social and cultural capital, and families who may or may not rank lower in the caste hierarchy, but who have more recently gained access to the material goods and lifestyles understood to be middle class. The housing conditions as well as the level of consumption of students' families varied accordingly.

In what follows, I use ethnographic material collected through informal conversations with male BVM students inside and outside school. The core of this material derives from interactions during the afternoon walks at the end of the school day, which was a prime moment for students to spend time in the company of friends. I also draw upon my observations of the daily interactions amongst students and between students and school staff.

Experiencing and evaluating schooling

In this section I focus on the different ways in which three young men talked about their experience as BVM students. My aim is not to create a typology but to illustrate different meanings and values attributed by students to one of the city's most reputed schools, and to think about how these valuations are bound up in the crafting of different and competing class identities.

Having an 'ego'

A number of students who participated in this research critiqued the school for allegedly being too concerned with trying to enforce teacher authority. These students argued that the school's emphasis on discipline risked undermining the development of autonomy amongst students, which they considered an essential attribute of a 'good' education. These narratives portrayed BVM as severely losing standards in face of the recently established 'international' or 'global' schools in the city, where autonomy was, according to these students, appropriately valued. One of these students told me that his parents should have shifted him to one of these new schools and expressed concern about the 'quality' of students entering BVM, implying a discomfort with the admission of less-well-off, presumably lower-caste students.

Vidwath, a higher caste student from a wealthy family, was one such student. He represented what anthropologists have analytically described as the 'established' middle class. His parents, both fluent English speakers, were successful medical doctors and entrepreneurs. Vidwath and his younger brother, both raised in an English-speaking home, lived in a luxurious flat in a middle-class neighbourhood in the heart of the city and possessed a range of durable goods associated with the ideal middle-class consumerist lifestyle: flat-screen TVs, car, motorbike, PCs, washing machine, fridge and expensive mobile phones. Able to afford a family holiday in Europe and more recently the expensive student exchange programme offered in the school, Vidwath and his family had the 'exposure' to foreign cultures that is characteristic of upper-middle-class or elite lifeways, which are increasingly emblematic of middle classness in dominant depictions.

When talking about his everyday experience at school, Vidwath and many of his close friends often emphasised a sense of being subject to constraints, which were experienced most forcefully with respect to the possibility of talking back and expressing opinions in classrooms. In conversations with Vidwath and other friends, frustration emerged at how teachers discouraged these behaviours and instead rewarded students who remained deferential to teachers' authority by talking of the impossibility of showing their 'ego'. Vidwath's best friend, Rency,[2] once told me:

> She [teacher] hates me. They basically hate any student who has an *ego*. You know these awards they give every year, like the 'best all-rounder', best reader, and stuff? They have to give these awards to someone … So they just give them to their favourite students, who are the students who study well, those who get high marks. For example, the guy who got the best reader award read one-fifth in a year of what I read in a month! So because he studies well [scores high marks], he is the teacher's favourite and gets awarded … Well Vidwath, for example, gets really high marks and he got the 'best all-rounder' when he sucks in sports!!! Yeah but teachers hate him too because he's *arrogant* too … you can't show no ego. For example, I don't like to go on stage and act and stuff … and every time the teacher calls me to participate in something like this, I say no, simply no. And they don't like this … You see, they believe that ego should be directly proportionate to age … for them age is what divides societ … So for them, they are always right just because they are older than you. So, they believe that because you're younger to them you have to show respect to them and stuff … If they say something and you say 'why' … they don't like you anymore … If you show some arrogance they don't like you, *in the UK* it is completely different, there people are encouraged to do what they want.

Having an 'ego' or 'being arrogant' – the English words were used for both – here referred to a capacity to manage oneself, to speak out and do things confidently and according to one's criteria and less to the demands of teachers and established social/school norms. They spoke of the school as thwarting their egos; their capacity to fulfil their own potential through their own endeavour and to determine the course of their development through acts of choice. As a foreign researcher concerned with their experience and aspirations, I was perceived as someone who would appreciate this capacity to exercise agency. Although directed at their private school, their discourse rehearsed wider neoliberal arguments about the rigidity of the state education system and its dependence on orthodox, rote learning, which prevents creativity and rewards only those who are ahead in the marks race (Chakravarti 2013: 52). Crucially, their narratives resonated with the conceptions of personhood that now dominate the Indian public imagination: Indians as culturally endowed with an entrepreneurial acumen responsible for the recent spectacular economic growth of the nation (Gooptu 2013).

The use of English was an integral part of communicating 'ego'. Vidwath's mastery of English was far superior to that of most teachers and many fellow students. Within his group of friends, English was the main language spoken inside and outside school, using contemporary American slang with ease. Extensive exposure to foreign English-language media and their social ties with youth in the UK added to their inherited competence. When addressing other peers who lacked that distinctively embodied competence in English, they often resorted to

Malayalam, drawing a gap with other students. Because of the de-indigenised quality with which they spoke the language (Fernandes and Heller 2006: 513), Vidwath, Rency and friends were often asked to take part in all sorts of regional and national debating or oratory competitions. In this way, they were fundamental for the school's image, which promised high-quality English language education.

An area where a sense of constraint was sometimes expressed by boys was that of being subject to pressure and control in terms of mobility and interaction with girls and, by extension, the areas of sexuality and marriage.[3] Vidwath and his friends complained of the gender segregation enforced in school, by which, for example, boys and girls were not allowed to share classroom benches and boy–girl interaction in hallways was discouraged. There was an ongoing clash between teachers and Rency, who kept insisting on sharing a bench with his girlfriend. This sense of constraint went beyond the school. Vidwath complained that 'here [Kochi] we can't even walk with a girl. This is why I want to go far away [when he goes to college]. You see, Kochi is not a Metro, in places like Bangalore you begin to see that people are more liberal. But for me this is the last generation that is like this, when I'm a father I'm going to let my kids date and go out'.

Arjun, Rency and Vidwath maintained *lines* [romantic relationships] and engaged in flirtatious 'dialogues' with girls inside and outside of school, especially in the new breed of fashionable coffee shops mushrooming in the city; spaces that reshape the interaction of gender and class status in courtship practices (Nisbett 2007: 944). This caused further tension between the school and youth such as Vidwath.

There were two sides to displaying 'ego'. On one hand, this was a fruitless endeavour for 'having an ego' generally went unrewarded in school and the undeferential attitude it entailed created undesired tensions with teachers. On the other hand, narratives of non-compliance, such as their stories of having and displaying an 'ego', were central to these social actors' efforts to give meaning to their cultural worlds and in turn to construct themselves as *connoisseurs* of worldly or metropolitan practices in the realms of education and personal affairs. For Vidwath, self-realisation was achieved not through the acceptance of externally imposed norms and values, but through resistance to these norms and values (Grimshaw and Sears 2008: 265). By telling stories of revolt against school norms that linked their social skills and interests to an imaginary 'UK' – where teacher–student relations are more equal and schools encourage students to do things 'their way' – and an Indian metropolis – where boys and girls can mingle in public more freely – Vidwath and his friends aimed to project themselves as modern individuals endowed with a more worldly or cosmopolitan orientation.

Importantly, displaying an ego was one of the ways in which many established middle-class students communicated and reinforced their social status vis-à-vis other students. In telling stories about their autonomous selves, endowed with worldly egos, underappreciated by the school, they not only critiqued the school but also distanced themselves from their imaginary others, whose lapse through school they deemed as inferior and devoid of autonomy. In other words, their strategy entailed disparaging others. In the context where the school has seen the increasing entry of new middle-class people of low-caste background, whose habitus lacked the undeferential attitude, their intimate familiarity with foreign places and the erudition shown in Vidwath's manner of speaking, his stories are rare but acts of rebellion were also a way of dealing with the uneasiness in a changing school context. If Indian new middle-class people have been most commonly characterised by experiencing a sense of inferiority, Vidwath and his peers experienced a marked sense of superiority.

Having 'balance'

But, what did other youth, in particular those of less well-off backgrounds make of the schooling landscape in Kochi? In light of the emergence of a new breed of expensive 'global' schools, of which elites have quickly availed themselves as a means to reinstate privilege on the face of new middle-class students entering the schools that were formerly their preserve, some middle-class students in my research sought to contest this shift by taking recourse to moral discourses. In conversation with Jacob, a high-status Christian boy, he succinctly explained that I had made the right decision in coming to his school to conduct my study by outlining a moral landscape of private English-medium schools in Kochi. Jacob said:

> There are some people that love *our culture*, some others that don't love it but don't regret it, and there are a third kind of people who regret our culture ... you see, culture is the only thing balancing this modernity thing. That is why I think you have come to the right place, because in our school there is balance between these two, in Chinmaya [another school], the balance is a bit off ... [What about these new 'international' schools? I asked]. Oh there is no balance there [accompanied by a facial expression that showed severe condemnation].

Unlike Vidwath, Jacob stood out as one of the most highly esteemed youth amongst teachers and staff. His conduct and academic achievements throughout eleven years in school resulted in him being named as the school's head boy. He was an all-round emblem of the school, a teacher's 'favourite', as Rency would argue. His words 'school attention' and 'school disperse' gave a solemn aura to every morning and afternoon assembly.

Jacob was the son of English-speaking Syrian Christian parents. Although endowed with inherited cultural and social capital, his family was not as comfortably positioned as Vidwath's in the economic sphere. They lived in an old block of apartments in a less-affluent yet middle-class neighbourhood north of the school. His mother, a lawyer by qualification, worked in an NGO providing legal assistance to scheduled castes and other backward sections of society. His father worked for a furniture factory in Qatar. Although a Christian, Jacob echoed the school's rhetoric when it came to his vision of Indian culture. He defended that Hinduism was fundamentally more than a religion, Indian people's 'way of life'.

For him, BVM stood as morally superior to the new schools, which he articulated as decadent, giving way to 'westernisation' and leading to the abandonment of Indian culture under the imperative of globalisation, echoing the school's rhetoric. He imagined himself in the same light as he valued the school – competent at balancing modernity and 'tradition' – or as he himself put it: 'modern too, but with a touch of tradition'. Importantly, the way he narrated the schooling landscape echoed the way he talked about the differences between him and wealthier students such as Vidwath, whom he described as 'look[ing] up to the Americans and what they do'. As I now show, he stressed his moral superiority to students like Vidwath in a number of spheres, a contestation of power that went beyond a mere vocal evaluation and entailed a more embodied critique.

An area where a sense of moral superiority was expressed was that relating to consumption. He counterpoised a vision of his group of friends' frugal and plain living with the ostentation and wastefulness of wealthier, 'posh' peers: 'They are into this branding; they cannot wear something without a brand. They have to have original Reebok flip-flops'. Jacob tried to project a sense of frugal living through wearing simple clothes and not purchasing expensive or branded snacks and drinks. 'Look at my bag', he said, showing me an inexpensive-looking bag he had received at a science competition. Jacob and most of his friends avoided going into the new trendy coffee shops, so attractive to many of his peers. He laughed at the idea of paying Rs75 for a coffee. As with Liechty's (2003: 73) depiction of Nepali middle classness, Jacob's account highlighted the need for middle-class restrain and 'suitable' behaviour, distinct from the vulgar and uncontrolled upper-class other.

Another area where Jacob voiced and acted a critique towards wealthier students was that of romance and marriage (Dwyer 2000). He liked to project the trendy coffee shops that students such as Vidwath frequented as the quintessential place of loss of values in these realms. In disdain, he asked:

Have you seen Kerala boys and girls hanging out [in public]?
This kind of pattern is confined to these 'cool' places [trendy coffee shops], like Barista in the Bay Pride Mall. There you can see boys and girls together, changing and exchanging boyfriends and girlfriends. This is supposed to be one of the coolest spots to hang out in the city. I don't believe in this thing. In traditional Kerala, one man is supposed to love only one woman, so I don't buy this whole dating thing.

Jacob aimed to project a sense of righteous living by eagerly participating in the festival of Raksha Bandhan[4] held in school; a day in the Hindu month of Shraavan on which girls as fictitious 'sisters' tie *rakhis* (a protective talisman made of thread) on boys'/brothers' wrists. Through this festival, the school tried to impose a vision of pupils and staff as family, mainly as a way to position itself against school romance (Lukose 2009: 117). In this celebration of brother-sister relations, the rakhis are said to symbolise a bond in which sisters give asexual/fraternal care and affection to brothers, while brothers provide protection to their sisters. For Jacob, Raksha Bandhan provided a morally acceptable context in which to spend time together in physical proximity to his 'sister' (*penggal*), with whom he shared 'a special sentimental relationship'.

Jacob's role-model status within the school was strongly linked to his mastery of the English language. In countless speeches, events and competitions, he displayed his competence in English and benefited from possessing that highly valued form of cultural capital. However, the use of English was an important dimension through which he sought to undermine the status of wealthier peers. He categorised students into three groups according to the language spoken amongst friends: 'Some are posh, who tend to speak in English, some people speak Malayalam, and then there are those who stay in between, they can hang out with both Malayalam gangs and English gangs'. Despite his mastery of English, which not all in his group shared, he classified his group of friends as Malayalam speaking, for they always spoke in Malayalam amongst themselves. For Jacob, English was 'out of place' when it came to interacting with friends outside formal school situations. 'It is not that we don't know English, we do, but we speak Malayalam amongst us', he explained. Echoing local scholars' criticism of the middle classes for becoming isolated and unsympathetic of the lives of the less privileged (Kumar and George 2009), Jacob expressed concern about an 'increasing tendency' amongst English-speaking groups to exclude and ignore those who speak Malayalam. He explained that while in previous years 'we all talk to each other, in the 11th and 10th [standard] there is a lot of difference between them, those who speak English don't even look at what the others are doing'. For him, there was nothing intrinsically immoral in knowing English, but it was its use as exclusionary means that they criticised as a sign of amoral 'westernisation'. Speaking Malayalam amongst peers was the central way through which they projected themselves as distinct from, and morally superior to, wealthier peers like Vidwath.

Jacob's strategy was a highly rewarding one for it adopted the moral and nationalist commitments enshrined in the school's pedagogy. In the face of the overall currency of the styles of wealthy youth, he succeeded in maintaining his status by cultivating a righteous identity, while depicting 'the class above' as immoral, vulgar and anti-patriotic (Liechty 2003). In elaborating his superiority, Jacob displayed a particular vision of 'masculine acuity' (Jeffrey *et al.* 2008: 72) and demureness that contrasted with notions of male prowess of boys such as Vidwath, based on undeferential conduct, sexual boldness (Osella and Osella 2002) or the display of expensive consumer goods (Osella and Osella 1999). This masculine vision allowed him to critique wealthier peers through images of moral 'lacks' linked to 'westernisation' processes. In particular, he deployed a vision of peers like Vidwath as engaged in immoral exclusionary practices and 'immodest' conduct.

Having 'sophistication'

Now let me turn to my third and final case study: that of Srijith, a seventeen-year-old Hindu Ezhava[5] boy. While Vidwath and Jacob had attended BVM since an early age, Srijith was new to BVM. Unlike Vidwath and Jacob, who lived in middle-class neighbourhoods near the school, Srijith lived in a village north of the city, 27 km away. Until his tenth standard he attended a private English-medium school, under the same national curricula as BVM, in a town near his home. Having scored an outstanding 91 per cent in his class ten board exams, he persuaded his parents to help him seek admission to an urban private English-medium school catering to the urban middle class in Kochi, following the steps of an elder cousin in a different city.

Recent literature has shown how non-urban 'new middle classes' – those who have recently experienced social and economic ascension often as a result of agrarian reforms, positive discrimination policies or the opening of employment markets overseas prior to economic liberalisation – have often resorted to intensifying their search for valued private English-medium education in urban centres to establish cultural distinction and to shore up their recently acquired economic position (Fernandes and Heller 2006; Jeffery *et al.* 2005). Rich Jat farmers in Uttar Pradesh, for example, have increasingly enrolled their children in secondary schools in urban areas, and like the Jats described by Jeffery *et al.* (2005), Srijith believed that only city schools could deliver the kind of 'civilisation' he desired.

In Kerala, this has been a central strategy to defend economic gains of families on the verge of social ascension, most commonly as a result of migration to the Gulf region since the 1970s. Srijith's father worked as an operator at an oxygen plant near Riyadh, Saudi Arabia. Having completed his SSLC (Secondary School Leaving Certificate) and a machinist technical diploma, his father reached Saudi Arabia at the height of Gulf migration in the 1980s. His overseas income allowed him to purchase land, build a house and pay for his son's private education in Kerala. Savings would be suffice to cover Srijith's new school fees – Rs10,000 (£100) higher than his previous school – and the need to pay for transport to school outside the village. Admission at this stage is difficult: applications to top schools outnumber places available. In the absence of social connections, access requires extraordinary marks and passing an English interview. Srijith's father recalled feeling uneasy about his son's change of school in the absence of any connections in Kochi.

As I will now examine, his story is about crossing boundaries. In the rapidly liberalising educational markets in India, middle-class abandonment of state schools for private schools has resulted in the rise of fully private schools that are differently funded and operated by international agencies, entrepreneurs or local communities/actors. Such developments have led to the increasing atomisation of the schooling population into various levels of access, as described earlier. Such fragmentation of the student population is likely to relate to the increasing separation of lower and higher castes into different schooling streams (Jeffrey *et al.* 2008). Srijith's story is about the relevance and implications of crossing significant class and caste boundaries mapped onto the schooling system.

The success of particular low-caste families and individual students in moving across these boundaries and climbing to a more unequivocally middle-class standing was an exception. No one else travelled 27 km every day to attend school like him. On a 'normal' weekday, Srijith got up before 6 am to begin the long journey; it took him nearly two hours of riding buses and walking to reach the school. The journey home usually took longer than the morning ride, often involving having to stand for hours in overcrowded evening buses.

At the most obvious social level, Srijith's evaluation of the schooling landscape of Kochi and his urban educational experience was an image-building strategy directed towards the Others. Neighbours in his home village, some of them former school peers, could not escape noticing him going and coming back from school wearing his new uniform. He explained:

> BVM has a name, it is reputed. BVM is known all over India. If you say that you study in BVM, the next question is: which BVM? But if you say that you study in Infant, the next question is: is that a CBSE school?

The ostentatious dimension of consuming urban private schooling was certainly important from the perspective of his parents. At a different level, there was an instrumental dimension to his quest for urban schools. As I show elsewhere (Sancho 2013), schools' reputations in Kerala and elsewhere in India rest greatly on their ability to produce excellent results in school board final examinations. The schools where Srijith applied for admission were long-established private schools that for many years had produced outstanding academic results. The new 'international' schools in Kochi did not feature in Srijith's strategy to seek an urban education. However, it would be too simplistic to consider his experience from these perspectives alone.

For Srijith, the shift of school was fundamentally an answer to a more central preoccupation with his lack of cultural capital and how to spur a long-term transformation of himself in the light of the 'urbane sophistication' of the city's middle classes. His 'big dream was to come to the city' and learn the ways of the city, and he valued the school as a site for providing exposure to certain demeanours, orientations and tastes that he desired to acquire to better educate himself. In our conversations he talked about his decisions to change school and to come to the city to learn interchangeably. This preoccupation with how to secure and maintain his newly acquired status in the future through changing his very own habitus is typical of many new middle-class people, especially of low-caste background, who are faced with the problem of social identification: how to gain social esteem in the new situation. They have to prove themselves constantly. As Willis (1977) argues, young people seek to legitimate their practices and strive for better futures, not only through their economic and political actions, but also at the cultural level through repeated and energetic stylistic practices, which sometimes transform broader structures and escape the confines of a class habitus. But as I will show, moulding one's embodied social and cultural location (Bourdieu and Passeron 1977) so as to perform the urban styles of accomplished masculinity (Jeffrey *et al.* 2008) – to demonstrate 'affinities of habitus' (Bourdieu 1984) – of dominant groups is not an easy task.

Essential to Srijith's self-transformation strategy was being able to cultivate new relationships with urban peers. Almost from the beginning of the academic year, Srijith befriended another fresher, Neelanjan, an upper-caste boy from West Bengal who was also new to the school. Both gradually joined the popular group constituted by Vidwath and his friends. By the time I began to spend time with Vidwath and his friends, especially when the school day was over, Srijith and

Neelanjan already lingered around the group. Srijith felt particularly drawn to hang out with youth of markedly wealthier backgrounds. He developed a sort of admiration for some of them and what he saw as their 'sophisticated' (he used the English word) thinking and demeanour, which he actively sought to appropriate.

Srijith yearned for being able to gain his urban peers' competence in English. His English was much less eloquent and confident than his new peers' language skills. Before coming to BVM, 'I thought I could talk in English with ease ... but soon in school I found I was wrong', Srijith told me. His friendship[6] with Neelanjan, who did not speak Malayalam and spoke quite fluently in English, became a very positive resource for Srijith. With him, Srijith practiced and probed new English skills. At the end of the academic year, he gratefully spoke of having improved substantially as a result of being his friend. Similarly, he refused to speak to me in Malayalam as he saw in me an opportunity to improve his language skills. Slowly, Srijith began to rework his use of English and the body language linked to it, introducing American slang words such as 'dude' (frequently used by Vidwath) into his speech repertoire. Through this sort of practice, Srijith aimed to gain recognition amongst his new urban peers and to distance himself from his old peers, seeking to affirm his new social identity through difference (Bourdieu 1984). 'In my village they don't know what it [dude] is. They also think I have changed', he said. He then told me: 'I use these words on purpose to show I have changed'.

Likewise, Srijith treasured being exposed to, and strove to take on, a number of his peers' practices and taste. Early in the academic year, he showed me his new playlist on his mobile phone; this was tailored to the likings of his new BVM peers. He showed me how he had replaced his entire list of Malayali songs with American English songs. He spoke of how he had become interested in Hollywood films. The afternoon walks after school often led to the Cool Dale, a movie-rental/snack shop where his peers not only bought and shared snacks but frequently shared opinions on Hollywood films. Srijith's participation in treating as well as in sharing film knowledge was limited by his lack of pocket money and exposure to English and Hindi movies. On one occasion, while in the Cool Dale, Srijith asked me if I could rent a film so that he could take it home. That afternoon, he chose *Quantum of Solace*, a James Bond film. He told me that unlike his BVM friends, he did not know anything about James Bond and hence he wanted to watch the film. Later in the evening, Srijith sent me a text message that read: 'it was all right. But I didn't understand a word in it! [I] might have to watch it several times to get it'. Srijith also took on his new peers' passion for the English Premier League and Facebook.

According to Srijith, one of the most challenging transformations that stood ahead of him was being able to embody the 'bold' way boys like Vidwath interacted with girls. For him, the way in which some urban boys and girls flirted and engaged in sexualised 'dialogues' (Lukose 2009: 116) was the best example of their 'sophisticated' ways. 'Guys in Infant [his previous school] are very much *conservative* in this issue, while BVM guys are too *forward*', he stated. He continued, saying:

I mean they [peers at his previous school] are sort of having a view that prevents them from having good relationships with girls. Many don't know girls can be good friends, and manage to keep distance from girls fearing of embarrassment from mates.

Srijith often spoke of the myriad differences separating him, the urban schooled, from those educated in the village.

Later in the academic year, Srijith struggled to muster courage to interact with girls in the confident way in which Vidwath and other peers did. 'I still have to improve that aspect, here girls go for the boys and get close, I have not got used to this yet', he said. Srijith blamed his lack of success on this front on his 'natural' disposition in matters of romance, which he described as being more from 'the village'.

Although he was successful in establishing bonds across significant class and caste boundaries, Srijith continued to receive unequal treatment from peers (with the exception of Neelanjan). Within the friendly environment of Vidwath's English-speaking group, he was treated politely; interaction with his new peers lacked the teasing characteristic of more intimate friendships, which Neelanjan did receive. As we walked through the streets, he participated in friendly interaction, yet he usually remained quiet and slightly distant from the group. Importantly, boys automatically switched from English to Malayalam when addressing Srijith. Although Srijith maintained that caste differences held no meaning amongst his friends, caste difference seemed to shape his entire experience in school. 'In my old school I can talk to everyone the same, there is no difference [amongst students]', he said. Moving his hands to illustrate horizontal layers stacked one above the other, he spoke of there being different groups of students in BVM, each requiring a different style of engagement: 'There are some people you can treat as equal ... but there are some people I have to engage differently'. Like the Hyderabadi new middle classes described by Saavala (2003), Srijith was especially cautious in his interactions with peers he knew to be of higher class and caste backgrounds.

Despite his caution, Srijith was ridiculed at various moments of the academic year for his background: an experience he found utterly humiliating. According to him, a group of BVM students mocked him because of 'the standard of his previous school' and his village background. 'They say I am a burden to them', he said. He spoke sadly of how everything he said or did was ridiculed by a group of class-mates, boys and girls, who felt 'superior' and treated him as if he was 'inferior'. 'They tell me that they do not know how I manage to be your friend', Srijith told me. During a bullying episode, Srijith, clearly in distress, felt like an 'uninvited guest' and as lacking the 'qualities' to be a BVM student. That day he considered leaving the school. He was struggling to negotiate the new social space and his aspirations to 'better' educate himself (as he claimed) and become more sophis-ticated by coming to the prestigious school in the city seemed like a mistake. He said, 'I wanted to change my outlook and attitude but ended up ruining my hopes, ambitions and desire to live. What's the use of changes that destroy you? I failed terribly'. For Srijith, gaining recognition from his new peers had an important role in his self-refashioning project. Failing to achieve such approbation from a group of classmates threatened to demoralise him.

Through subtle and more violent means, Srijith was reminded of his social position and his inability to 'pass'; to embody a middle-class, urban style so instinctive to his high status Hindu and Christian peers (Osella and Osella 2000). As he developed a sense of his social position and the relatively degraded value of his own cultural-linguistic resources amongst his peers, he also developed a sense of his social limits. A victim of 'symbolic violence' (Bourdieu 1984) like many others in the school, he learnt when to self-censor and self-silence in the new school field. Although Srijith insisted that caste had no meaning in his life in school, it was his deferential and demure attitude and his lack of erudition – a habitus that hinted at a low-caste background – that sparked suspicion and triggered the mocking of his 'way of saying and doing things'.

Conclusion

In this chapter I have explored how three higher secondary students tell stories about themselves and their school within the context of a globalising and increasingly privatised schooling sector. Their stories speak of the myriad ways in which young students created and challenged representations of themselves and of one another. Throughout the chapter, Vidwath, Jacob and Srijith tell stories of themselves vis-à-vis the school as a crucial strategy to carve out a sense of identity. Vidwath told stories of himself as someone whose attitude and demeanours were little understood, or had no place in school. Through his narratives he projected a sense of superiority, which to my understanding allowed him to deal with the feeling of being left behind as many of his socioeconomic equals have shifted to the recently established 'international' schools. On the contrary, Jacob spoke of the school as a symbol of moral propriety, undermining the growing hype around the new schools, which he described as 'lacking balance' (read as immoral). He actively sought to project a sense of himself in the image and likeness of the school's moral undertaking, emphasising the importance of striking the right balance between 'modernity' and 'tradition', directly contesting the status claims made by wealthier peers such as Vidwath (Sancho 2015). Finally, Srijith spoke of attending BVM as being a dream come true; a reality that has allowed him to gain the aspired social and cultural capital to refashion himself into what was deemed to be a sophisticated urban man. Crucially, his stories spoke of how attending the urban school distanced him from his semi-rural background and peers. My intention has not been to create any kind of typology or clear-cut school-based identities according to differentiated socioeconomic 'backgrounds': there were lower caste boys with 'egos' and elite boys who did not describe themselves as arrogant.

Over the last few decades, growing numbers of families and individuals across India have acquired the paraphernalia of middle-class life, including consumer goods, large homes, urban employment and, importantly, private English-medium schooling (Bloch *et al.* 2004; Dickey 2013; Jeffrey 2010; Liechty 2005; Osella and Osella 1999; Rutten 1995). Private schooling has expanded and become available as a means to realise middle-class identities for people of increasingly diverse economic capabilities. I have sought to add to the literature that examines how new middle-class families (and those aspiring to become and be seen as 'middle class') have intensified their search for valued private English-medium education in urban centres to buttress their recently acquired social and economic position by examining the lived experienced of the young people involved in those strategies. Accounts of strategies to acquire urban education have tended to allow little room for the role played by young people themselves.

Two important insights emerged from this chapter. First, it emphasises the agency of young people themselves in decisions made concerning educational choices (Sancho 2015). It was Srijith who took the lead in the quest for urban educational opportunities, not his parents. His desire to break away from his semi-rural background and transform himself into an urban 'sophisticated' persona was inspired by a cousin.

Second, this chapter allows for a better understanding of the complex and contingent processes of transformation of the self-implicated in strategies towards urban educational opportunities (Sancho 2015). The interaction between Srijith and his peers is crucial here. His is a story of a seventeen-year-old boy who actively sought the opportunity to transform his family's financial capital and the capital gained from his academic results into the prestige of studying at a reputed urban school. Howeveer, attending an urban, private English-medium school became primarily an answer to the shortcoming felt in his recently acquired social position as a result of his dearth of appropriate 'sophistication'. However, his transformation was contingent to his interaction with his new school peers, which many times undermined his efforts and made him feel inferior and as though he didn't fit.

Notes

1   Viewed as a Hindu school by many in the city, there were very few Muslim students in the school.
2   Rency was a high-status Christian boy, son to successful entrepreneurs. Like Vidwath, he was also among the few who had gone to the UK with the students exchange programme.
3   Donner (2002) and Fuller and Narasimhan (2008) examine the notion and experience of love marriage among middle-class urban Indians. For comparison, Grover (2009) offers an ethnographic account of love marriages among poor women in Delhi.
4   Although this is generally perceived as a Hindu festival, recent research shows how it has rapidly been taken up by youth of varied religious, class, caste backgrounds as part of 'Indian traditions' (Sinha-Kerkhoff 2003: 432).
5   Ezhavas, the biggest single community in Kerala, are an ex-untouchable community, who, throughout the twentieth century pursued mobility in many social arenas, both as a caste group and as individual families (Osella and Osella 2000).
6   For a review of the anthropology of friendship, see Bell and Coleman (1999) and Osella and Osella (1998).

Bibliography

Arnold, D. and S. H. Blackburn 2004. *Telling Lives in India: Biography, Autobiography, and Life History*. Indiana University Press.

Balagopalan, S. 2005. An ideal school and the schooled ideal: Education at the margins. In *Educational Regimes in Contemporary India* (eds) R. Chopra and P. Jeffery, 83–98. Sage.

Bell, S. and S. Coleman (eds) 1999. *The Anthropology of Friendship*. Berg 3PL.

Bloch, F., V. Rao and S. Desai 2004. Wedding celebrations as conspicuous consumption: Signaling social status in rural India. *The Journal of Human Resources* **39**, 675–695.

Bourdieu, P. 1984. *Distinction: A Social Critique of the Judgement of Taste*. Harvard University Press.

Bourdieu, P. and J. C. Passeron 1977. *Reproduction in Education, Society and Culture*. Sage.

Chakravarti, P. 2013. Fantasies of transformation: Education neoliberal self-making, and Bollywood. In *Enterprise Culture in Neoliberal India: Studies in Youth, Class, Work and Media* (ed.) N. Gooptu, 42–56. Routledge.

Chopra, R. and P. Jeffery 2005. *Educational Regimes in Contemporary India*. Sage.

Ciotti, M. 2006. In the past we were a bit 'Chamar': Education as a self- and community-engineering process in northern India. *Journal of the Royal Anthropological Institute* **12**, 899–916.

Dickey, S. 2013. Apprehensions: On gaining recognition as middle class in Madurai. *Contributions to Indian Sociology* **47**, 217–243.

Donner, H. 2002. One's own marriage: Love marriages in a Calcutta neighbourhood. *South Asia Research* **22**, 79–94.

Donner, H. (ed.) 2011. *Being Middle-Class in India: A Way of Life*. (1st edition). Routledge.

Dwyer, R. M. J. 2000. *All You Want is Money, All You Need is Love: Sexuality and Romance in Modern India*. Continuum International Publishing Group Ltd.

Fernandes, L. and P. Heller 2006. Hegemonic aspirations: New middle class politics and India's democracy in comparative perspective. *Critical Asian Studies* **38**, 495.

Froerer, P. 2007. Disciplining the saffron way: Moral education and the Hindu Rashtra. *Modern Asian Studies* **41**, 1033–1071.

Fuller, C. J. and H. Narasimhan 2008. Companionate marriage in India: The changing marriage system in a middle-class Brahman subcaste. *Journal of the Royal Anthropological Institute* **14**, 736–754.

Gooptu, N. (ed.) 2013. *Enterprise Culture in Neoliberal India: Studies in Youth, Class, Work and Media*. Routledge.

Grimshaw, T. and C. Sears 2008. 'Where am I from?' 'Where do I belong?' The negotiation and maintenance of identity by international school students. *Journal of Research in International Education* **7**, 259–278.

Grover, S. 2009. Lived experiences: Marriage, notions of love, and kinship support amongst poor women in Delhi. *Contributions to Indian Sociology* **43**, 1–33.

Holliday, A., M. Hyde and J. Kullman 2004. *Intercultural Communication: An Advanced Resource Book for Students*. Routledge.

Jeffrey, C. 2010. *Timepass: Youth, Class, and the Politics of Waiting in India*. Stanford University Press.

Jeffrey, C., P. Jeffery and R. Jeffery 2005. When schooling fails: Young men, education and low-caste politics in rural north India. *Contributions to Indian Sociology* **39**, 1–38.

Jeffrey, C., P. Jeffery and R. Jeffery 2008. *Degrees Without Freedom?: Education, Masculinities, and Unemployment in North India*. Stanford University Press.

Jeffery, P. 2005. Introduction: hearts, minds, and pockets. In *Educational Regimes in Contemporary India* (eds) R. Chopra and P. Jeffery, 13–38. Sage.

Jeffery, R., P. Jeffery and C. Jeffrey 2005. Social inequalities and the privatisation of secondary schooling in North India. In *Educational Regimes in Contemporary India. New Delhi: Sage Publications* (eds) R. Chopra and P. Jeffery, 41–61. Sage.

Kumar, N. A. and K. K. George 2009. *Kerala's Education System: From Inclusion to Exclusion?* Centre for Socio-Economic and Environmental Studies.

LaDousa, C. 2007. Liberalisation, privatisation, modernisation, and schooling in India: An interview with Krishna Kumar. *Globalisation, Societies and Education* 5, 137–152.

Levinson, B. A., D. E. Foley and D. C. Holland 1996. *The Cultural Production of the Educated Person: Critical Ethnographies of Schooling and Local Practice.* State University of New York Press.

Liechty, M. 2003. *Suitably Modern: Making Middle-Class Culture in a New Consumer Society.* Princeton University Press.

Liechty, M. 2005. Carnal economies: The commodification of food and sex in Kathmandu. *Cultural Anthropology* 20, 1–38.

Lukose, R. A. 2009. *Liberalization's Children: Gender, Youth, and Consumer Citizenship in Globalizing India.* Duke University Press Books.

Nambuthiri, S. 2004. *Cost of Schooling in Kerala: A Study of Private and Institutional Cost Under Different Types of Management.* (KRPLLD Discussion Paper). CDS.

Nisbett, N. 2007. Friendship, consumption, morality: Practising identity, negotiating hierarchy in middle-class Bangalore. *Journal of the Royal Anthropological Institute* 13, 935–950.

Osella, C. and F. Osella 1998. Friendship and flirting: micro-politics in Kerala, South India. *The Journal of the Royal Anthropological Institute* 4, 189–206.

Osella, C. and F. Osella 2002. Contextualising sexuality: Young men in Kerala, South India. In *Coming of Age in South and Southeast Asia: Youth, Courtship and Sexuality* (eds) L. Manderson and P. Liamputtong, 137–162. Curzon.

Osella, F. and C. Osella 2000. *Social Mobility in Kerala: Modernity and identity in conflict.* Pluto Press.

Osella, F. and C. Osella 1999. From transience to immanence: Consumption, life-cycle and social mobility in Kerala, South India. *Modern Asian Studies* 33, 989–1020.

Rutten, M. 1995. *Farms and Factories: Social Profile of Large Farmers and Rural Industrialists in West India.* OUP India.

Saavala, M. 2003. Auspicious Hindu houses. The new middle classes in Hyderabad, India. *Social Anthropology* 11, 231–247.

Sancho, D. 2012. 'The year that can break or make you': The politics of secondary schooling, youth and class in urban Kerala, South India. Doctoral thesis, University of Sussex (available online: http://sro.sussex.ac.uk/43282/).

Sancho, D. 2013. Aspirational regimes: parental educational practice and the new Indian youth discourse. In *Enterprise Culture in Neoliberal India: Studies in Youth, Class, Work and Media* (ed.) N. Gooptu, 159–174. Routledge.

Sancho, D. 2015. Ego, balance, and sophistication: Experiences of schooling as self-making strategies in middle-class Kochi. *Contributions to Indian Sociology* 49, 26–51.

Sarangapani, P. M. and C. Winch 2010. Tooley, Dixon and Gomathi on private education in Hyderabad: A reply. *Oxford Review of Education* 36, 499–515.

Sinha-Kerkhoff, K. 2003. Practising Rakshabandhan: Brothers in Ranchi, Jharkhand. *Indian Journal of Gender Studies* 10, 431.

Tooley, J. 2005. Private schools for the poor. *Education Next* 5, 22–32.

Tooley, J. and P. Dixon 2006. 'De facto' privatisation of education and the poor: Implications of a study from sub-Saharan Africa and India. *Compare: A Journal of Comparative and International Education* 36, 443–462.

Willis, P. 1977. *Learning to Labour: How Working Class Kids get Working Class Jobs.* Ashgate Publishing Limited.

6   Education at the fringes

Schooling in the Kerala backwaters

It is early in the morning and Phil rides to school on one of the few city buses that run from Ernakulam to Kothad, located some 6 km on the northern outskirts of the city. Until recently Kothad was an islet in the Periyar backwaters with no roads linking it to Ernakulam's mainland. Although it was located so near to Kochi's urban buzz, the only way in and out of Kothad was by country boats, especially adapted to carry two small cars, a few motorbikes and pedestrians at a time. The journey across the backwaters to reach the mainland, and hence public services such as the nearest hospital, was time consuming and at times troublesome. In February 2005, a 180-metre-long bridge was built, finally connecting the islet to the city. Kothad Bridge was built to facilitate the construction of a section of a new highway that will cut across the islet, which is part of one of the state's most, if not the most, ambitious development projects: the Vallarpadam International Container Transshipment Terminal.[1] The terminal, dubbed by the state government as the 'hub of Kerala's development', was built and is now ineffectively operated by Dubai Port World Pvt. Ltd with the collaboration of the central government of India. As per the contract between the two parties, the central government was to invest nearly Rs1,000 crore (£100 million) to develop the shipping channel and railway and road links connecting the terminal to the hinterland. The International Container Terminal (ICT) Road, NH 966A, or Vallarpadam-Kallamassery Road, is the still-under-construction link between the ship terminal and India's NH47, the national highway connecting some of the most important cities of Kerala and Tamil Nadu. In short, Kothad was turned into a construction platform of a small part of one of India's mega projects to improve Indian exporters' competitiveness in the global market.

Apart from bringing lorries and construction workers to the islet, Kothad Bridge has transformed the locality in much more profound ways: water pollution, loss of ancestral land, skyrocketing land values and abundant employment opportunities (mainly on the construction site) are some of its more pervasive effects. The main concern of this chapter, though, is the rapid and very significant changes the construction of the bridge between the backwater area and the city has had on education. These changes became most evident in the increasing flow of students along the bridge from Kothad to Ernakulam and vice-versa. It is precisely these movements, negligible before 2005, that I trace in this chapter. First, I turn to the rising number of mini-vans and auto-rickshaws loaded with school children of all ages flowing from Kothad to the city. As I demonstrate, this flow reflects the spread of educational practices and aspirations that are generally seen as typically middle class amongst the relatively wealthier semi-rural families of Kothad. Emulating urban middle classes, Kothad's 'rich' families increasingly seek the market of private, English-medium, CBSE curriculum schools and coaching centres outside the islet as the most adequate provider of education. In their quest for urban private education these families produce new social distinctions between themselves and those whose children remain in the local school. I show how, through new practices and discourse, new values such as competitiveness and 'communication' become relevant to these local elites, who use them to (re)think and (re)assess education. This phenomenon, by which better-off families opt out of local state schools, is translated in an overall *residualisation* (Jeffery 2005: 27) of public sector schooling in India, and very recently, Kothad, leaving only sections of the poor labouring classes to attend these institutions.

The second movement of youth, embodied by Phil riding a city bus onto the islet, signals the reproduction, or rather the entrenchment of old spatial and social inequalities: those that pit the Periyar backwater areas against Kochi's metropolitan centre. Ideally, the opening of the bridge would have enhanced Kothad youth's educational prospects by providing them physical access to highly reputed state schools in the city. Despite a new educational policy[2] that increased the number of merit seats available to higher secondary applicants, I demonstrate how the poor educational background of the majority of Kothad's families has entailed that local youth continue to stand a poor chance at accessing these better, long-established schools. In contrast, the physical linkage established with the construction of the bridge has resulted in a surge of students flowing in the opposite direction. Like Phil, the majority of newcomers to Kothad's school – the government-aided Higher Secondary School of Jesus – also failed to benefit from widened merit quotas as a result of poor individual academic performance. Phil also lacked the capital to buy his access into a reputed state school, let alone into private institutions. Focusing on Phil's story, I argue that his relocation to Kothad illustrates a broader phenomenon whereby students belonging to sections of the financially and educationally poor, and mostly lower-status Latin Catholics, end up attending marginal schools. The geographical rearrangement of these students seems to be turning them into an ever-more socioeconomically homogeneous group, effectively making local Kothad youth the object of a double residualisation; the product of new and old inequalities.

Before turning to the flows of students back and forth, I focus on the continuities between this and the previous generation of residents of Kothad to show how, in line with various works on the coastal peoples of Kerala, their geographic marginality vis-à-vis the city continues to be a metaphor of their socioeconomic marginality. Then, drawing from a survey of sixty households, fieldwork in the local Kothad school and interviews with parents in Kothad and its surrounding areas, I move on to explore the practices and discourses of those leaving and entering the islet.

The political economy of Kothad

Kothad is the main village of the Kadamakkudi grama panchayat,[3] containing the majority of its 21,000 inhabitants. With regard to community and caste, the population has a diverse composition, although Namboodiri Brahmins and Muslims are missing. Hindu Ezhava, Kudumbi and Pulaya, and a small number of Syrian Christians, complete the Latin Catholic majority of over 12,000 people. This majority is even greater on Kothad, where I only surveyed two Hindu Ezhava and two Hindu Pulaya households. The islet is divided into three residential parts, showing a certain degree of residential segregation. The residents of the southern and western parts of Kothad, known as Kodampadam and Kothad respectively, are Latin Catholics. There are few Hindu Ezhava and Pulaya families in Kodanad, on the eastern part of Kothad.

Most of the islet's population belong to the Latin Catholic community. Catholics in Kerala date back to the visits of St Francis Xavier in the sixteenth century, whose missionary undertaking led to various waves of conversion of mostly fisher castes (Mukkuvans and Arayas) along the coastal belt of Kerala (Fuller 1976). Many became Christians or Muslims as a result of the burden of low status derived from being involved in the 'polluting' acquisition and processing of flesh food, according to the perspective of the dominant caste order (Ram 1991). Until the nineteenth century, conversion of other lower castes, such as Hindu Pulayas, took place.

As a number of works (Klausen 1968; Ram 1991) exploring the coastal peoples of Kerala show, large sections of Latin Catholics on the Travancore coast, descendants of fishing castes converts, are still in the fishing profession. In Kothad, though, fishing appears less prominently (as an occupation for at least the last two generations). Located deeper into the backwater, the people of Kothad have been less dependent on sea resources, which Kerala fishermen have so intricately depended upon. In Kothad, one generation ago the majority already worked as carpenters, masons or sand miners, while some were agricultural *coolie* workers (casual labourer). This might be, as Klausen (1968) already noted in the 1960s, the result of an inclination amongst Catholics to break the frame of the caste professions. He showed how Catholics from a fishing village on the Kollam District were involved in (non-fishing) salaried positions in and outside the village almost twice as much as their Hindu Arayan neighbours (Klausen 1968). By the mid-twentieth century, the people of Kothad were engaged in a variety of salaried employment not linked to local resources (or caste professions). Some of these salaried occupations were fitter, mechanic, construction worker, factory worker, teacher, tailor, auto driver, crane driver, clerk, tea/stationary shop owner, *kathakali* artist, toddy shop owner, military, health inspector, watchman, coir worker, merchant, painter and engine retail shop worker. Many of these only engaged single persons, but all together constituted a sizable cohort. Work was often found in large private or central government enterprises, such as the Cochin Shipyard, the Cochin Port, FACT, Indian Rare Earth Company Ltd (sand mining), the India Aluminium Company and TATA.

Except in a few cases, in which advanced educational qualifications were required, work for these large employers consisted of manual labour, demanding very little formal education. My survey shows that there were at least two people holding university degrees amongst the parents of the current head of households' generation. A few others held industrial training courses (ITCs) or teacher training courses (TTCs), while a handful got schooled up to matriculation (class ten). This is not to say that education was not sought after. On the contrary, obtaining at least some educational qualifications has been central to the social life of Kothad since the early twentieth century, when the school was inaugurated. As in any other region exposed to missionary endeavours, the islet's people have long been exposed to a combination of new notions of society, morality, aspirations of mobility and strong critical appraisals of local society and its entrenched powers and hierarchies for a long time (Devika 2007). With the inauguration of what later became HSS of Jesus in 1917, they were also introduced to modern education institutions. Yet the large majority would not study past lower primary school (classes I–IV). Upper primary (classes V–VII) was sought after by very few people, like the forbearers of the families that today send their children to private schools. In the Ernakulam District, with the highest Christian population in Kerala (and India), Christian churches have been instrumental in making this the first totally literate district in India (Tharakan 2004). In urban Ernakulam, Christian-run schools have not only been the utmost provider of education, but are landmark institutions that embody the power of the Christian community in the district.

However, a number of studies have shown that Kothad's geographical exclusion, recently disrupted by the construction of Kothad Bridge, is a metaphor of how its people, like most fishing communities in Kerala, have remained marginalised socially and politically from the mainstream population (George and Domi 2002: 16; Hoeppe 2007; Klausen 1968; Ram 1991). Moreover, shattering the image of Kerala as a development model, these works have shown how state achievements in education have failed to benefit Kerala's fisherfolk, amongst whom high dropout levels and low achievement levels are a common trend (George and Domi 2002). A look at the slow development of the Higher Secondary School of Jesus illustrates how Kothad's Catholics have not only been geographically marginal but have been made educational 'fringe-dwellers' (Ram 1991). As early as 1917, the Latin Church's local authority in Kothad, the Archdiocese of Verapoly (Vazhapuzha), inaugurated a lower primary school, which later became HSS of Jesus. Although the school has long been there, its development has been markedly sluggish when compared to schools in Kochi. In 1963, almost fifty years after its foundation, the school opened its upper primary section. Subsequently, in 1982 and 1998 respectively, the high school and higher secondary school were inaugurated. In short, students in Kothad were only able to complete class ten for the first time half way through the 1980s. In the meantime, the archdiocese, under the direction of Joseph Attippetty, its first Indian archbishop, had already been running numerous high schools and two colleges (St Teresa's and St Albert's College) since before Independence, fastidiously catering to and fuelling the demand for education amongst the urban dwellers. In Kothad, the minority who had attended school beyond primary levels had done so outside the islet, most of them in a school run by Muslims in the neighbouring residential area called Cheranalloor.

While Kothad remained marginal to the mainland in many ways, the development of backwater prawn fishing in the 1950s was of great importance to the economy of the area. Early in the decade, the governments of Norway and India had signed an agreement for a fisheries development project: the Indo-Norwegian Pilot Programme (INP), under the auspice of the United Nations. While the Norwegians aimed to introduce fishermen to new and 'more efficient' technology, the central government entered the agreement under the condition it would provide food for the rural poor, and not export (Hoeppe 2007: 140). At that time the government of Kerala had also taken steps towards improving the organisation of fishermen and productivity by introducing nylon nets. Both approaches to fisheries development were based on raising the productive capacity of existing facilities by developing artisanal (caste-bound) fishing. However, it was the initiative of a private merchant, who independently began to export tons of frozen prawns to the United States, and later to Japan, that changed the face of the local economy (Hoeppe 2007; Klausen 1968). By 1962 the exports reached more than 2,000 tons and continued to rise thereafter (Hoeppe 2007: 141). The rush for the 'pink gold' spread hugely and 'fisheries development in Kerala soon became synonymous with increasing prawn harvest and earning foreign exchange' (Kurien and Achari 1990: 2011). The opening of the international prawn market had a direct impact on Kothad's economy.

One of the islet's leading families today made its current wealth and its high local status through prawn fishing.[4] While the majority of residents in Kothad were landless labourers, not all were poor. A small group of families owned land, most of which were in the form of freshwater low-lying *Pokkali* rice fields, which used the age-old prawn filtration practice (*chemmeen kettu*). With the booming international demand for prawns in the 1960s, these families turned their paddy fields into relatively successful prawn farms. Slowly they accumulated wealth, property and education, boosting their relative status in the locality, more in conformity with a class society than with caste (Klausen 1968: 96). In Kothad, there were also some key differences that distinguished these families from less-privileged households. Amongst these leading families, now referred to locally as simply the 'rich' families, it was more common to find men occupying salaried jobs in the city. Likewise, they were more able to marry their sons to highly educated women holding degrees or even post-graduate degrees, from Kochi families, whose parents had steady salaried employment in government posts in Kochi or worked in the Gulf.[5] They were also keener to educate their sons and daughters slightly more than the average Kothad family.

Thus far, I have explored the social, educational, employment and economic context from which the current generation of residents emerged. Now, drawing from data derived from a variety of methods, I turn to the families whose sons and daughters are *staying*, *leaving* or *coming* to Kothad for education. I focus primarily on how they, with their own experiences in hindsight, engage with their children's education in the face of the newly 'bridged' relationship to the mainland.

Staying: Reproducing continuities

In the previous section I showed how Kothad has been marked by geographic, social and educational marginality with reference to the mainland, as well as by internal inequalities, mainly with regard to wealth, and less markedly, education. In what follows I refer to parents (fathers and mothers) as the current generation of head of households of Kothad with sons and daughters of schooling or college age. As I demonstrate, after the construction of the Kothad Bridge in 2005 there have been marked continuities between this and the previous generation. In addition, their contemporary strategies of employment, education and marriage signal important continuities between these two generations and the upcoming one. With the exception of the 'rich families', the overall majority of families in Kothad continue to belong to lower classes, in the broader context of urban Kochi. As with the previous generation, the large majority of fathers are manual labourers. Masons and carpenters, as well as sand miners, made up 60 per cent of the working population, while agricultural and fishing workers constituted another 25 per cent. They were employed both outside and inside the islet. The construction of the ICT road provided relatively long-term employment for construction workers in the vicinity. The remaining fathers were engaged, like their predecessors, in a variety of salaried employment in factories, the retail sector, as well as menial jobs in the government sector.

There has been a change in the educational qualifications between generations, with the current generation of parents being more likely to have reached class ten than the previous one. Although nearly half of fathers and a third of mothers still held less than a class ten pass, around a third of Kothad's parents did hold a Secondary Schooling Leaving Certificate (SSLC) pass. This is directly linked to the local school becoming a high school, introducing classes VIII to X in the early 1980s, a late yet direct response to a rise in entry-level requirements for basic jobs, similar to that in 1970s Bangalore (Holmström 1976; Nisbett 2007: 938). An SSLC pass was required for many sought-after factory and government jobs. In Kothad, many parents agreed that 'at that time, if we passed 10th [SSLC] it was considered good education'. But many recalled that as little as four years of formal schooling would have sufficed to move into (labour intensive) government or factory jobs.

The approach of the current generation of parents towards their sons' education and employment foretells key continuities between this and the upcoming generation. The bottom-line for most Kothad parents I interviewed remains the same: sons' education is loosely fastened to the perceived minimum qualification required to enter basic jobs. This strategy derives from an overarching parental desire for sons to get a job and 'make money' as soon as possible. Ironically, parents almost always spoke about their strong willingness to support their sons' study 'up to what they want'.[6] The over-supply of SSLC graduates in the job markets where their parents competed led to the further inflation of entry-level qualifications for basic jobs (in, for example, the construction sector, factories, or at the Cochin Shipyard). Before, 'tenth standard was enough' and 'now more qualification is needed for a good job'. The SSLC pass has inflated to ITCs or university degrees. The majority of Kothad families send their children, both sons and daughters, to the local HSS of Jesus. After completing their schooling, many sons are sent to the nearest industrial training institute. This means that many young men do leave Kothad in search of the qualifications that would help them gain access to the most common jobs. In short, this educational strategy remained almost the same; the change was only in the qualification required for basic jobs (Nisbett 2007: 939). However, many male children often continued to drop out of school after failing their SSLC, and to take on occupations (for example, mason and carpenter) that were likely to be the same as their fathers.

Many parents expressed a sense of frustration with education and employment. The rise of entry-level requirements has translated into a myriad of private colleges that cover the demand for education, for which the dwindling seats available at government colleges (in the most sought after courses) do not suffice. For some parents the extended practice of donations – to enter school, to enter college, to get a job – adds to this frustration, making it seem pointless for some to invest in education when 'donations' ahead are insurmountable. 'Now education and employment is like a business, if we have to get good education or job we have to pay money'. Another parent commented 'before the value of money was more; with little education we got a good salary and we could live with that money'.

Here it is important to comment on the internal discrepancies in Kothad. As it was expected, there was an overrepresentation of the fathers and mothers belonging to the well-to-do families (for example, the prawn entrepreneur family) amongst the few parents who studied beyond high school. Amongst this small, dissonant cohort fathers were more likely to have attained a PDC (Pre-Degree Course[7]) or other job-oriented qualifications (i.e. ITCs). Amongst them I found two households that had asked for bank loans in order to send their sons to engineering colleges. Mothers were more likely to have studied at university; there were at least thirteen mothers holding bachelors or post-graduate degrees. This was a result of two trends. First, the leading families had started educating their daughters. For example, the daughter of the most senior prawn entrepreneur, now a full-time housewife, completed a master's degree in commerce when the majority of Kothad mothers only passed class ten. Second, the current generation of fathers amongst the most influential families were married to highly educated women from outside Kothad, and whose fathers held salaried jobs in government, the private sector or the Gulf. I discuss the implications of this latter trend in the following section. The lack of formal higher education amongst local elite fathers, and the highly educated background of mothers, shape the educational strategies of sons, who are made to climb up the educational ladder through professional coaching and degrees, mostly in engineering. I interviewed two fathers who had either taken a sizeable bank loan or sold the house to be able to afford donations of over Rs50,000 (£500) and yearly fees of Rs1 lakh (£1,000) at reputed engineering colleges.

Unlike sons' education trajectories, daughters' education has gone through more substantial changes (De Neve 2011). The educational profile of the daughters of Kothad's average families mimicked those of the richer families. As a mother explained to me, daughters now 'study up to their marriage', which means that they are likely to have a much higher level of education than their male siblings.

One of the families I interviewed illustrates this change. The mother and father had been schooled up to class ten and class five respectively. The latter worked as a construction worker reportedly earning Rs500 (£5)/day. They had two daughters and a son. The eldest of the daughters held a bachelor's degree in commerce (BCom) and had already been married; she was now a full-time housewife. The second daughter already had a BA in sociology and was currently working towards the completion of a bachelor's degree in education (BEd). Once completed, the father told me, there will be a *kalyani* (wedding). On the contrary, the son had stopped studying after failing class ten and was working in the construction field. The father was looking to send him to Dubai to work as a mason. He had already managed to get him a passport and had asked for help from his cousin, currently employed in Dubai.

Unlike the leading families, whose efforts to educate daughters are based on status considerations, education amongst the more average families in Kothad is more complexly shaped by a mixture of status and income considerations. As in the previously described family, daughters were usually encouraged to obtain university degrees, like 'rich' families had begun doing in the prior generation. Daughters studied in colleges in and around Kochi. Degrees were sometimes enhanced with BEd, or post-graduate degrees, usually followed by marriage. The purpose of daughters' education is a lot more complex than that of sons' formal education. In the following statement, Neelu, a key informant/collaborator in her early twenties, demonstrates how girls' education is shaped by ideas about marriage, income prospects and child rearing:

> The trend among the girls of my generation is to be educated to the level of a graduate. But they [girls] don't care about the studies, they just care about becoming a graduate, they don't care if they don't pass, they just care about being able to say 'I'm a graduate'. That means that when they finish the course work of the BA, for example, they'll get a certificate saying that they are graduates even if they failed the final examination of the degree. It's just a prestige issue. This is the reason why there are so many private colleges now (i.e. to cover this demand for degree and professional courses). For the boys it is a prestige issue to say that my girl is a graduate, so that they can give a good education to their children. And if the girl is educated like this then the dowry is less, for the girl can work and the family can earn from her salary, plus if you are educated like this you get good marriage proposals. That is, a good educated girl can also receive proposals from higher status families with like engineers and doctors.

In this statement Neelu raises many important questions regarding the ways in which daughters may assess the education they receive. I return to these questions in the final section of this chapter. Let me turn to the education of daughters as a means to enhance marriage prospects. Ideally, having a highly educated daughter means that she could potentially be married off to the son of a highly educated, higher-status family, as it was widely assumed that grooms should be equally or more educated than brides. In other words, marriage was used as a calculated strategy for social mobility amongst Kothad families (Osella and Osella 2000: 59). However, more often than not this strategy did not pay off and daughters were frequently married to grooms of similar social status and lower educational qualifications.

Amongst well-to-do families (for example, the prawn entrepreneur family) neither parents nor husbands intended to let their daughters (or wives) enter paid employment (De Neve 2011). By contrast, income considerations – the idea of daughters contributing an extra salary to the household – are increasingly shaping ideas of education and marriage amongst the majority of less-well-off families in Kothad. During fieldwork, Neelu, still single, found a job in Kochi as an accountant. Generally, parents agreed that daughters should ideally be married off after education. But they too recognised the benefits of having them enter salaried employment as a way to provide cash to the household, often paying for the debt created by their own qualifications, and as proof for potential grooms of their potential bride's ability to generate an extra income. After marriage though, parents believed that it is entirely up to the husband to decide whether their new wives should seek or continue paid work. The over-qualification of some daughters deterred many local young men from proposing, scared off by the possibility of having a wife who earns a higher salary than them. A young man told me, 'this generation's trend is that boys are ready to send wives to work, both salaries are coming to the home, right?'. However, he stressed that 'having a wife that makes more money than the husband is causing some problems, tensions'. In Kothad, young men realised the importance of an extra salary, but putting wives to work risked affecting their masculine respectability, closely dependent on their role as breadwinners, and their overall family status. Jinu (aged twenty one and single) insisted: 'the importance of education (of women) comes after they are married so that they can give coefficient [knowledge] to the children'; in other words, so that mothers can support children's school education. Childrearing considerations are also an essential part of marriage as a strategy of social mobility, as it is widely assumed that better-educated grooms of higher status are looking for well-educated brides who possess the knowledge and familiarity necessary to guide and manage their children's educational careers (Parry 2005).

Apart from income considerations there were some other important ways in which the education of daughters amongst the more affluent families differed from that of the less-well-off majority. In the case of daughters seeking professional degrees (i.e. nursing), the education of daughters of local elites was much more local. Amongst poorer families the degrees studied by girls often did not require the investment of large sums of capital. At times, when daughters demonstrated great willingness and aptitude to study through school marks, parents invested more heavily in their education. This often meant that a professional degree in nursing, highly coveted in Kerala for its income and migration prospects, would be considered. Girls have to 'be very bright' and 'show her talents', like a mother said to me, in order for parents to consider their wishes to pursue a costly nursing degree. However, the exorbitant cost of nursing schools (both donations and fees) in Kerala turned these courses into a preserve of the well-to-do families of Kothad. Other families seeking to turn their daughters into nurses sent them to private colleges in other Indian states such as Uttar Pradesh or Madhya Pradesh. In these places the combined cost of the course and the accommodation was still much lower than in Kerala. Similarly, there was also a qualitative difference when girls attended college in Kochi. The daughters of a poorer background tended to attend new institutions, the quality of which was still uncertain (De Neve 2011). On the contrary, because affluent parents could afford hefty donations, the daughters of the 'richer' families went to more prestigious and established colleges in Kochi.

While these distinctions marked everyday life in the islet, what I aim to highlight now is that the construction of the bridge in 2005 offered an unprecedented opportunity to use school education as a means for the production of difference. After the construction of the bridge most of the families in Kothad continued to send their children to the local HSS of Jesus. However, this event saw the rapid exodus of the children of the more upwardly mobile families towards private, English-medium schools outside the islet. This shift triggered a debate over the meaning of good education. The discussion centred on the standard of the local school in the face of English-medium schools having become physically more accessible after the construction of the bridge. Parents whose children remained in HSS of Jesus agreed that 'everyone should speak good English because every job in Kerala is asking for English'. But not only 'good English' figured in parents' discourses of a good education; other elements, such as proper behaviour, good general knowledge and computers skills, figured too. Similarly, I frequently heard parents talk about teaching methods as the core element of good-quality education. When comparing methods used when they were students to those used now, many parents praised the recent changes in classroom methods from older approaches based on rote learning and towards new practices that encourage the application of knowledge to problem solving. Many also highlighted the obvious benefit of not having to pay hefty fees charged in the private English-medium sector. In short, English-medium education was not simply equated with quality education.

Faced with the increasingly socially residual character of HSS of Jesus, many parents launched vocal critiques on other parents who opted out of the local school. As a way to resist new exclusionary practices through schooling, they criticised these parents' choices as being only 'a prestige issue', as 'they are only concerned about the name of the school and the standard of English'. Dismissing the relevance of the kind of school parents chose for their children, some other parents simply argued that if a student is good in studies, there is no difference between whether they go to a private, government or aided school; they 'will reach whatever they want'. Naturally they questioned 'if there is a good local school why go somewhere else?'. Local teachers were also very outspoken about some parents' decision to opt out of government-aided schools like HSS of Jesus and enter private English-medium schools.[8] One of them vehemently complained that these parents sending their children to private school outside Kothad 'are not worried about what's happening inside the school, if teachers are prepared or not, they are only bothered about the name of the school and the standard of English'. She argued that the quality of teachers and the teaching methods used in such schools is poor for 'in those schools the teachers are not trained, they only have a good level of English; they receive the training after they are hired'. A teacher at HSS of Jesus critiqued the approach at CBSE schools: 'In CBSE schools they are spoon-fed; they are given the notes by the teachers to study'.

A sizeable number of parents whose children remained in the local HSS of Jesus were clearly feeling resentful as a result of the new trends. The linking of Kothad to the mainland and its concomitant opening to a broader and more stratified field of schooling meant that existing inequalities were not only amplified but that they had also become more strongly felt by those belonging to the lower echelons of Kothad society. While many valued the construction of Kothad Bridge and the ICT road as bringing development to the region, they also were increasingly faced with the fact that 'today, good education changes according to each family. If a family has good financial capacity, they can spend money. If parents have no finance, good education is limited'. The mother of a poorer household illustrated this point when she, evidently feeling embarrassed, apologised for lacking 'proper' education, which prevented her from 'talking [with me] freely'. 'Bright children are going to waste because of lack of financial capacity'. A new sense of being left behind was acutely felt by Kothad's less-well-off families.

Figure 6.1 On the recently built Kothad Bridge

Figure 6.2 In Kothad

Figure 6.3 HSS of Jesus students

Figure 6.4 HSS of Jesus, Kothad

Figure 6.5 HSS of Jesus, Kothad

Leaving: Producing distinction through schooling

The physical link established through the construction of Kothad Bridge has rapidly brought about an exodus of students from Kothad onto the mainland. Before 2005, moderately well-off families, like those from the prawn fishing business and those from the bottom of the working-class ladder, sent their children to the local HSS of Jesus. At present, the wealthiest families of Kothad have opted out of the local school and now invest hefty sums of capital in private unaided schooling and entrance coaching closer to the city. Schooling and EC have thus become new tools central to the production of distinction amongst families on the islet. I heard of other families boosting their reported incomes on their ration cards so that they could demonstrate the sufficient financial capacity to pay fees and hence get admission to private schools. Ironically, an informant told me, some of these very same families used to undervalue their incomes so as to qualify for government concessions (of rice and fuel, for example) reserved for the poorer section of the population.

The movement of students across the bridge has unleashed a debate over the appropriateness of HSS of Jesus to deliver quality education vis-à-vis private schools outside Kothad. The debate between those deserting the school and those remaining in it is highly reflective of the changing status of the islet's upwardly mobile families. At the time I conducted the household interviews a minority of families had already opted out of the local school, considering it of 'low standard'. These included six households who belong to the now extended prawn entrepreneur family. The recent construction of the bridge spurred them to reconsider their relationship with the local school, which was now thought to be inappropriate for their children's education. Joseph (aged forty-one), an established prawn businessman, was the head of household in one of those families. His two elder sons, in years nine and six, attended the local HSS of Jesus, while his youngest daughter had just started first standard at the private SBOA Public School across the bridge. Glossing over varied local strategies of education, Joseph made the following statement:

> People who are financially able send their children to private school. People who have no money also send their children to private because of its standard. I stopped my education at tenth standard. That was good because I learnt how to do business and make money. Now I'm financially stable. If I had gone for further education I would have lost time and money. 10th standard was enough, now there's no limit to education. Now things are different. Now I should give proper education for children otherwise they can't get any good job. Some people claim to be concerned about Malayalam [the language]. So this people send to Malayalam-medium. I'm not concerned about this, in today's world we should get good education otherwise we cannot face competition. Now Kothad is different, we can send our daughter to SBOA, a car comes to pick her up.

He explained that his sons were not being sent to SBOA because the bridge had not been built when they started school. But he proudly told me that it was his eldest son who compelled him to place his third child at the private school. Joseph recalled his son urging him not to let his sister 'suffer' the same 'language problems' he had been going through. Therefore, Joseph sent his youngest child to a private, English-medium school. Joseph's story, whether or not it actually took place, portrays him as somewhat naïve of pervasive pressures to send children to private, English-medium schools and expensive entrance coaching common to many middle classes across India. This helped highlight his narrative about a 'simple beginning' (De Neve 2011) and the fact that he carved out his wealth and social status by learning to manage the (already successful) family venture rather than as a result of formal education. Fathers, like Joseph, possessed similar or slightly higher educational qualifications than the poorer male heads of households of Kothad. But these families, mainly as a result of having highly educated mothers, had a keen knowledge of and familiarity with the available coaching courses, higher education institutions and admission processes necessary to climb up the educational ladder. In other words, they knew how to go about producing potentially mobile youth out of Kerala's educational maze. His account also attempted to de-emphasise the consumption of these forms of education as a way to stake social status by simply putting it as common sense or responsible parenting whether you are financially able to access them or not. What matters from this story is that Joseph saw the physical connection to the mainland as an enabling link, allowing him to provide his daughter with what he saw as an education of higher standard.

Although missing in Joseph's account, mothers were centrally active in the pursuit of 'quality' education amongst these families. Their often extensive educational experiences were the core of these families' familiarity with the educational field, which in turn shaped their expected role as mothers as guides, managers and organisers of their children's school careers[9] (Donner 2005: 129). Mothers, unlike fathers, spoke more openly about how educating their children outside Kothad contributed to making them more competitive in 'today's world', and hence why local elite families felt a pressing need to direct all available resources towards certain forms of education (Donner 2005: 127). Mothers' focus was drastically changed by the construction of the bridge in 2005, after which they began to strategise and talk about education in terms of the acquisition of English-language skills. The 'standard of English' was rapidly cited by almost all mothers as the reason behind schooling their children in a private school outside Kothad. Language skills also became the basis for these mothers' critique of Kothad's local school. HSS of Jesus was deemed of 'low standard' because Malayalam-speaking teachers were allegedly[10] imparting English lessons. Soon after being introduced for the first time to English-medium schools, educating children in English from the lower kindergarten rapidly became synonymous to giving one's children a good education (De Neve 2011; Donner 2005). A mother defined her aim as a parent as doing everything it takes so that her son does not 'face communicative problem in his career'. This often involved grappling with new challenges, such as the sense of inadequacy and anxiety Malayalam-educated mothers felt in supporting and supervising children's English schoolwork. Apart from adequate English skills, parents also sought EC for professional courses outside Kothad. Mothers were in charge of compiling information about entrance coaching centres and managing all decisions concerning these.

Besides a sound knowledge of English, sending children to schools outside Kothad was frequently talked about as enabling youth to benefit from 'mingling with good educated children'. That is, schooling became understood as the site of cultural capital, where cash is converted into the possibility of establishing relationships with the 'right' class and changing the habitus of the schooled in consonance with the culture of the dominant (Osella and Osella 2000: 141). When probed about the HSS of Jesus, 'that is where the locals go', 'Kothad's standard is very weak, there is no competition amongst them [students]' and 'the circle of friends is no good' are quotes from mothers about the school and its students. In short, schooling beyond Kothad was understood as an immediate new marker of social status and distinction.

Most of the families who opted out of HSS of Jesus sent their children to SBOA, deserting the state/vernacular school system all together. The school embodied the new educational aspirations of Kothad's wealthiest families. SBOA Public (Senior Secondary) School, located on the northern outskirts of Ernakulam, was privately managed by the State Bank of India Officers' Association Educational Trust. There are some important similarities between SBOA and city schools like BVM. Like many of the most recent private schools in India, it appeals to a 'modern' constituency by incorporating 'Public School' into its name (Jeffery *et al.* 2005: 54). SBOA, like most schools of its kind (i.e. outside the privileged world of metropolitan private, elite schools) is an English-medium, unaided school, in which students appear for examinations held by the CBSE. This syllabus is widely believed to provide better English training than the state syllabus. Both SBOA and elite urban schools boast having transportation facilities and their infrastructure is usually comparable. The eye-catching aesthetics of SBOA's uniforms, with ties and shiny belt buckles with the school insignia cast on them, resembled that of city schools. In their vocal approach to education they too frame their objectives in terms of 'all-round' personality development. They claim 'to inculcate in the pupils social, moral and aesthetic values based on the Indian culture and heritage' and to produce citizens 'with a keen sense of commitment, responsibility, self-confidence, honesty, social consciousness and initiative'.

There are some important ways in which SBOA differs from top urban schools.[11] The reputation of institutions like SBOA is much more localised. Like in Advani's Rajya Mahal School (2009: 17), the school was a symbol of higher status amongst many families in and around Kothad. For Kothad's elite, it stood as a school of reputation and a central part of their new middle-class project, while seen from the perspective of an urban middle-class dweller it would probably not stand out as a highly reputed institution. In SBOA almost all students are first-generation learners of English, unlike the majority of students in top city schools, many of whom speak English at home. Although relatively upscale, SBOA and other schools of its kind charge lower fees, ranging from around Rs15,000 (£150) per annum, with 'donations' near Rs10,000 (£100) for admission to the Plus Two level (between 2009 and 2010).

Let me now turn to how these nuanced layers of relative status, which map onto both the region and schools, are perceived by the local Kothad elites seeking private schooling in Kochi. During a round of household interviews, my research assistant and I spoke to the mother of a Latin Catholic family. A full-time housewife with an MA in commerce, she was the daughter of a senior prawn entrepreneur. Her husband held an electrician diploma from a local ITI (industrial training institute) and had been working as a fire alarm technician in Dubai for the last seven years. Like the children of her five siblings, her two daughters attended SBOA. She proudly elaborated on this decision as a move to provide better education to their children, which later in the conversation became synonymous with giving them an English-medium education. The mother delivered a recurrent discourse about government teachers' inefficiency and sloth to justify the decision to desert the government-aided system. This discourse, which has been used by the Indian state to distance itself from the deteriorating standards of government and some government-aided schools (Balagopalan 2005), was deeply entrenched in public opinion. Parents in Kerala frequently reproduce the idea that government school teachers lack commitment, being paid by the government while they go on strike, as a way to justify their opinion regarding the local school and their decision to choose the private sector (Balagopalan 2005: 95).

As our conversation moved on, the mother enquired more deeply into the nature of my research, as a result of which she learnt that I was simultaneously conducting research at BVM, a reputed urban private school. Clearly feeling self-conscious (or embarrassed), she went on to say:

> Chinmaya is a nice school, a top school like BVM. Only students with high standard go there, [those] *who speak very good English*. No *locals* can go there. They can't admit us there; they take *parents of reputation* … Children have to *know Hindi* … Students are bright there. In schools like SBOA they know English, but don't know! Understand? And [at Chinmaya Vidyalaya] the donation fee is Rs40,000 [£400].

Sending their children to a private urban school, SBOA, allowed them to transform economic capital into cultural capital, producing new symbolic distinctions between them and the 'locals' who continued to attend the HSS of Jesus. If considered within the wider private schooling sector of Kochi, and against 'parents of reputation' (read: urban, middle class and higher caste), attending SBOA heightened a sense of social and economic inadequacy, rather than entailing experiences of mobility and privilege. In other words, the effects of the move towards urban private schooling were relative. As a Latin Catholic from a fishing community, her degraded community and geographical background (coded as 'local' or 'lacking reputation') acquired a renewed salience. Older hierarchies (of caste/community) were now mediated by newer hierarchies according to different types of private education. Private, English-medium education has thus become a ladder offering families the possibility to climb higher than those educated in the local language. At the same time, though, it is a ladder from the bottom of which families like this look up at other inaccessible private schools. Despite this, knowledge of the English language, attained through English-medium schooling, was seen as pivotal to reinventing herself along the lines of the urban middle-class imagination. Against the option of vernacular education in government-aided schools, these schools emerge as an alternative, which matched more closely their aspirations and tastes of a socially mobile, semi-rural family. This suggests, as Advani (2009) notes, the continuous penetration of the metropolitan, middle-class imagination amongst relatively affluent semi-rural families, who seek to stake a claim in its new cultural standard.

Coming to Kothad: Ghettoisation

The opening of the bridge has not only unleashed the exodus of youth from Kothad, it has also resulted in the large movement of higher secondary students in the opposite direction. Before its construction, only students from Kothad and the neighbouring backwater areas attended the school. Now the physical proximity of Kothad to the city has resulted in the inclusion of HSS of Jesus in the list of schools being considered by broader applicants. Thus, students from areas near the city today travel north to attend Kothad's HSS of Jesus. In what follows, I examine the process by which these young people end up attending the HSS of Jesus. Their reassignment to Kothad's school is bound to the complexities of the admission procedures in Kerala state schools (i.e. government or government-aided schools), whereby students – having passed their SSLCs – can apply to proceed into higher secondary school through merit, management or community quotas. In other words, students can enter the final two years of school education either as a result of their Class 10 exams (SSLC marks), their economic situation (which allows one to purchase, or not, a 'management' seat) or their religious/caste identity (often requiring the payment of a 'donation' too). In other words, if a student cannot afford a management seat and fails to get high marks in the Class 10 exam, the only way she can 'choose' a school in which to do higher secondary is through a community seat: seats allocated by government-aided institutions to students of particular communities. This means that many students, mainly the less privileged, are left without a choice, and end up packing out marginal schools.

The flow of students into Kothad has increased as a result of the implementation in 2008 of a new educational policy, the so-called single window system. The policy, which affects only the state system, is in turn nothing but the continuation of numerous waves of state reforms oscillating between attempts to play into the interests of communities[12] and efforts to undermine[13] the autonomy of aided schools' managements. The bill sought to increase the number of 'merit' seats allocated to higher secondary school through a centralised government-controlled process. In other words, it aimed to undermine school managements' discretion to allocate seats to students by broadening the quota of seats assigned solely according to students' performance in the SSLC, a centralised examination. As a result, seats assigned through either management or community quotas were reduced. Hence, ideally, the opening of the bridge and introduction of the single window policy would have enhanced Kothad youth's chances of gaining access to highly reputed Christian schools in Kochi.

But far from substantially changing the educational prospects of Kothad's youth, the physical connection to the city and the implementation of the single window system have resulted in the ghettoisation of the HSS of Jesus (Jeffery *et al.* 2005: 59). Kothad youth have failed to benefit from having a broader school system with more merit seats at their disposal. The unwillingness to opt out of Kothad's school, together with their lack of strong educational backgrounds, extra tuition and coaching, as well as the much lower competence in English amongst local families, have meant that Kothad's youth continue to stand a poor chance at benefiting from merit seats. On the contrary, the bridge has facilitated the inflow of students from a broader area outside Kothad, who belong mostly to sections of Kochi's poor labouring classes. The reason behind this is that amongst all Kochi schools, the HSS of Jesus, ranks low in the preferences of higher secondary applicants. Long-established schools, such as St Albert's or St Teresa's and many others in Kochi, have a better reputation and rank high in the list of school preferences handed out with students' higher secondary applications. As a result, students that perform well in their SSLC tend to remain in their school or get access to 'better' schools, while those with poorer SSLC results end up attending schools lower in the hierarchy,[14] as with HSS of Jesus. This is further complicated by management or community quota applicants. What is important to note here is that the poor results of most of Kothad's newcomers are reflective of their poor educational background, marked by a lack of exposure to extra coaching and tuition courses and lack of independent access to English similar to that amongst most Kothad families. This lack is in turn reflective of their families' somewhat similar social and financial backgrounds, which impinge on their capacity to afford management seats elsewhere, extra coaching or private schooling. Thus, the bridge and the policy have translated into a broad movement of students whereby only sections of the financially and educationally poor and mostly lower status Latin Catholics attend HSS of Jesus. Adding to the residualisation from the outward movement of wealthier students towards private schools, this inward movement seems to be doubly residualising for Kothad's school: first because only the local poor are left to attend the school, and second, because educationally and financially poor Latin Catholics are flowing in from outside Kothad. As a result, Kothad students became an ever more socioeconomically homogeneous group, reinforcing existing educational inequalities.

Teachers often commented on the negative impact of this phenomenon of double residualisation. One of them said:

> The problem is that all bright children are going to CBSE schools; all educated parents are sending their children there. And this is affecting the proper functioning of our [government or government-aided/state syllabus] school. If we get a group of bright students, we'll be effective. We are only getting the *standard and below average students*. That's why we are not functioning properly, and we could bring good results if we got good bright students. [emphasis added]

The teacher vehemently complained of how students seem to be geographically rearranged and segregated into schools according to their brightness. As it became evident in the account of the mother in the previous section, and in the following excerpt, having brightness or being bright, locally used to describe academic ability or a student's ease at scoring marks, was often conflated with being wealthier, and sometimes, belonging to a higher-status community group. More specifically, brightness was always associated with speaking 'good English', being from the city, knowing Hindi, having parents of 'reputation' and having 'financial capacity'. The teacher continued:

> Almost all the students here come from Malayalam medium. There are maybe three or four students in a class who come from an English-medium school. But when I teach the class, I have to come down to the level of the rest. I cannot teach to these few students. In the schools like St Teresa's and St Albert's they get better students, from English-medium backgrounds. You know I taught in St Albert's for eight years ... This Kothad is another school managed by the same management, the Archdioceses of Verapoly. You know

St Albert's is a boy's school, so they will be naughtier ... But in terms of teaching in St Albert's is much easier, they come from the city you know, many come from English medium. So it is easier to teach them. Here it is really a challenge; it is difficult to teach them. When I taught in a private school students come from a better financial background. The parents send their children also for tuition class. So we don't have difficulties to teach them. They come here to learn, they go home, study, and they will do well in the exam. They have educated parents; that makes a huge difference. The parents are better placed they have good jobs, you know these children here in Kothad their parents have ... not so good jobs.

Many local parents felt alarmed by the challenges posed by the inflow of city youth. Parents expressed their trust in Kothad's school, but felt that being con- nected to the city in this new way posed a threat to their children. Their fears resonated with the parental narratives of city youth as aimless and as a moral danger, as described by Jeffrey *et al.* (2008: 180). One father said:

According to me, Kothad is a good school. After studying there no one in my family has gone wrong. When we were students, only students from Moolampalli, Pizhala [neighbouring islets] were coming to Kothad. Now students from different schools, from different places are coming, having different nature and they are using drugs and all.

Importantly, although the HSS of Jesus was hardly ever at the top of the new- comers' preferences for higher secondary, they rarely experienced coming to Kothad as detrimental. Phil, a Latin Catholic boy, was in Class 11 when we first met. An entirely new batch had been opened to accommodate all the students who had just arrived from various city schools. His father, mother and younger sister lived in a small concrete house in a residential area to the north of Vaduthala, between Kothad and Kochi. Phil's father failed his SSLC and has since then, like many fathers in Kothad, worked as a mason. Phil's mother only studied up to Class 6 and was a full-time housewife. Up to his Class 10, Phil attended Sree Narayanan Higher Secondary School (SNHSS), a government-aided school. After appearing for the SSLC examination he applied to continue studying in this school. Fearing he would not get the merit seat at SNHSS, he applied for a community seat at the HSS of Jesus. 'So I opted for it', Phil recalled. Many of his new peers had actually been relocated to HSS of Jesus from various schools as a direct result of their SSLC results. He wished he could have continued his studies at his old school. In our last conversation Phil talked about missing his friends and complained about the daily complications involved in reaching the islet using public transport, being used to walking to school. However, when asked to compare his experience in SNHSS to that in HSS of Jesus, Phil did not discern any major difference about attending either school. When asked about the difference of studying in their previous school and attending the HSS of Jesus, many of Phil's friends agreed that 'this [Kothad] is the city now'.

Like Phil, the majority of the newcomers to Kothad came from families that were very similar to the average Kothad family. The educational qualification of these families' head of households, both fathers and mothers, was often below SSLC. Many parents frequently expressed frustration for feeling unqualified to guide their children's educational careers, as a result of their lack of knowledge and familiarity with educational institutions, courses, coaching centres, as well as with their inability to speak English. Despite this, newcomers' parents always expressed a willingness to help their sons and daughters study 'up to what they want to study'; 'Now parents are ready to give good education', 'however much they want to study, we are willing to support them'. Parents often talked about 'being ready' to take on financial challenges, such as selling property or land, as a way to demonstrate their willingness to support their children's higher education. Their discourse of willingness was often accompanied by accounts of the previous generation of parents as 'poor' and 'ignorant' of 'the value of education' (Parry 2005). However, like amongst Kothad families, when it came to sons, willingness to educate was contingent on the necessity to have their sons enter paid employment sooner rather than later.

Paul's case was an important exception to this trend. He was a seventeen-year-old Latin Catholic boy who came from a relatively well-to-do landed Latin Catholic family. Until his Class 10, he attended the prestigious government-aided St Albert's school in Kochi. His parents, who studied up to their PDC, owned a prawn and coir business. With hindsight, Paul's father now regretted not having continued studying and learning English, which he claimed would have allowed him to start exporting prawn directly without having to pay commissions to intermediaries. 'After getting to business we came to know that we did not get proper education', he said. He regretfully recalled receiving a letter from a client in English and not being able to understand it. Now, he told me, 'they [his sons] have to gain maximum education'.

Paul, who had applied to continue his studies in St Albert's after his SSLC, felt a strong resentment towards the single window system for having forced him out of St Albert's school and into HSS of Jesus. He recalled how after failing to get a seat in the first two rounds of allocations, he applied to Kothad's community quota and got admitted. Only after having accepted the seat were they offered a management seat at St Albert's for Rs10,000 (£100), but it was too late. Having failed to capture that seat in St Albert's, Paul liked to talk about his ambitions and aims as a way to distance himself from his class peers, whom he described as those who 'are only interested in jobs' (see Chapter 7). Paul, like all newcomers to Kothad, missed his old school and friends and resented the daily bus journey to the islet. He particularly missed the way he and his ex-schoolmates used to enjoy the life in the centre of the city, window shopping for the latest mobile phone and going to the cinema during school intervals.

Conclusion

It is clear that schooling has changed in significant ways since the construction of the Kothad Bridge. What I have endeavoured to document in this chapter is how, since the construction of the bridge, schooling has become a new means for the production of difference amongst the inhabitants of a backwater islet at the fringes of urban Kochi. With this aim I described the flow of students from Kothad into Kochi and vice-versa, and showed how these shifts are the outcome of new educational policies and physical linkages – roads, terminals, connections to boost India's global trade – and old inequalities being reproduced. Furthermore, I demonstrated how these inequalities are reflective of old spatial – the coastal backwater region against the urban centre – as well as social differences, which pits low-status Latin Catholic groups against other higher-status communities. As a result, schooling has become increasingly differentiated.

Wealthier prawn-fishing families live in hope that their sons and daughters will reproduce their status within the local context or perhaps attain a position of higher prestige and wealth in the city; they realise that in order to do so they must get the right sort of school education. This unequivocally means leaving the local school and using their incomes to send their children to a private English-medium school closer to the city. Concomitantly, the poor and marginalised increasingly become subject to ghettoisation in Kothad's school (Jeffery *et al.* 2005: 59). Its intake now consists of the poorer section of the locality and students discarded by city schools. As these students are mainly low-status Latin Catholics (OBC), this chapter further demonstrates how regardless of policies of positive discrimination in higher education, their chances to access and benefit from higher learning will continue to be marginal, particularly as a consequence of the marginalising effect of higher secondary school (Osella and Osella 2000: 142). In short, this chapter illustrates how schools catering to the lower strata of society may become sites where long-standing inequalities are not just reproduced but further entrenched.

Notes

1   In 2011 the ICTT became India's first hub port despite delays in the deepening of the channel, as well as in restrictive laws that continue to limit foreign flag vessels to operate freely. The terminal was built to reduce India's dependence on neighbouring hub ports – mainly that of Colombo in Sri Lanka – to haul container cargo. Like many other development projects in the city of Kochi, the terminal has raised expectations. In 2004 the government's magazine, *Kerala Calling*, wrote 'the possibilities are mind boggling and it is suffice to point out the example of Singapore, which thrived to the status of a developed nation thanks mainly to its port'. India's exporters and importers incur extra costs of at least Rs1,000 crore (£100 million) per year on trans-shipment of containers through ports outside the country, according to the shipping ministry. In fact, India's traders pay an additional Rs600 crore (£60 million) every year to ship their containers through Colombo alone.

2   This 2008 policy, known as *single window system*, aimed to centralise through a government-controlled process, and increase the quota of HSS seats allocated through 'merit' (i.e. according to the mark students secure in the also centralised secondary school final examination) without any reference to socioeconomic difference.

3   This is a local self-governing unit at the village or small town level. Kadamakkudi panchayat is divided into three residential villages or *karas*, which are also three different islets: Moolampalli, Pizhala and Kothad (Klausen 1968: 69). Grama

panchayats constitute larger bloc panchayats. Multiple bloc panchayats in turn form district panchayats. The Kadamakkudi, Cheranalloor and the Trikkakara grama panchayats constitute the Edappalli bloc panchayat.

4   The social stigma attached to fishing, a 'polluting' occupation of lower castes, pre-vented free entry of capital and persons from outside the traditional fishing communities into the fishery. However, this caste-bound nature of the fishery sector ceased to be a barrier in prawn fishing (Kurien and Achari 1990).

5   Marriage alliances in which wealth is traded off against urban and educated status and prestige in Kothad and elsewhere in India have been shown to be a common calculated move (Jeffrey 2008: 520; Osella and Osella 2000: 59).

6   Jeffrey *et al.* (2008: 170) document a similar reported intention from parents to encourage youth to stay in education for 'as long as possible'.

7   PDC refers to two years of formal education before college. These used to be taught in colleges themselves, but starting in the late 1990s they became what is now known as higher secondary school (i.e. eleventh and twelfth standards).

8   I must note here that other local teachers were sending their children to private schools, too.

9   This has been described as a distinctively middle-class practice (Kumar 2011: 230).

10   This is not really the case. I was able to corroborate that English teachers at the HSS of Jesus were fully competent and qualified.

11   Mehrotra and Panchamukhi (2006) argue that most private schools at the lower end of a segmented private sector do not contribute to gender and social equity. They show that although they often dispose of better physical facilities, they offer a poor alternative to low-quality government schools as a result of having poorly paid and trained teachers.

12   As Lieten (1977) rightly notes, restrictive policies have continuously been interspersed with policies promoting private schools without too much supervision, thus allowing for the expansion of private (mostly church-run) schools responsible for a great deal of Kerala's renowned literacy record. In Ernakulam, Christian government-aided schools constitute the core of the state education system. These schools and colleges have not only been a key site for radical social transformation, responsible to a great extent for shaping Kerala's modernity (Devika 2007), but also an important economic resource for Christian communities, whose interests have become intertwined with these institutions. As such, education has become an object of political contestation between Christians (and other community identities with a vested interest in education) and the established sociocultural and state forces (Jeffrey 1992; Lukose 2005). The former have actively negotiated with the state to corner material and cultural resources (Devika 2007), while successive state governments have oscillated between complying with community forces, in exchange for political support, and trying to undermine Christian control over the state education sector. In other words, education has become inextricably linked to Kerala's political modernity.

13   The 1957 Education Bill, which sought to centralise teachers payments (Lieten 1977), was one such attempt. Resembling the logic for launching the reforms in 2008, the 1957 policies were allegedly an attempt by the government to prevent private manage-ment from utilising school seats to collect donations and to favour people of their particular religious community.

14   The admission process thus produces a *de facto* hierarchy of state schools, which are known by parents and students as schools that take students who have scored in the 60s, 70s, 80s or 90s. The most reputed urban government-aided schools benefit from this change: a great part of their student intake now consists of the youth with top marks.

Students who perform outstandingly in the SSLC do better in HSS and stand a better chance at securing some of the scarce merit seats in desirable university courses, hence furthering the reputation of these schools. This allows them to lure in parents and charge even higher donations for the shrinking and increasingly coveted management and community seats.

Bibliography

Advani, S. 2009. *Schooling the National Imagination: Education, English, and the Indian Modern*. Oxford University Press.

Balagopalan, S. 2005. An ideal school and the schooled ideal: Education at the margins. In *Educational Regimes in Contemporary India* (eds) R. Chopra and P. Jeffery, 83–98. Sage.

De Neve, G. 2011. 'Keeping it in the family': Work, education and gender hierarchies among Tiruppur's industrial capitalists. In *Being Middle-class in India: A Way of Life* (ed.) H. Donner, 73–99. Routledge.

Devika, J. 2007. *En-gendering Individuals: The Language of Re-forming in Early Twentieth Century Keralam*. Orient Longman.

Donner, H. 2005. Children are capital, grandchildren are interest: Changing educational strategies and parenting in Calcutta's middle-class families. In *Globalizing India: Perspectives from below* (eds) J. Assayag and C. J. Fuller, 119–139. Anthem Press.

Fuller, C. J. 1976. Kerala Christians and the caste system. *Man* **11**, 53–70.

George, M. K. and J. Domi 2002. *Residual Literacy in a Coastal Village: Poovar village of Thiruvananthapuram district*. (KRPLLD Discussion Paper No. 45). CDS.

Hoeppe, G. 2007. *Conversations on the Beach: Fishermen's Knowledge, Metaphor and Environmental Change in South India*. Berghahn Books.

Holmström, M. 1976. *South Indian Factory Workers: Their Life and their World*. Cambridge University Press.

Jeffrey, C. 2008. Kicking away the ladder: Student politics and the making of an Indian middle class. *Environment and Planning D: Society and Space* **26**, 517–536.

Jeffrey, C., P. Jeffery and R. Jeffery 2008, *Degrees Without Freedom?: Education, Masculinities, and Unemployment in North India*. Stanford University Press.

Jeffery, P. 2005. Introduction: Hearts, minds, and pockets. In *Educational Regimes in Contemporary India* (eds) R. Chopra and P. Jeffery, 13–38. Sage.

Jeffrey, R. 1992. *Politics, Women and Well-being: How Kerala became 'a model'*. Macmillan.

Jeffery, R., P. Jeffery and C. Jeffrey 2005. Social inequalities and the privatisation of secondary schooling in North India. In *Educational Regimes in Contemporary India*. Sage (eds) R. Chopra and P. Jeffery, 41–61. Sage.

Klausen, A. M. 1968. *Kerala Fishermen and the Indo-Norwegian Pilot Project*. Universitetsforlaget.

Kumar, N. 2011. The middle-class child: Ruminations on failure. In *Elite and Everyman: The Cultural Politics of the Indian Middle Classes* (eds) A. Baviskar and R. Ray, 220–245. Routledge.

Kurien, J. and T. R. T. Achari 1990. Overfishing along Kerala coast: Causes and consequences. *Economic and Political Weekly* **25**, 2011–2018.

Lieten, G. K. 1977. Education, ideology and politics in Kerala 1957–59. *Social Scientist* **6**, 3–21.

Lukose, R. 2005. Empty citizenship: Protesting politics in the era of globalization. *Cultural Anthropology* **20**, 506–533.

Mehrotra, S. and P. R. Panchamukhi 2006. Private provision of elementary education in India: Findings of a survey in eight states. *Compare: A Journal of Comparative and International Education* **36**, 421–442.

Nisbett, N. 2007. Friendship, consumption, morality: Practising identity, negotiating hierarchy in middle-class Bangalore. *Journal of the Royal Anthropological Institute* **13**, 935–950.

Osella, F. and C. Osella 2000. *Social Mobility in Kerala: Modernity and Identity in Conflict.* Pluto Press.

Parry, J. 2005. Changing childhoods in industrial Chhattisgarh. In *Educational Regimes in Contemporary India* (eds) R. Chopra and P. Jeffery, 276–298. Sage.

Ram, K. 1991. *Mukkuvar Women: Gender, Hegemony and Capitalist Transformation in a South Indian fishing community.* Zed Books.

Tharakan, P. K. 2004. Ernakulam revisited: A study of literacy in the first totally literate district in India. In *Paradigms of Learning: The Total Literacy Campaign in India* (ed.) M. Karlekar, 48–92. Sage.

7   Living the final year of school

It was January and the twelfth standard students of Brahmacharya Vidya Mandir and Higher Secondary School of Jesus were two months away from the end of their school days. However, the atmospheres in the urban and the peripheral schools were markedly different. In the city school, teachers had rushed through their 'portions' to finish by November (having started in June), which meant that students had been officially on study leave in order to prepare for their final exams for quite a while already. Students had long finished their first and second 'models' (mock final exams), practical models, the actual practical Board exams, and were on study leave preparing for the Boards. They came to school for clarification and revisions on set times and dates. The ambience of these sessions was solemn. On one occasion, I was able to catch a glimpse of a maths revision session through one of the few classroom blinds that was not fully shut. Students, with absolute concentration, stared at the blackboard where the teacher went over some problems. The imminence of the Boards kept everyone tense and focused.

In Kothad, the timetable was not as rushed and exam oriented as it was in the city. Here the portions had not been finished yet and students kept coming to school every day; I was told they would continue to do so during their study leave. A teacher told me that because this is a rural school they come every day. 'At home they'd sit in front of the TV, and not study at all; here they are made to study', he explained. On the day after I saw the city youth cloistered in that classroom, I went to HSS of Jesus in Kothad. The ambience was much more relaxed amongst final year students even though their 'models' were soon to start. While some students were indeed attending a maths revision in a classroom, others were busy finishing one of their final chemistry reports, neatly handwritten, in the corner of an otherwise unused classroom. Others were leisurely hanging out in classrooms or roaming into the *chayakada* (teashop) opposite the school gates. They come to study, do revisions, but also to 'enjoy', as another teacher explained. In a classroom towards the back, a group of female students was enthusiastically writing farewell messages on each other's leavers' books. I was asked to join, so I spent quite a nice afternoon amongst them writing my best wishes for what was to come. The nostalgia of finishing school and calmness in the daily sessions made it feel more like a prolonged farewell celebration, transmitting a different emotion about this moment of their lives.

Before getting to the final stages of the academic year, I imagined youth in Kothad and Kochi would reveal similar sorts of anxieties, joys and hopes, which I presumed to be associated with the end of one's schooling years. But as the picture just portrayed shows, there was a markedly different ambiance at BVM and Kothad's HSS of Jesus. To a large extent, the differences speak of differences in terms of types of school (aided/unaided), location of the school (urban/semi-urban) and syllabi (Salim 2004).[1] They are also revealing of the particular ways in which the final year of schooling was understood and hence structured by these particular schools (see Chapter 3 for the case of BVM) under the impetus, or not, of parental demands (Chapter 4). But on another and perhaps more important level, these differences speak of the distinctive ways in which two groups of youth – one that according to socioeconomic definitions may strictly be classified as 'middle class' and another that may not – actually inhabited the final year. These differences between students' experiences of the final year at school in turn spoke of the various ways in which they envisaged their futures in twenty-first-century India. This chapter examines how schooling is differently experienced across social groups. In particular it consists of a comparative exploration of how young men and women at both the top and the bottom of the educational ladder inhabit the final year of school and articulate vision of the future. The argument is simple: the degree to which education is experienced as beneficial varies widely across social groups.

In what follows I describe the HSS of Jesus youth's idealised visions of the future, focusing primarily on the educational aspect of these visions. In the subsequent section, I juxtapose these with their more realistic aspirations and their strategies to get to them as they cropped up in conversations at the end of the academic year.

Transitions: Sketching fantasies of the future

Early in fieldwork, as I sought to appease the inherent anticipation generated by my presence in the school and establish my research as a worthwhile endeavour, I decided to engage with a topic I sensed would be of relevance to institutions and students at the final year of school: higher education and career aspirations. During one of my first encounters with the Class 11 and 12 students at the school in Kothad, I designed and conducted an activity, which I called 'transitions', with the intention of generating a carefree conversation about career choices and future life plans and aspirations, and building rapport with students and teachers. In the activity students were asked to represent diagrammatically their 'aims' in life, indicating their own idealised life trajectories from aged fifteen to seventy on which they marked the various important transitions. After sketching their life trajectories, students were encouraged to present their transition lines to the rest of the class, which was then followed by an open discussion of career and job preferences.

Many students took the activity more seriously than I had anticipated and began to work on their diagrams diligently; for others it became nothing more than a lark. Several worked in groups, agreeing on a mutual transition; others worked individually, with many requesting assistance from the teacher who collaborated with me on that day. Despite this, the diagrams that emerged displayed enormous similarities.

They all drew straight lines at the top of their sheets of paper. Below each line students wrote a sequence of numbers signifying age below which neatly arranged boxes filled with one-word labels represented the various events and achievements that constituted the dream-like lives of their imaginary selves. Arrows then shot from box to box signifying the connection and sequence between events. Their pictures portrayed themselves moving seamlessly through time acquiring higher-education credentials, jobs and driving licences; purchasing cars, motorbikes and houses; achieving 'love success' and getting married; having children (one or two), educating and subsequently marrying off their children; and finally, retiring. Everything took place at the right time, place and order. Drawings showed no signs of difficulty, struggle or idleness, like the sort of relatively purposeless time periods characteristic of the lives of many educated unemployed or under-employed youth across India (Jeffrey 2010).

The transition activity did not, by any means, amount to any systematic effort to grasp students' 'true' life aspirations, yet what their sketches did offer was a strong indication that these pupils had understood what constituted the 'right' kind of trajectory. This was ultimately a bourgeois or middle-class trajectory, whereby education stands out as the primary route towards desired white-collar jobs and consumption-inflected lifestyles.

The diagrams reflected a disposition to stay in formal education for a long time,[2] almost always accumulating the graduate and postgraduate degrees expected of commerce stream students in middle-class Kochi. The proscriptive autobiographies captured in their diagrams anticipated the sort of 'strategic credentialing' (Fernandes 2000) that has been shown to be a central part of middle-class life, often used as a form of strategic 'waiting' in situations of uncertainty as a way to acquire or maintain one's middle-class status (Baviskar and Ray 2011; Jeffrey *et al.* 2008). The investment on a variety of educational credentials has been recently described as a strategic way of characteristic amongst the lower-middle classes (Jeffrey 2010). Amongst their sketches, the majority shared an almost script-like educational strategy, by which after finishing school most of them pictured their ideal selves acquiring Bachelor's degrees in commerce (BCom), followed by master's degrees in commerce (MCom), chartered accountancy courses[3] or MBAs.

Their sketches reproduced the pervasive notion of education as intrinsically beneficial and as a driver for change, propelling them out of manual wage labour – a field that employed most of their parents – and towards white-collar jobs and middle-class lives. No boy pictured himself working as a mason, and no girl imagined herself being a full-time housewife. In contrast to the caste-based occupations of their parents or grandparents (Busby 2000: 52; Osella and Osella 2000: 38; Ram 1991: 143; Rogers 2008: 82) they all imagined themselves gaining some form of non-manual secure source of income, which many described simply as becoming 'accountants'. A few imagined themselves acquiring government jobs in the police or as teachers, while others depicted their imaginary selves acquiring high-flying jobs in the Indian Administrative Service, a pre-eminently elitist job since Independence. As shown in Chapter 6, these sorts of high status government jobs[4] have rarely been accessed by Kothad's Latin Catholics.

In the middle-class trajectories education was not valued only with reference to employment, it also emerged as central to their ideal marriage strategies. Many girls imagined their future ideal husbands not just as removed from manual labour but in possession of specific educational qualifications and secure forms of employment. In their sketches, girls depicted themselves achieving higher education and post-graduate degrees as a way to access better grooms, who must ideally be equally or better qualified than brides. Sherin, for example, saw herself getting an MCom and marrying an MBA graduate and businessman. Simmy pictured herself marrying an engineer after completing an MCom degree. On the contrary, a few boys sketched their ideal selves marrying teachers.

Education also had a bearing in their depiction of themselves as parents. With an eye already put on their ideal future families' educational strategies, many of them depicted their imaginary selves as parents devoting enormous resources into private, English-medium schooling for their imaginary children. Neenu painted her imaginary children as attending a highly reputed private English-medium school in Kochi. Her choice matched the most pervasive understanding of quality schooling amongst the city's middle classes described in Chapters 3 and 4. This signals the extent to which these schools stand as markers of prestige and wealth across classes. Never having been part of such a space did not preclude their strong sense of the symbolic value that attending these schools holds (Balagopalan 2005: 93). Neither did their exclusion from government jobs[5] and middle-class trajectories preclude Kothad student's strong sense of these trajectories.

There were some exceptions to the dominant imaginary trajectory of prolonged education and white-collar employment. A dozen of the almost eighty students who participated envisaged themselves getting only one educational credential after finishing school. Their imaginary post-school trajectories seemed to respond to more pragmatic considerations than their peers. They depicted themselves acquiring highly specific job-oriented credentials that in the face of pervasive unemployment or under-employment appeared to offer them new and better opportunities. Akhil, for example, sketched himself getting a fire and safety diploma and subsequently finding work as a fire and safety technician in the Gulf region. Most of them had learned about these sort of credentials through teachers and the many educational fairs that pack out the city in May. However, these choices may also turn out to be too expensive or simply futile as many of these service-sector jobs may not exist or offer the earnings they tend to promise (Baviskar and Ray 2011: 5).

In addition, the few students who belonged to wealthier business families, like Paul (Chapter 6), had a different take on the activity all together. Rather than depicting what seemed like an ideal trajectory, they sketched themselves acquiring degrees in commerce or business in order to gain skills to further develop a family business. Paul, for example, aspired to acquire a business education and improve his English language skills in order to expand his family's coir business to the

Figure 7.1 Sign advertising job-oriented courses

Figure 7.2 Educational fair in Kochi centre

international markets. Belonging to a successful business family gave them a certain entrepreneurial acumen and a different understanding of an ideal trajectory.

Aspirations revisited: Strategies at the brink of post-school life

Throughout fieldwork, students' plans for the future or their life and career aspirations emerged countless times during more informal conversations with many of my close, and not so close, informants, especially towards the end of the academic year. In what follows, I juxtapose these aspirations with the dominant imaginary trajectory of prolonged education and white-collar employment portrayed earlier with the aim of capturing the tension or gap between them.

Gayathri

Gayathri belonged to a Dheevara[6] family from Cheranelloor, a neighbouring town. She was determined to acquire a diploma in animation after completing her higher secondary. Gayathri was amongst those who during the transition activity had come up with an 'alternative' path, different from the almost script-like trajectory the majority had depicted. As I wrote my best wishes on her leaver's book she ran back towards her backpack, from where she pulled out a glossy brochure from the private institute where she was planning to get her animation training. Amongst the various courses offered at the institute, which ranged from five-week to one-year courses, Gayathri wanted to complete the one-year diploma in animation, costing Rs80,000 (£800). 'It is very expensive', she acknowledged. But she had already thought of a plan, bold as herself, to collect the fee money. 'I will go visit one uncle, his son is a doctor there; I am going to go see them'. Excited, she carried on talking about the potentially very rewarding jobs she imagined awaited her as an animation graduate. 'The starting salary will be Rs20,000 (£200) for someone with this diploma. You have seen Avatar? That film is full of animation, 3D animation; like that I want to do'. She had been deeply inspired by the film as well as by the increasing number of television ads on Indian channels using animation. She had already identified an animation studio in the city, precisely dedicated to producing advertising. Her reading of education, employment and of her future in general was highly pragmatic.

Youth like Gayathri were full of wit. Gayathri vocally critiqued, and at the same time shored up status, against those who claimed to want to follow a more conventional trajectory and acquire a degree in commerce after completing school as people with 'no aims in life'. This discourse, and her orientation towards an alternative sort of trajectory, spoke of her awareness that the 'ideal' educational trajectory depicted in the transition activity at the beginning of the academic year had rarely led to the middle-class lifestyles to which they were supposed to lead. Instead of rejecting education, what appeared more crucial to students like Gayathri was to recognise the inadequacy or failure of such 'ideal' trajectories and devise alternative strategies that conceive education in new ways, something students like Gayathri prided. She imagined her strategy towards the field of animation as leading to job opportunities, higher salaries, greater consumer choice and a better quality of life. She viewed her own educational strategy as more adapted to current times and thus more effective to crafting a transformed future. Gayathri located her aspirations in the private sector and saw no promise in the government sector, a typically middle-class attitude in contemporary India.

However, Gayathri's strategy may in the end prove futile. Her dreams of an alternative route to a middle-class lifestyle were inspired by the many private, job-oriented institutes that have appeared in the city. These sell their educational alternatives at prices that often turn out to be either too expensive or that are incapable of living up to the hype and the promised employment or earnings advertised by them (Baviskar and Ray 2011: 5). Job-oriented courses, like the one that had captivated Gayathri, are aggressively sold in a number of educational fairs that pack many venues in the city in May. These feature not only a wide range of private vocational and job-oriented course providers, but also a wide range of banks and other financial institutions promoting education loans for students. Sales representatives from these institutions also visit schools such as HSS of Jesus, disguised as career counselors, to advertise their courses amongst possible new clients.

Her parents, a fisherman now working in a cement factory and a fish vendor, thought the course that Gayathri wished to pursue was too expensive. They saw no job prospects for it, and hence thought it would be too risky for Gayathri to undertake it. Instead, they thought it would be sound for Gayathri to complete a BCom 'since she is doing +2 in commerce'. When I interviewed Gayathri's father, Gayathri's eldest brother was completing the final year of his BCom degree. 'After BCom, he has to start working; the salary I get is not enough to educate them more', he explained. He expected Gayathri to follow a similar path, plus having her complete a degree to which most local parents were acquainted would allow him to navigate the marriage market more confidently.

The experiences of Neelu and Jinu, both of whom assisted my research in Kothad while waiting to find employment, shed light on the outcomes these sorts of courses offered local young people. Like Gayathri, Neelu (Chapter 6) was a HSS of Jesus graduate. She dreamt of becoming a flight attendant, however, her father managed to persuade her to complete a BCom degree right after finishing school. After acquiring her degree, she persevered and got a loan to pay for the Rs125,000 (£1,250) fee to attend an air-hostess course. After completion, she recounted sadly how she would not be able to qualify for a job interview as her arms bared a birthmark that would be visible when wearing the flight attendant uniform. She then signed up for a Master's in Commerce degree at a private institution. When Neelu agreed to collaborate with my work in Kothad, she had finished that degree and was searching for work. Months of waiting passed until she was employed as an accountant at a small *godown* (a warehouse) owned by her father's friend. The poorly paid work allowed her to begin to pay back her loan, while (intentionally) delaying marriage. Jinu had completed a marine science diploma a year ago, costing Rs400,000 (£4,000). He had been placed on a waiting list for a placement as an officer on board a merchant ship. During his wait he has been largely engaged in the sort of 'timepass' described by (Jeffrey 2010; Jeffrey *et al.* 2008) amongst Uttar Pradesh Chamars. With the exception of the work he did with me, Jinu spent his time roaming around on street corners, doing family errands once in a while and waiting for that call from the employment agency. He would also have to start paying back the huge loan sometime soon.

Pious

Pious belonged to a Latin Catholic family in Vaduthala. His father worked as mason in a construction site outside the city. When I first met Pious, while conducting the transition activity, he was sitting on the left of the classroom and the first few buttons of his shirt were unbuttoned, showing his muscled chest adorned with a pendant. On that day he took the activity well. He and a group of friends sitting around him took on their sketches together making a comment on every bit and often joking amongst themselves. At the end of the class period Pious and many of his friends had produced similar transition-lines depicting their ideal selves completing BCom and MCom degrees, and subsequently finding jobs, which he generically described as 'jobs'.

Like Gayathri, Pious and his close friends effectively foreclosed themselves of the trajectories identified as 'ideal' early in the school year. But, unlike Gayathri, Pious showed no intention to adopt them in any way. Pious' academic skills and knowledge of English were not above the average in the class. In fact, Pious and a few of his peers showed little enthusiasm and motivation for school work. Towards the end of their final year, when class portions were nearly finished and mock final exams were soon to start, Pious and his peers spent most days hanging out and roaming between the school and the *chayakada* opposite the school gate having *bondas* and tea.

One morning, as he gave me a few '*goonda* bands' to wear (plain black plastic bracelets), I chatted informally with Pious and his friends about their life plans after school. Unsure if he would even pass the twelfth STD, Pious did not envisage himself moving seamlessly through desired degrees and acquiring respectable white-collar employment. Rather than seeming concerned about their futures, Pious and his friends joked about their predicament. Like the Dalits described by Jeffrey *et al.* (2008), humour and jokes signalled a sense, although subtle, of them failing to embody the pervasive notions of idealised trajectories: of hard-working students who acquired good salaried jobs. Pious joked about having to become a mason after all, while one of his friends jested about his future work as a '*goonda* manager'. For Pious and his friends, the uncertainty looming ahead only reinforced the possibility of having to rely on the familiar. Manual wage labour, the source of employment of the majority of their close kin, appeared to provide a more plausible possibility within which to imagine their futures.

Their awareness of their predicament did not seem to lead to a sense of personal crisis. Rather than developing a cultural style centred on a sense of failure or of being 'good for nothing' (Jeffrey *et al.* 2008: 181), Pious effectively carved out status amongst his group of friends. Amongst them (a group of around a dozen) status relied heavily, as made evident in their appearance and talk about being '*goonda*' (a ruffian or rogue), on their ability to construct hyper-masculine identities, a hierarchy of performance (Chopra 2004; Osella and Osella 1998), which rather than through hard work in studies and aim-talk was enacted around ideas concerning physical strength, the muscularity of their bodies and a particular style of fashion (Rogers 2008: 86). They devoted energy almost obsessively on body-building exercises at the gym and at home. At school, during the tea break, Pious once took me to a small empty room next to their classroom where he and some friends had been chalk-drawing on the walls. He told me: 'come see the muscle-mania'. On the walls, they had sketched a highly muscled male torso and a sign that read 'multi-gymnasium'. Pious' friends animatedly gathered around and prompted Pious and one other peer to show me their biceps and triceps. However, Pious' tactic, as that of the 'college rowdies' described by Rogers (2008), was self-defeating. As the economic structures, employment markets and markers of status are transformed in the conditions of liberalisation, their resistance strategy of developing *goonda* identities risked only reproducing their situation.

Shillu and others

Towards the end of the academic year, Shillu, one of closest informants in Kothad, remained committed towards the ideal trajectory depicted at the start of the year.

As with most students from their commerce batch, she unquestioningly envisaged herself getting a BCom. Shillu seemed slightly more determined than the majority when she spoke of wanting to become a chartered account: the most highly coveted profession amongst non-science streams. However, when I asked her about how she was planning to get charter accountancy qualifications, she barely had any knowledge of the intricate recruitment process leading to them. On the contrary, the commerce students in BVM possessed an excellent knowledge of application and recruitment processes and of how to micro manage such complex fields so as to act in a timely way (Jeffrey 2010: 20). But most of Kothad's students were first generations in their families to reach +2 and most of their parents were manual labourers, and they held very vague ideas as to the sort of job they should aspire to or might be able to secure. Moreover, many of them lacked the knowledge pertaining to the admission and recruitment processes to the degrees outlined.

There were a few exceptions to these experiences presented. One of them, perhaps the most salient one, was the case of Paul (Chapter 6). He was amongst the very few who sketched his idealised life leading to him becoming a large-scale entrepreneur. It was the end of the school year and nothing had changed: Paul's idealised future mirrored his real aspirations. Echoing his father's expectations, Paul aspired to become a successful businessman and to speak fluent English. He already spoke more fluently than any of his peers. He spoke resolutely of his life plan: completing a Bachelor's in business administration in Bangalore,[7] followed by an MBA. Paul had decided that he would pursue his higher studies outside Kerala because seats in the state are too scarce and because studying in a different state with a different language, and away from family, would force him 'to concentrate on studies, and improve [his English] language'. Like Gayathri, Paul liked to talk about his ambitions and aims as a way to distance himself from the rest. 'In Albert's [his previous school] they all have aim; they enjoy life but they concentrate on studies and get marks also. But in Kothad only 30 per cent have aims; some students even think plus two is enough'. He spoke of himself as having a superior set of aims than his peers. But unlike Gayathri, Paul's aspirations were backed by the economic, social and cultural resources of a well-established entrepreneur family. However, as Fernandes (2000) rightly notes, the attainment of an MBA requires a substantial financial investment that is out of the reach for most Kothad youth, even too costly perhaps for Paul's parents. Even though they may never be able to acquire MBA credentials, they may still turn to the vast field of private institutes that grant diplomas and certificates to provide credentials in an attempt to gain a foothold in the new middle-class dream of neoliberal employment (Fernandes 2000: 94).

Students at Kothad's HSS of Jesus asserted that their schooling experience was largely a positive one. Many valued the affectionate relationship with teachers and peers, and expressed their grief of having to part ways at the end of the year. Managing to pass their final exams and obtaining their SSLC – something accomplished by approximately half the students at Kothad's HSS of Jesus – was important and considered a necessity for the vast majority. Parents in Kothad often said that obtaining an SSLC was the minimum level of education one should attain.

This was indeed an important credential for accessing jobs and further education. However, they did not experience schooling as leading to a transformed future.

Future aspirations: A site of convergence amongst middle-class youth

The transition activity was also conducted in BVM. In what follows, I document the sketches produced in the urban middle-class school. To a large extent, their diagrams converged in very similar aspirations and ideal transitions to adult lives. Towards the end of the academic year the symbolic unity captured in their diagrams earlier infused their experiences of the final months of schooling, when peer group divisions of all kinds seemed to dissolve and an air of unity brought BVM pupils closer together (see Winkler Reid 2011 for a similar account).

The diagrams produced at BVM also portrayed lives characterised by bourgeois transitions from school, to higher education, postgraduate degrees and salaried employment. Their career choices were those leading to professions with opportunity for 'growth' as Sidu's father dubbed them (Chapter 4): engineering, medicine, law and chartered accountancy. The professions have been and continue to be a central project by which the middle class has been a defining feature of the dominant understanding of what means to be middle class (Baviskar and Ray 2011: 4). Amongst the professions there was a clear hierarchy with a preference for engineering (BTech), in particular IT-related varieties. This was also reflected in the fact that computer/mathematics was the most sought after higher secondary stream, which was perceived to better equip students for their engineering degrees. Due to high demand, the number of computer/mathematics places doubled the number of seats offered in the biology/mathematics and commerce streams. This also meant that many of the students who had failed to secure a computer/ mathematics place and had only managed to enter the commerce stream – the least popular option – had to contend with stereotypes that portrayed commerce students as less intelligent or capable. Apart from engineering degrees, they all envisaged themselves acquiring postgraduate degrees: mostly MBA degrees. The combination of BTech plus MBA was talked about as the 'basic degrees' needed in today's job market. One important difference between Kothad and Ernakulam youth was that while the former only sketched their ideal selves attending local colleges, the latter envisaged themselves attending colleges and universities in urban centres across India.

Beyond education, their diagrams depicted their imaginary selves moving seamlessly from college into their first jobs in 'private firms',[8] many of them in the IT sector. Similar to the young Bangalore men described by Nisbett (2009), there was almost an obsessive orientation towards forms of learning, and subsequently working, linked to the IT industry. In conversations with some of them, they were often specific in their imagined future employment, naming companies in the local IT park, or some of the most prominent IT companies in India (Wipro or Infosys) or abroad. Many of them imagined the IT sector as a thriving employment field, in which to forge one's riches. The imaginary lives portrayed in their diagrams evinced the shift in aspirations that Fernandes (2000) describes as a defining feature of what she calls the 'new middle class'. In symbolic terms, she argues that 'while for the old middle class the cultural and economic standard may have been represented by a job in a state bank or Indian civil service, the new middle class would aspire to a job in a multinational corporation or foreign bank' (Fernandes 2000: 92).

These jobs and the imaginary wealth generated by them were in turn imagined as enabling high levels of consumption. When I asked Balram about what he expected from education, he replied 'a good job, a good income'. Their visions of the future involved high salaries and purchasing of pets, motorbikes, cars, houses (abroad and in India), penthouses, flats in Bangalore and family holidays in Europe. Their visions resonated with images of prosperous urban Indians occupying expensive suburban homes, equipped with all modern conveniences that increasingly circulate in the Indian media (Jeffrey 2010: 8). In Fernandes' words, they adopted the 'social practices of taste and commodity consumption that mark a new cultural standard that is specifically associated with liberalisation and the opening of the Indian market to the global economy' (2000: 3).

The cultural and economic standards of their middle-class dream were not just represented by a job in a corporation and the associated practices of taste and commodity consumption. Upon a closer exploration of their diagrams, these reflected that for the majority of urban middle-class youth the ideal life trajectory had come to be cast in the language of enterprise. In a recent, seminal volume, Nandini Gooptu (2013) examines how the promotion of an enterprise culture and entrepreneurship in India in recent decades has come to recast mindsets and individual subjectivity, with profound social and political implications far beyond the economic sphere. Contributors in that volume delve into various narratives and discourses of enterprise and the enterprising self as increasingly expressed and promoted by the private sector, the public media and the state. They present the current historical conjuncture in India, initiated with the launch of economic reforms in the early 1990s, as marking an epochal shift, the chief significance of which lies in the creation of new Indians, whose dreams, passions and desires fuel growth and development in India today, and whose powerful newly liberated capacity to aspire is itself an asset. This new enterprising citizen, endowed with 'aspirational capital' (Gooptu 2013: 3–4), shaped the ideal life trajectories captured by BVM's students.

Their diagrams spoke of a profound sense that in present-day India 'the sky is the limit'. They shared a vision of India as a fertile and potentially very rewarding ground for individual creativity, innovation and leadership. If the previous middle-class generations aspired to become professionals as a means to capture a job in the Indian civil service, in the new context becoming a professional, primarily an engineer, was seen as a fundamental first step towards becoming an entrepreneur. Their ideal life trajectories were marked by a clear impulse towards producing or leading some form of independent creation or innovation that would lead to much greater prestige, recognition and wealth, as well as the overall development of India. They were inspired by powerful company foundation stories that increasingly circulate in India, such as the well-known one of N. R. Narayana Murthy (co-founder and former chairman of Infosys Technologies). Born in the dusty village in Karnataka, Murthy was one of eight children. Son of a poor school-teacher, he rose to great fame and wealth as the leader of one of the most successful IT companies in India. He managed to secure admission to the prestigious IIT, what many BVM students aspired to, yet had to be content with attending a local engineering college as his family could not afford the fees. Equipped with his degree, the story tells us, he pursued a postgraduate degree at IIT Kanpur then worked several years abroad and in India (Upadhya 2011: 180). Muthry and six other friends quit their jobs and founded Infosys in their apartment in Pune, with Rs10,000 (£100) of capital. The company rose after 1991 and in 1993 was listed in Nasdaq, bolstering the image of the Indian software industry and putting it on the map of the global economy (Upadhya 2011: 180). His and others' rags to riches stories, which form a crucial component of consciously crafted publicity strategies of the organisation, have garnered immense symbolic power for the aspiring middle classes, specially the youth (Upadhya 2011: 190). Mirroring the story of N. R. Narayana Murthy, many of their sketches depicted both their technical education and first salaried employments as stepping stones towards all sorts of entrepreneurial projects. Many of them envisaged themselves opening new firms, starting new business, resorts, hospitals, dental clinics or law firms; in other words becoming catalysts of new enterprises.

They demonstrated a wider disposition towards leading new enterprises not just as a means to generate wealth, but also for intellectual/knowledge and social change. Jacob (Chapter 5), for example, pictured himself as a future catalyst of scientific knowledge. When I first met him, Jacob aspired to access the reputed Vellore Institute of Technology in Tamil Nadu to pursue a degree in biotechnology. He dreamt of finding the cure for cancer. He spoke of being deeply concerned for the brain drain affecting India. He felt the duty to stay and 'do something' to push India in what he called 'the final stretch' to becoming a global superpower. Like Jacob, others aspired to become a best-selling author, making a major discovery in fields such as history, medicine or nano-technology, all forms of knowledge entre-preneurship. In short, there was an entrepreneurial duty that defined their understanding of citizenship.

Similarly, many envisaged themselves engaging in various kinds of social entrepreneurship. This included, for example, engaging in charity work, starting a home for rescued animals, doing social work, adoption or voluntarism. They all aspired to become known for these individual achievements and endeavours, which they, in turn, identified as the sort of contribution responsible for India's develop-ment into one of the world's superpowers.

Finally, some middle-class youth envisaged their future selves engaging in politics. The drawings of a small yet equally important group of students depicted their ideal selves 'getting into politics' after having become successful engineers and entrepreneurs. These students often talked about 'politics' and 'politicians' as the reason India has not yet become fully 'modern'. These were often mocked through jokes and SMS messages that centred on the lack of education of many politicians.[9] These drawings gave evidence of how within the social world of the urban middle classes there is a sense that public civility, middle-class material aspirations in modern urban life, and the country's development at large are being thwarted by a rise of 'plebeian' politicians, drawn from peasant communities and lower caste-groups (Hansen 1999: 56). This critique was linked to a broader disdain towards public-sector employment and institution, mainly government schools (older middle-class aspirations and values). They expressed what has been described as a distinctively middle-class moral duty to become active in politics and to 'lead India' out of the predicament of corruption (Baviskar and Ray 2011: 6), going against Varma's (2003) idea that the middle classes have become disinterested in the poor, inequality and politics.

Just as amongst the Kothad students, the transition activity also elicited a dominant understanding of what constituted an ideal life trajectory, which involved a particular set of practices (for example, technical education, private-sector employment and consumption) and dispositions (for example, entrepreneurial acumen). The values of individual responsibility, initiative, self-(re)making and goal-oriented, self-directed self-development, associated with enterprise culture, were the defining features of their subjective understanding of success. These particular sets of practices, dispositions and values constituted the tastes (and distastes) and fantasies (and phobias) that created the unconscious unity of a class (Bourdieu 1984: 77). In other words, BVM students adopted a set of ideal aspirations that mark a new cultural standard that is specifically associated with neoliberal policies and ideologies.

Living in 'the year that can break or make you'

'Middleclassness relies heavily on imagery and on the production and consumption of images of spaces, [achievement], sites and practices that are not necessarily ever fully realisable' (Donner and De Neve 2011: 13). Through the informal realm of peer-group interactions explored in Chapter 5, I showed how higher secondary middle-class students constructed different middle-class subjectivities, for example, the English speaking and the Malayalam speaking. I demonstrated how intersecting categories of distinction – caste, class, gender and religion – were manifested and reworked through different social practices, and forms of worth and status – language proficiency, consumption, particular tastes and styles – offered an alternative to formal education. However, as the year came to an end and their post-school lives were increasingly imminent, a growing sense of unity overshadowed those experiences of difference.

The pervasive sense of unity amongst the final year students at BVM was premised on the convergence of projects and aspirations and the joint struggle to achieve these. The struggle was based on the idea that the twelfth STD (not so much the eleventh STD) was a determining year for their life-long projects. A few months before the end of their school days, the twelfth STD students seemed to talk mostly of a common dream: doing well enough in the Board and entrance exams so as to secure seats in the desired higher-education courses and universities. They united, literally, in revision sessions like the one described at the introduction of the chapter. But most importantly they united in the common experience of hardship and sacrifice. Even though the struggle towards their projects was ultimately an individual experience, the collective sense of hardship 'we are put through' was an important element in these students' collective experience. This involved giving up 'leisure', including going to the cinema, playing football and the use of internet and mobile phones; what a student defined as putting himself on 'house arrest'. It also included the self-imposition of pressure and studying routines that involved long hours of studying at home alone or in groups. This sense of unity in sacrifice was premised on the idea that only through hard work and merit would they successfully achieve their dreams. This in turn formed the basis for their shared self-disciplining into the set of practices and motifs that constituted the experience of the twelfth STD, what they described as 'the year that can break or make you'. One afternoon in the middle of fieldwork, on the walk home, Srijith (Chapter 5) wanted, once again, to go over some of the essential questions of my research and to know whether or not I had learned what I had come to find out. He told me that if my aim was to look at youth's experiences of education I must write about the pressure '*we are put through*'.

I first came to hear of 'the year that can break or make you' from Vijay (Chapter 4). He was quoting one of his entrance coaching tutors, who described the way they should understand their predicament as twelfth STD students. 'You should be like a bird in a cage', the teacher explained to them. But later, once they had reached the study leave period before Board and entrance exams, the phrase cropped up as students rationalised the sacrifices and strenuous routines they disciplined themselves into. Vijay, who early in the academic year described himself as being 'lazy', although as he said '[in India] you can't say you are lazy', exemplified the process of embodying that heightened sense of hardship/sacrifice and the drive to work hard. Midway through the year, he told me how 'the entire mood ha[d] changed'. At first, 'my mother used to wake me up very early in the morning', but now he 'would just wake up on his own at 3.30 in the morning to study'. 'The people of the back benches are coming to the front benches to take notes', Vijay added. I asked him, 'like whom?', to which he replied 'me! I'm serious now, I'm feeling the pressure'. In the revision session described at the beginning of the chapter, Vijay sat in the front row, surrounded by students from his and other peer groups; they all looked ahead more focused than ever.

Like Vijay, many youth talked about this regime of hardship, especially about the sacrifices related to managing school and entrance coaching. Asked about their daily studying routine, many talked about being 'exhausted and hungry'. 'We finish class at 3 and have to be there [entrance coaching] by 3.30 p.m., until 5.30 p.m.'. Many students complained about the way EC was conducted by various centres but never hesitated to acknowledge the importance it had for their futures. For example, Priti (Chapter 4) complained that:

they [tutors] give a question and the top five brilliant guys shout the answer, while many of us feel inferior. Finally, when they [the top students in the class] reach the IIT[10] they do well, and they [the EC institute] say oh, we have done it again: we have made someone get admission to a top institution.

Although she strongly regretted the pressure and stress EC produced in students, she valued the sort of skills gained in her coaching class. Similarly, Sameer was said to have become depressed by the pressure generated by Mr Nandakumar, his EC teacher: 'At the beginning of the session Mr Nandakumar said that in the group there were only ten students who were on the right track to get into the IITs and that the rest needed to work', Sameer explained. The teacher read the names and Sameer was not amongst them. So, Sameer left soon after the class, feeling disheartened. After that incident, Sathya, Sameer's school and EC peer, helped him regain confidence and return to his studying routine. Both Priti and Sameer continued to attend and embrace their coaching classes. Enduring these hardships together, providing support and empathy for each other, became a prominent unifying experience towards the end of the school year.

Their sense of sacrifice was premised on the idea that life-long projects and aspirations were at stake, and depended on one's level of sacrifice and hard work in this one year. At this stage their aspirations and their family and wider social expectations blended into a more or less seamless whole. There was truly a feeling amongst many youth that their entire adult life was at stake in this one crucial year, leading to important exams that determined to a large extent how far one could 'grow'. Hence, it was understood that if they worked extraordinarily hard at this stage, a great deal of the years to come were taken care of. In an address to his fellow seniors during their farewell ceremony at school, two months away from exams, the head boy reminded his peers that:

> This may probably be the last day, remind you, the last day that we get to enjoy ourselves for some amount of time, because in the next two months we have a lot of *pain to undergo*, we have to concentrate, we have to *sacrifice*, we have to avoid all leisure. And if we become successful, then, you guys know the rest.

What was most interesting perhaps was that although the experience of 'undergoing pain' and 'sacrifice' to acquire merit served as the basis for a growing sense of unity amongst them, in reality some students' projects and aspirations were much more at stake than others. By compounding students of unequal backgrounds, with different cultural, social and economic resources (i.e. of divergent middle classes), the shared regime of hardship, hard work and merit performed the cultural task of concealing inequality (Baviskar and Ray 2011: 7). For some, those who belonged to the more dominant fractions of the middle class, this year was not as much of a crossroad – a 'year that can break or make you' – as it was for others. Following Deshpande's (2006: 2443) reading of Galanter (1984):

> Three broad kinds of resources are necessary to produce the results in competitive exams that qualify as indicators of merit: (a) economic resources (for prior education, training, materials, freedom from work, etc); (b) social and cultural resources (networks of contacts, confidence, guidance and advice, information, etc); (c) intrinsic ability and hard-work.

Let us go back to Vijay now. Belonging to a Hindu Nair family of successful entrepreneurs, he possessed the key material, social and cultural resources that would certainly pave his way into the degrees, jobs and lifestyles of his choice. Parents such as Vijay's were willing to pay large amounts for specialised coaching that had the best success rates in the market. As a rule of thumb, the higher the fees, the better the chance to success in competitive entrance exams. Moreover, youth like him had the financial backing to get them into the desired professional and postgraduate degrees in case their efforts to achieve these through 'merit' failed them. Moreover, and perhaps more importantly, youth like Vijay possess the sort of social skills and cultural knowledge (i.e. the 'exposure') that have been shown to be critical for dominant middle-class fractions' ability to reproduce their social status through new forms of employment like jobs in leading IT companies (Fuller and Narasimhan 2006). Vijay's attitude, sharp English and 'communication skills' – predominantly vested in the educated, professional, urban middle class – will probably allow him to face interviews and become part of a highly paid IT professional minority, before he takes on the reigns of his father's multiple enterprises.

For many other middle-class young men and women, like Parvathi, Priti or Srijith for example (Chapters 4 and 5), whose projects and aspirations depended more heavily on places in state-run colleges and universities, and on their intrinsic ability and hard work, their post-school predicaments were more uncertain. For them, securing a 'merit' place in government institutions was more critical. Take, for instance, the case of Visakh, a BVM graduate and first-year student of pharmacy at a private local college. Visakh belonged to a Hindu Nair family from Kozhikode. The family's sole provider was his father, who was employed as a welding technician at the Cochin Shipyard. Visakh's father held an SSLC and a diploma in welding from an ITI. Like many others in his batch, Visakh aspired to become a medical doctor. Likewise, he had embodied the regime of hardship and hard work of 'the year that can break or make you' a year ago. However, he failed to acquire one of the limited number of merit seats available in government colleges. In addition, his family lacked the social and cultural resources that would have guided him into alternative routes, as well as the exorbitant economic resources required for accessing a place at a private medical college. Visakh opted to study pharmacy instead; a much cheaper option.

Girls, too, embodied these regimes in very similar ways, actively imposing hectic studying regimes and restrictions on leisure activities on themselves with the aim to achieve similar goals to boys. Inequality with reference to gender was concealed by the experiences of unity in hardship. Girls' aspirations, and their embodying of hardship and hard work, were conditioned by parental decisions. These were, in turn, shaped primarily by ideas of morality and of girls' future role as mothers (Mills 2003). For example, when conversing with Priti's father, in the presence of Priti herself, he explained what, for him, the ideal career choice was for Priti: that she should aim for engineering, and not medicine, because jobs in the former field would allow for time for the family. On the contrary:

If you are a famous doctor, you will never have time for the family … But, engineering is OK, you work in a company or she can go as a teacher, especially for girls. If it was a boy, it is a different stand you'd have to take [as parent]. Girls got certain limitations; we consider family setup very much important. Children, she should be able to look [after]. There are couples both of them go to IT, their children psychologically are gone. The value system, the family should have a strong foundation. Then they [the children of that sort of families] grow and they don't know what affection is.

While her father did try to inspire her to aspire to join the ranks of young IT professionals, this came from an understanding that this choice was compatible with her responsibilities as a future wife/mother. Girls' choices of colleges or universities were also shaped by morally based limitations imposed by parents. A few girls spoke of not being allowed to go outside Kerala for college, while boys were not subjected to any sort of spatial limit other than that of their parents' economic resource to cover the cost of college, accommodation and living expenses beyond Kochi. Likewise, when it came to attending EC, girls would never be allowed to attend evening sessions, greatly reducing the number of coaching sessions available to them. In the coaching lessons I audited, three quarters of the class were boys. In some families, parents skimped on their daughters' EC, sending them to a less-known centre, while their sons attended a more expensive option.

Finally, I would like to highlight how the rhetoric of hard work and merit was not only used to talk about their final year of school, but was often deployed to think through wider social debates. For instance, the discourse of hard work and merit was used by many to oppose positive discrimination policies based on caste. In a classroom discussion (about the relative importance between school and EC for achieving their goals), students recognised that EC gave students a competitive advantage over those who were not exposed to coaching, but because EC involved hard work it was nevertheless a legitimate form of acquiring merit. Vinay expressed sorrow for those 'bright people who can't get into high positions because they can't afford the [EC] fees'. Students talked, almost entirely agreeing, about the need to dismantle the caste-based reservation system and to create instead a reservation system based on families' income level. Their rational reproduced 'creamy layer' arguments;[11] those that suggest that caste-based reservations are unfair for they discriminate against poor Bhramins and benefit rich OBC people who can afford EC. 'Is not that he [someone] deserves a seat because of his caste, you have to work hard!', Vedu declared, when one of her peers suggested caste-based reservations made sense. She felt that her right to be identified as meritorious of professional education was being infringed by caste reservations. They emphasised merit and hard work, measured through examination results/ranks, as the only legitimate criteria to discriminate those with merit and those without. Together, narratives of sacrifice and merit concealed any other factor shaping people's capacity to use higher education as a means to craft better futures for themselves and their families. Through their imagery of hard work and merit (as opposed to little work and caste-based quotas) everyone was assumed to be competing directly to demonstrate one's individual merit, in one single ranking. This imagined illusory 'equality' was, for them, the legitimate basis upon which they could compete to stake their rightful claim on the best degrees the nation has to offer, that is, their 'right' to put themselves on the right track to become beneficiaries of and contributors to the development of the Indian economy.

Figure 7.3 Sign advertising a popular entrance coaching institute

Figure 7.4 Sign advertising a popular entrance coaching institute

Conclusion

In this chapter I have examined the experiences of the final year of school and the life aspirations of two distinct groups of young people in Kerala. In Kothad, life aspirations were varied, yet they reflected how middle-class values and aspirations have captured the minds, at least partially, of a widening range of social groups (Ahmad and Reifeld 2001; De Neve 2011) at the fringes of privileged groups. Yet what is perhaps more salient in the stories captured in this chapter is how, unlike BVM students, pupils in Kothad did not experience the final year as being crucial. For Kothad's students there was no crucial year that could 'break' or 'make' them, and nor was there a similar experience of unity at the end of the year. In middle-class urban Kochi, youth of disparate middle-class backgrounds united themselves under the same aspirations, however, the outcome of their shared experience of sacrifice will be one marked by inequalities. Today, a disproportionate number of families and youth imbibe the middle-class dream that in India, through sacrifice and merit in education, 'the sky is the limit'.[12] In the final year, students actively united and oriented themselves towards a common struggle to improve their prospects in the face of competitive entrance examinations, without which larger dreams would be rendered unachievable. Although their prospects to succeed in these examinations and in the professional lives that follow are heavily shaped by their structural position and family background, their efforts made no reference to such differences and actively hailed their equality in the face of their quests ahead. Sacrifice and merit conjured up a unifying experience of 'the year that can break or make you' that concealed differences and inequalities, and thus rallied legitimacy for projects and lifestyles achievable for those in the dominant middle-class, upper-caste minority. Disguised as an equal quest for success, their fantasies only risked reproducing inequalities. In a similar way to the boys described by Willis (1977), the higher secondary students at BVM reproduced their middle-class position through their participation in school and EC, and their active adoption of the key symbolic resources of hard work and sacrifice.

Notes

1   This study by Salim (2004) shows how the quality of education, understood according to parameters such as type of school, medium of instruction, location of school, syllabi, is a determining factor in students' ability to secure admission to professional courses. He demonstrates how urban, English-medium, unaided, Central syllabi schools account for the large majority of students who were able to secure admission to these courses.
2   See Jeffrey *et al.* (2008) for a similar example.
3   The formulaic shift from +2 commerce to BCom (and MCom) may be viewed as a result of the fact that in Kerala, only ten years ago, higher secondary (the final two years of formal schooling) was not part of the school education system as it is today. It was indeed attended in colleges already as part of one's degree – what used to be called PDC or 'pre-degree'. As a commerce pre-degree student, one would normally advance towards the degree in commerce once having completed the PDC.
4   This is the sort of government post that inspired social reform movements and encapsulated the most pervasive ideas of acquired prestige and wealth among middle classes in the early twentieth century.
5   This sort of government occupation matches the sort of jobs that in the decades after Independence have been traditionally monopolised by the English-educated middle class (Varma 2003).
6   This is an inland fishing Hindu community.
7   All others referred to local colleges.
8   Today the middle classes locate their aspirations in the private sector.
9   These critiques were mainly directed towards Kerala politicians and not so much at political figures in the central government.
10   Here IIT refers to the Joint Engineering Entrance Exam. This is considered to be the most challenging and sought after all-India engineering entrance exam, leading to a seat in the most prestigious institutes of technology in the country.
11   Creamy layer arguments are self-defeating for in their very nature, quoting Deshpande (2006: 2441), higher education presupposes access to a minimum level of economic, cultural and political resources. Thus, indiscriminate use of these risks disqualifying precisely those segments of socially disadvantaged castes that have a good chance of succeeding. Deshpande argues further that heavy handed use of creamy layer arguments would end up admitting students whose cumulative disadvantages make it highly probable that they will fail, thus discrediting the affirmative action programme itself (2006: 2441).
12   Authorities in India claimed to be concerned about the manifold difference between the number of candidates and admissions in professional degree courses. Many blamed

the rising number of applicants on the alleged Rs2,000 crore (£200 million) coaching industry and the promises and the methods used in these centres, allegedly teaching students to 'memorise concepts' or 'track answer patterns' without understanding the concepts. Measures have been put in place to curb the number of students appearing for these major public examinations, for example, the use of the twelfth STD final examination result as screening for appearing for the Joint Engineering Entrance Exam. Further proposals include the introduction of a section in examinations aimed at testing 'language skills', to allegedly avoid people who do not understand lectures from entering top professional institutions (that is, to stop non-English-medium students from accessing these institutions).

Bibliography

Ahmad, I. and H. Reifeld 2001. *Middle Class Values In India And Western Europe*. Social Science Press.

Balagopalan, S. 2005. An ideal school and the schooled ideal: Education at the margins. In *Educational Regimes in Contemporary India* (eds) R. Chopra and P. Jeffery, 83–98. Sage.

Baviskar, A. and R. Ray 2011. *Elite and Everyman: The Cultural Politics of the Indian Middle Classes*. (1st edition). Routledge.

Bourdieu, P. 1984. *Distinction: A Social Critique of the Judgement of Taste*. Harvard University Press.

Busby, C. 2000. *The Performance of Gender: An Anthropology of Everyday Life in a South Indian Fishing Village*. Berg.

Chopra, R. 2004. *South Asian Masculinities: Context of Change, Sites of Continuity* (eds C. Osella and F. Osella). Kali for Women.

De Neve, G. 2011. 'Keeping it in the family': Work, education and gender hierarchies among Tiruppur's industrial capitalists. In *Being Middle-Class in India: A Way of Life* (ed.) H. Donner, 73–99. Routledge.

Deshpande, S. 2006. Exclusive inequalities: Merit, caste and discrimination in Indian higher education today. *Economic and Political Weekly* 41, 2438–2444.

Donner, H. and G. De Neve 2011. Introduction. In *Being Middle-class in India: A Way of Life* (ed.) H. Donner, 1–22. Routledge.

Fernandes, L. 2000. Restructuring the new middle class in liberalizing India. *Comparative Studies of South Asia, Africa and the Middle East* **20**, 88–112.

Fuller, C. J. and H. Narasimhan 2006. Engineering colleges, 'exposure' and information technology professionals in Tamil Nadu. *Economic and Political Weekly* **3**, 258–262.

Galanter, M. 1984. *Competing Equalities: Law and the backward classes in India*. Oxford.

Gooptu, N. (ed.) 2013. *Enterprise Culture in Neoliberal India: Studies in Youth, Class, Work and Media*. Routledge (available online: www.routledge.com/books/details/978 0415705417/).

Hansen, T. B. 1999. *The Saffron Wave: Democracy and Hindu Nationalism in Modern India*. Princeton University Press.

Jeffrey, C. 2010. *Timepass: Youth, Class, and the Politics of Waiting in India*. Stanford University Press.

Jeffrey, C., P. Jeffery and R. Jeffery 2008. *Degrees Without Freedom?: Education, Masculinities, and Unemployment in North India*. Stanford University Press.

Mills, M. B. 2003. Gender and inequality in the global labor force. *Annual Review of Anthropology* **32**, 41–62.

Nisbett, N. 2009. *Growing up in the Knowledge Society: Living the IT Dream in Bangalore.* (1st edition). Routledge.

Osella, C. and F. Osella 1998. Friendship and flirting: Micro-politics in Kerala, South India. *The Journal of the Royal Anthropological Institute* **4**, 189–206.

Osella, F. and C. Osella 2000. *Social Mobility in Kerala: Modernity and Identity in Conflict.* Pluto Press.

Ram, K. 1991. *Mukkuvar Women: Gender, Hegemony and Capitalist Transformation in a South Indian Fishing Community.* Zed Books.

Rogers, M. 2008. Modernity, 'authenticity', and ambivalence: Subaltern masculinities on a South Indian college campus. *Journal of the Royal Anthropological Institute* **14**, 79–95.

Salim, A. A. 2004. *Opportunities for Higher Education: An Enquiry into Entry Barriers.* (KRPLLD Discussion Paper). CDS.

Upadhya, C. 2011. Software and the 'new' middle class in the 'new India'. In *Elite and Everyman: The Cultural Politics of the Indian Middle Classes* (eds) A. Baviskar and R. Ray, 167–192. Routledge.

Varma, P. K. 2003. *The Great Indian Middle Class.* Penguin Books Australia.

Willis, P. 1977. *Learning to Labour: How Working Class Kids Get Working Class Jobs.* Ashgate Publishing Limited.

Winkler Reid, S. 2011. 'Growing up, growing together': Processes of year group unification in secondary school. Unpublished conference paper: Anthropology and Schooling: Learning the 'Modern Way'. Brunel University.

8 Conclusions

In this book I have sought to portray a middle-class cultural life in Kochi using, as a departing point, the recent work of Mark Liechty (2003) amongst the middle classes in Kathmandu, as well as the work of Pier Bourdieu (Bourdieu 1984). Like them, I think of class in terms of a 'practice' or 'project', which emphasises a processual conception of class – a perpetual work-in-progress that is fluid and contested – rather than a passive and objectifying definition. Therefore, I have presented parents, students and educational institutions joined together through a range of class practices and discourses. Liechty (2003: 265) rightly concludes that if class is not an objective category, then we ought to move past the immobilising question 'What *is* class?' to the active question 'What does class as cultural practice *do*?'. Ultimately, he argues that what class practice in Kathmandu *does* is carve out a new cultural domain that he calls the middle-class 'cultural space', in the imagination of urban middle-class dwellers as well as imbuing 'real', physical space with class meaning.

For Liechty (2003: 256), consumption practices and the way people talk about middle-class consumer goods and consumer desire are especially important in the production of class-cultural space. He is not alone in this stance. Since 1991, representations of the middle class by advertising and the media, as well as by studies of the middle classes have focused – almost exclusively – on their engagement with new forms of consumption, leading to the theorisation of new forms of consumer citizenship (for example, Fernandes 2006; Lukose 2009; Mazzarella 2003). In particular, studies of Indian youths have brought to the fore the emergence of and engagement with specific consumption practices that are apparently constitutive of novel aesthetics and subjectivities, and at the same time, reproduce politics of class, community, caste and gender. Against this backdrop, drawing on Liechty's frame for analysing middle-class cultural life, and focusing on education as a lens, this book has sought to accomplish two things. First, I have aimed to challenge, or rather, complement the emphasis that has been placed on the importance of consumer practice in the collective performance of middle-class culture. I have attempted to provide a complete picture that highlights how the middle classes are situated and situate themselves in economic processes not just as consumers, but also, crucially, as producers. Second, I have aimed to further this line of analysis of middle-class life with an exploration of the internal politics of the middle-class cultural space through a comparative analysis. If what middle-class practice ultimately does is carve out a 'middle' cultural space, what does this culturally constructed space actually do? In this book I have argued that the space of education – as an imaginary middle-class space and the actual physical space – helps to uphold, and at the same time conceal, inequalities between the established and the emergent middle classes.

Education: Consumption and production

The language of consumption was crucial to the narrative strategies that middle-class people in Kochi deployed to locate themselves and others, to discursively produce cultural space. I have shown how for established or new middle-class parents, talking about themselves as parents who send their children to private schools and entrance coaching institutions was an important recourse to discursively construct a shared (imaginary) space for the middle-class social self, as well as to differentiate themselves from the class others above and below. In Chapter 4, parents' narrative about the consumption of private schooling and expensive entrance coaching allowed them to ground an understanding of middle-class, modern parenthood as 'detached', portraying parents as being absorbed by their jobs or professional careers and hence only able to materialise their deep concern for their children's educational careers through spending money. Consuming private, English-medium schooling and expensive entrance coaching were important acts in the performance of class; things that were understood to be more about participation in a child's life and in the collective performance of middle-class parenthood than about possession. Similarly, the stories of resignation to consumer pressures that emerged from some middle-class parents in Kochi show that sometimes the consumption of private education is less about the goods themselves than about sociality and the social imperative to consume. The Malayali saying *nadodumbol naduve odanam* ('when people are running, you should run in the middle'), recurrently used by parents to talk about the decision to send their children to EC, captures 'the sense of how members of the middle class constitutes consumption less as a domain of goods, objects or passive possession than as an active communicative sphere' (Liechty 2003: 256).

But that is only one side of the coin. As detailed in Chapter 4, the collective performance of middle-class parenthood through consumption practice was sustained or made possible through other narrative practices, wherein a particular language of *production* was especially important. Most middle-class people I met in Kochi, parents and school staff alike, discursively constructed the middle-class child through the language of active entrepreneurship. The everyday linguistic construction that portrayed young men and women as naturally endowed with enterprising qualities, such as ambition, self-reliance and the willingness to sacrifice, primarily manifested through education, points to the importance of a particular productive orientation in the collective performance of middle-class culture. This language resonates with a now-dominant imagination that celebrates the supposed emergence of a new 'pulsating' India: an active and aspirational society whose passions and ambitions propel the development of the nation. The everyday language of urban middle-class youth echoed these narratives and worked to create an inclusive, collective social space constructed through shared educational, employment and entrepreneurial aspirations. The language of individual merit, hard-work and personal sacrifice, which was central to their collective performance of middle-class culture, underpinned an understanding of their lives as the enterprise of themselves. This discursive production of the middle-class child was often discursively juxtaposed to stories that characterised previous generations as passive and dependent.

It is essential to look beyond the narrative strategies that middle-class people used to carve out a social space for themselves, and to give equally important consideration to the material practices, embodied experiences and actual objects that contributed to the middle-class project of carving and claiming a middle-class cultural space. In Liechty's terms, it is important to consider how class-cultural practice takes place, not only in the sense that it actually *occurs*, but also in the sense of how actual physical space comes to be dominated by the cultural values and bodies of a particular class collectivity (Liechty 2003: 257). Chapter 7 described in detail the middle-class notions of the 'house arrest' and the 'year that can break or make you' as embodied practices fundamental to the collective performance of middle-class culture. Performing the 'year that can break or make you' was about embodying the enterprising qualities of passion, initiative, energy, independence, hard-work and willingness to sacrifice and to accept responsibility for one's own well-being. Middle-class educational, employment and entrepreneurial (productive) aspirations colonised the minds and bodies of urban young people at BVM with visions of successful trajectories that were almost unimaginable to the youth in Kothad.

Moreover, the book has also examined how class cultural practice transformed specific places – the school, but also the city at large – into arenas or stages for the performance of middle-class cultural logic. Chapter 3 explored precisely how the school was *taken* by the middle-class cultural logic of 'the year that can break or make you', which imagines the final year of school as a decisive moment wherein much of the students' paths to professional, middle-class and globally oriented citizenship was at stake. The private, English-medium school and the EC institute, with its systematic, exam-oriented teaching regimes, became the 'natural' space for the enterprising middle-class student, as well as for the wider aspirational middle-class society. The proliferation of private schools and other educational institutions across in Kochi, imbued the city with not only this particular middle-class aspirational logic, but also with a distinctively middle-class discourse of 'suitability' (Liechty 2003: 256). Middle-class schools in Kochi advertised and promoted themselves in a language that explicitly constructed a socio-moral landscape and pitted themselves against both the local elites, associated with the immorality of global modernity, and the local poor, associated with the inappropriateness of the old government-aided schools. The book described how middle-class schools portrayed themselves as producing competent subjects for the global economy, who were both modern and traditional, safely away from the immorality of elite international schools and the low-quality education said to be found in government-funded institutions. This language of propriety helps produce a middle-class space between the poles of upper- and lower-class deficiencies that deflected attention away from the economic advantages of the middle class, and gave a moral weight to their aspirations and strategies of mobility (Liechty 2003: 256).

I have sought to locate education at the centre of an understanding of middle-class cultural life in Kochi. Education offers an exceptional lens that doubles as a consumable good, as well as a primary locus of the aspirations and strategies of social and geographical mobility of the middle class. It allows us to bring out the importance of consumer practice in the ongoing construction of middle-class culture, and perhaps more importantly, it helps us see how the middle classes have always been situated in economic processes, not just as consumers, but also as aspiring producers. The middle classes are those oriented towards or struggling (some more than others) to secure the most privileged productive roles, which are in turn historically produced. Jobs in the Indian Administrative and Foreign Services once served as middle-class aspirational compasses. Today, the middle classes locate their aspirations in the private sector – iconically in the IT industry – and the management and engineering professions are the most sought after (Kumar 2011: 238). This understanding of middle-class life brings together the dominant fraction of the middle class, discussed within much of the scholarly literature and the media (for example, Dwyer 2000; Fuller and Narasimhan 2006), as well as the more 'down-to-earth middle-class status that premises this identity, not on unlimited access to the accoutrements of a globalised bourgeoisie, but on aspiration inhibited by a more humble access to resources and on a need to find work' (Nisbett 2009: 190). In short, the cultural meaning of being middle class is inextricably linked to the quest to embody success defined by a particular orientation towards modernity, being urban, professional, wealthy and the imagined relationship of these to the global economy (Upadhya 2011: 177); it is education that is said to hold the key to the success of this quest.

Using education as a lens to explore middle-class cultural life also allows us to historicise the middle class in India. As a prelude to its core chapters, the book started by revealing the history behind what is today a fragmented and complexly stratified schooling field in Kerala, arguing that it cannot be fully understood unless we examine it in the face of its historical link with its twin modernising enterprise: the middle-class project. Chapter 2 showed that in nineteenth- and twentieth-century Kerala, modern education served simultaneously to propel processes of social change and mediated the reproduction of previously existing inequalities. Early access to modern English education, the primary path to new economic and social roles, became the cultural base for the emergence of a Malayalee middle class from the ranks of rich and upper caste/community elites. Departing from the privileges inherited from their traditional status, they set out to access education and new employment opportunities and to rearticulate the basis of their status and wealth with reference to those educational achievements, through ideas of social mobility and competence, and no longer on social group membership. This quest, however, took the form of separate and competing communal struggles to become part of the new educated middle classes. As these progressed, different 'educational regimes' (Chopra and Jeffery 2005) emerged and developed, producing varied educational outcomes. In the meantime, the idea of competence, the banner of the modern person to emerge at the turn of the twentieth century, captured the imagination and aspirations of an ever-larger portion of society. Sometimes supported and at other times opposed by the state government, community-based schools helped spread this imaginary of progress across all social groups, eventually becoming part of Kerala's state rhetoric, while schooling became a profitable activity on its own. But what is most important is that out of these developments emerged a highly fragmented and stratified educational field offering different resources according to class, community/caste and gender. In other words, while education has been seen as a modernising tool able to displace social difference according to caste or religion, it has been a key site for the maintenance of those differences with a shift from direct to mediated reproduction. In short, caste and class remained entwined within twenty-first-century education. Most private English-medium educated Keralites are higher-status Christians and Hindus, as are most of those who get privileged access to EC centres and to professional degree courses. Today's wide array of government-aided and private schools is reflective of the long affair between the middle-class project and education.

Inclusive discourse, exclusive lives

Bourdieu's notion of field offers an important concept with which to make an analytical analogy with Liechty's idea of the middle-class cultural space; an analogy I believe can help bring out the implications of such space (Bourdieu 1984). In other words, the concept of field can help us understand what the middle-class cultural space *does*. For Bourdieu, a field was a social arena (crafted through cultural practice) in which people manoeuvre and struggle in pursuit of desirable resources; certain species of capital taken as significant by the people located in that particular field. Of course, significance is socially and historically constructed. A central idea in Bourdieu's writing is that the significance of symbols is connected with power, and that the dominant class in any society is the class that ultimately determines the ranking of symbols and the form of dominant discourse. In other words, the dominant class controls the criteria or specific 'rules' for good taste in any given social field. People in a disadvantaged position within a field (i.e. those whose habitus and capital do not match what is valued in the field) will struggle much more than someone in a privileged position; their fight will, tacitly or explicitly, in turn support the dominant criteria for understanding good taste or 'success'. The chapters in this book have composed a picture of a distinct field that we may call middle-class education, and which I juxtaposed with a more lowly education field, that inhabited by the school and the students in Kothad. I have explored a number of 'symbols' within the field of middle-class schooling; different varieties of private, English-medium schools, extra-school coaching institutes, undergraduate and postgraduate degree 'choices', English language competence, 'proper' attitudes towards education and academic results, as well as professional and life aspirations. Control over the more desirable varieties of these symbols (for example, access to top private schools, fluency in English, good marks and the ambition to become an engineer) are inextricably related to the everyday practices of people and their social backgrounds, as well as to economic inequality. This book has attempted to show that middle-class education favours and helps reproduce the power of the dominant and established fraction of the middle classes. The practices, values, aspiration and trajectories constructed as the most desirable within the field are ultimately hegemonic and the preserve of the middle-class elite. This middle-class education ultimately allows for the (re)production of inequalities amongst the established and emergent middle classes in Kochi and its surrounding areas.

Various chapters in this book provide insights into the expanding new private schooling sector and show how it is highly stratified, catering to very different economic capabilities, as well as fragmented according to various religious/secular orientations. At the top, we find the newly established 'international' schools, and at the bottom I presented the recently established private, English-medium schools to which the better-off families from Kothad sent their children. Somewhere in the middle, yet towards the top of this middle-class school hierarchy lies BVM. Such schools are extraordinarily different, yet they embody certain fundamental values and perceptions widely agreed upon amongst the people engaged with them. The high value placed on and the perception that English language is better taught in fee-paying schools, the disdain towards government-funded education and the associated orientation not to make any claims on the state, a particular understanding of 'good' parenthood, the idea that fee-paying schools are accountable and offer higher-quality education, are all shared perceptions amongst the people involved in this study. More importantly they were all involved in the collective conversion of economic privileged into the social currency of private education; a distinctively middle-class practice. But within this middle-class field, the economic authority of the dominant fraction of the middle class did not dissipate after its transformation into this social currency, but became culturally mediated as it was transformed into the most exclusive forms of education available. With changes in the private schooling landscape, such as the emergence of schools offering internationally recognised credentials or the subsequent 'international' turn of most of the top private schools, new forms of inequalities have emerged, allowing, in the end, the dominant fraction of the middle classes to reinstate its power.

Srijith's story, in Chapter 5, offered a glimpse into what could be considered a more extreme conversion of capital. He sought to transform the limited economic privilege of his family – gained through two decades of migrant labour in the Gulf – and the cultural capital acquired in his class ten Board exams, through which he gained considerable leverage, into the cultural privilege of studying in one of the most reputed private schools in Kochi. At BVM he struggled to gain control over the species of capital, such as English competence, that were most effective and held a high value in that particular schools. His lack of capital in the new setting threatened to jeopardise the entire transaction. However, seen from a more longitudinal perspective, accessing the urban school in Kochi allowed Srijith to occupy a significantly more privileged position than that of his ex-school peers.

Education as a form of middle-class social currency, as Liechty points out (2003: 253), serves to deflect attention away from economic privilege. In doing so, it conceals inequalities. For example, in Chapter 7 I showed how the middle-class social currency of merit serves to conceal the privilege derived from economic capital and social origin. The language of sacrifice and merit gave the final year of school at BVM a certain aura of unity, dissolving most peer group divisions. Despite the fact that the students' prospects of attaining the most coveted educational outcomes were markedly unequal, lower-middle-class students actively appropriated the language and conduct of equal sacrifice and merit of the 'the year that can break or make you' as a strategy to navigate the high level of (un)certainty and expectations placed upon them at this crossroad year. In that way, final year students actively united and oriented themselves towards a common struggle to improve their chances in competitive examinations. Making no reference to their markedly different levels of English competence (largely a result of their caste or religious backgrounds), as well as their families' capacities to afford EC (which shaped their chances to achieve 'success'), they emphasised their equality in the face of their quests ahead. In this manner, sacrifice and merit conjured up a unifying experience of 'the year that can break or make you' that concealed differences and inequalities, in the end rallying legitimacy for projects and lifestyles more feasibly achievable to those in the dominant middle-class (and predominantly upper-caste) minority.

At the opposite end of the spectrum, this book showed that schools catering to the lower strata of society have become sites where long-standing inequalities are not just reproduced but further entrenched. The book illustrated this point with the example of Kothad, an islet in the backwaters of Kochi's fringes. In Kothad, inequalities according to space (pitting the urban centre against its fringes) and community (pitting fisherfolk against urban Latin Catholics) became further entrenched. The local school's youth became the object of a 'dual residualisation' or ghettoisation: first, residual because only the local poor are left to attend the school, and second, residual because educationally and financially poor Latin Catholics are flowing in from the city. As a consequence the periphery became more deeply marked as educationally backward. The outcome being that old inequalities are being reproduced and intensified by new educational policies and physical linkages linked to the city's development.

Globalisation and education

The domain of education has become an ostensible manifestation of globalisation in a number of ways. The rising number of international students, the growing affiliation to internationally recognised credentials, and the intervention of international organisations within national education systems leading to the increasing promotion of an international agenda and concepts such as global citizenship, are some of the ways in which education has become most obviously internationalised

(Hayden 2011). In addition, recent studies point to the changing nature of international schools, which are said to be growing in size and influence, and expanding beyond their historical niche of elite expatriates to include postcolonial middle-class families in large cosmopolitan cities across the global South (Hayden 2011). For example, scholars have documented the establishment and functioning of international schools in cities such as Hong Kong (Bray and Yamato 2003; Yamato 2003), Shanghai (Yamato and Bray 2006) and Dubai, mostly by global commercial schooling providers such as the Nord Anglia Group, Global Education Management Systems and Taaleem. This book documents how internationalised schooling – as an aspiration and a marker of class status, as well as a practice that gives new meaning to urban spaces – has penetrated beyond metropoles into what has been described as 'second tier cities' (Markusen *et al.* 1999). Kochi is far from becoming an Indian metropolis. However, the city is growing rapidly and might soon turn the tide of hyper-urbanisation in cities such as Bangalore (Nair 2005). The elites and the middle classes are crucial to this transformation, setting the tone as to precisely how the city ought to develop. One such arena of change has been education. Underpinned by the desire to see Kochi attain the reputation and command the function of a metro of 'international standard', the city's schooling sector has seen the emergence of international schools and the internationalisation of old schools. These are said to better equip young people for a career in the global economy, while imbuing the city with a newly aspired global pedigree.

Although the internationalisation of education is a global cultural process, giving form to middle-class cultures worldwide, in this book I have shown how shared global cultural phenomena are far from simply the result of ready-made 'global forces' acting upon 'local places', as is often assumed. Assayag and Fuller (2005: 1) warn us that one should remain particularly critical of those developments that seem to be obvious manifestations of 'globalisation' and explore the ways in which they 'are actually driven endogenously by local, regional or national forces, which have often been in place since the colonial period or even earlier'. In this book I have argued that elites and the upper middle class in Kochi have, for the past two centuries, been active in creating cultural distinction from their class others below through education. The recent emergence of international schools is linked to this long-standing cultural strategy. I have also shown how the associated *pseudo* internationalisation of top private schools in Kochi can be read as a middle-class attempt to stake a claim at contemporary narratives of modernity, while creating a moral space that allows the middle class to deflect the 'evil emanations' (Liechty 2003: 251) of the modern. In one breath, BVM's staff voiced the need for radical change, the need for students to become world citizens, while simultaneously urging the need to live by India's 'fundamental' values, maintaining a balance with modernity. As Liechty (2003: 251) rightly notes, a 'fundamental part of the middle-class cultural project is precisely to *circulate* these tales of modern propriety and impropriety'. Throughout the book I have also highlighted how the transformations described – of privatisation and internationalisation of education – have been more pronounced in wealthier and migration-rich states, such as Punjab (Qureshi and Osella 2013) and Kerala. The desire for internationalised forms of education is also a by-product of a long history of migration, which has exposed educational entrepreneurs, parents and students to foreign forms of education.

One must also remember that these global cultural processes are actually extremely uneven. The growing privatisation and internationalisation of schooling in Kochi have created educational 'choices' that are heavily skewed against the poor and marginalised (Jeffery 2005), so that the growing diversity and number of private schools serves to exclude large sections of the population (Kumar and George 2009). More generally, the welfare consequences of the growth of second-tier cities such as Kochi may raise important problems from an equity point of view. While contributing to a lessening of regional inequality, new urban hier-archies may also lead to the entrenchment of the marginalisation of those inhabiting the fringes and the countryside surrounding new pockets of urban prosperity. This is precisely the case for the youth of Kothad, whose prospects of social ascension through education have become ever more disenfranchised, just at a time when education seems to promise it all to their urban, middle-class counterparts.

Bibliography

Assayag, J. and C. J. Fuller 2005. *Globalizing India: Perspectives From Below*. Anthem Press.

Bourdieu, P. 1984. *Distinction: A Social Critique of the Judgement of Taste*. Harvard University Press.

Bray, M. and Y. Yamato 2003. Comparative education in a microcosm: Methodological insights from the international schools sector in Hong Kong. *International Review of Education* **49**, 51–73.

Chopra, R. and P. Jeffery 2005. *Educational Regimes in Contemporary India*. Sage.

Dwyer, R. M. J. 2000. *All You Want is Money, All You Need is Love: Sexuality and Romance in Modern India*. Continuum International Publishing Group Ltd.

Fernandes, L. 2006. *India's New Middle Class: Democratic Politics in an Era of Economic Reform*. University of Minnesota Press.

Fuller, C. J. and H. Narasimhan 2006. Engineering colleges, 'exposure' and information technology professionals in Tamil Nadu. *Economic and Political Weekly* **3**, 258–262.

Hayden, M. 2011. Transnational spaces of education: the growth of the international school sector. *Globalisation, Societies and Education* **9**, 211–224.

Jeffery, P. 2005. Introduction: Hearts, minds, and pockets. In *Educational Regimes in Contemporary India* (eds) R. Chopra and P. Jeffery, 13–38. Sage.

Kumar, N. 2011. The middle-class child: Ruminations on failure. In *Elite and Everyman: The Cultural Politics of the Indian Middle Classes* (eds) A. Baviskar and R. Ray, 220–245. Routledge.

Kumar, N. A. and K. K. George 2009. *Kerala's Education System: From Inclusion to Exclusion?*. Working paper no. 22. Centre for Socio-economic & Environmental Studies.

Liechty, M. 2003. *Suitably Modern: Making Middle-Class Culture in a New Consumer Society*. Princeton University Press.

Lukose, R. A. 2009. *Liberalization's Children: Gender, Youth, and Consumer Citizenship in Globalizing India*. Duke University Press Books.

Markusen, A. R., Y.-S. Lee and S. DiGiovanna 1999. *Second Tier Cities: Rapid Growth Beyond the Metropolis*. University of Minnesota Press.

Mazzarella, W. 2003. 'Very Bombay': Contending with the global in an Indian advertising agency. *Cultural Anthropology* **18**, 33–71.

Nair, J. 2005. *The Promise of the Metropolis: Bangalore's Twentieth Century*. Oxford University Press.

Nisbett, N. 2009. *Growing Up in the Knowledge Society: Living the IT Dream in Bangalore.* (1st edition). Routledge.

Qureshi, K. and F. Osella 2013. Transnational schooling in Punjab, India: Designer migrants and cultural politics. In *Refugees, Immigrants, and Education in the Global South: Lives in Motion* (eds) L. Bartlett and A. Ghaffar-Kucher, 99–115. Routledge.

Upadhya, C. 2011. Software and the 'new' middle class in the 'new India'. In *Elite and Everyman: The Cultural Politics of the Indian Middle Classes* (eds) A. Baviskar and R. Ray, 167–192. Routledge.

Yamato, Y. 2003. *Education in the Market Place: Hong Kong's International Schools and their Modes of Operation*. Comparative Education Research Centre, University of Hong Kong.

Yamato, Y. and M. Bray 2006. Economic development and the market place for education dynamics of the international schools sector in Shanghai, China. *Journal of Research in International Education* **5**, 57–82.

Index